Acts of Surrender

a writer's memoir

Mark David Gerson

ACTS OF SURRENDER: A WRITER'S MEMOIR

Copyright © 2012, 2013, 2019 Mark David Gerson
All rights reserved

No part of this book may be reproduced, stored in a retrieval system or transmitted by any means, electronic, mechanical, photocopying, recording or otherwise, without written permission from the author, except for the inclusion of brief quotations in critical reviews and certain other noncommercial uses permitted by copyright law.

First Paperback Edition 2013. Second Edition 2019.

Published by MDG Media International
2370 W. State Route 89a, Suite 11-210
Sedona, AZ 86336

www.mdgmediainternational.com

ISBN: 978-1-950189-09-0

Cover Photograph: Kathleen Messmer
www.kathleenmessmer.com

Author Photograph: Kevin Truong
www.kevintruong.com

More information on the author
www.markdavidgerson.com

Resources for Writers
Books, Recordings, Coaching/Mentoring, Workshops/Retreats

*Whenever I feel blocked, I open this book,
read a couple of pages and feel inspired again.*
ANNA BLAGOSLAVOVA – MOSCOW, RUSSIA

*Without Mark David's inspiration, example and encouragement, I might
never have had the courage to publish my book.*
NANCY POGUE LaTURNER – AUTHOR OF "VOLUNTARY NOMADS"

A highly recommended guide from one of the most creative people around.
WILLIAM C. REICHARD – AUTHOR OF "EVERTIME"

Coaching with Mark David Gerson: Best investment ever!
CHRISTINE FARRIS – DENVER, CO

*I am filled with awe at how easy Mark David has made this.
No more writer's block!*
AZUREL EFRON – SEDONA, AZ

*I owe so much to Mark David! He helped me believe in myself enough to
write the book that got two wrongful murder convictions overturned.*
ESTELLE BLACKBURN – AUTHOR OF "BROKEN LIVES"

Memoirs
Pilgrimage: A Fool's Journey,
Dialogues with the Divine: Encounters with My Wisest Self

An absolute must for all fans of this immensely talented and generous writer.
PAOLA RIZZATO – HEYSHAM, UK

*I feel as if Mark David wrote this book just for me. Each page contains
wisdom I need to hear, over and over and again. What a gift this book is.*
KAREN HELENE WALKER – AUTHOR OF "THE WISHING STEPS"

*An honest dialogue between the human and the divine is a healing
reconciliation for many of us. Ultimately, we discover that our humanity
is part of our divinity. Mark David Gerson bridges the gap and heals the
separation with this book.*
REV. MARK POPE – AUTHOR OF "THE FINAL PRISON BREAK"

Self-Help & Personal/Spiritual Growth
*The Way of the Fool, The Way of the Imperfect Fool,
The Book of Messages*

It will transform your life!
Rev. Brendalyn Batchelor – Unity Santa Fe

Simple but powerful!
Dave Kerpen – author of "The Art of People"

A book that changes everything that's holding you back!
Ted Wiga – San Francisco, CA

The Legend of Q'ntana
*The MoonQuest, The StarQuest, The SunQuest,
The Bard of Bryn Doon*

Magic, music and universal truths masterfully woven into a gripping tale.
Betty Dravis – author of "1106 Grand Boulevard"

An exceptional, timeless novel.
"Mindquest Review of Books"

You will love this book!
Amy Robbins-Wilson – author, singer/songwriter

Leaves you turning every single page, hungry for more!
David Michael – author of "The United Series"

The Sara Stories
Sara's Year, After Sara's Year, The Emmeline Papers

Honest and heartfelt. Brilliant!
Joan Cerio – Host of radio's "Earth Energy Forecast"

Thrilling...bittersweet...triumphant!
Dan Stone – author of "Ice on Fire"

A classic in the making!
D'Arcy Mayo – Mittagong, Australia

What do dreams know of boundaries?
AMELIA EARHART

When the last dime is gone, I'll sit on the curb outside with a pencil and a ten-cent notebook and start the whole thing over again.
PRESTON STURGES

To all the ghosts I have befriended in revisiting my past, to all the me's I have rediscovered in setting these words to the page, to all the places and realms I have visited through the decades of my journeying, and to all those who have participated in my drama, knowingly or not, I dedicate this book.

Contents

Overture   11
  About This New Edition   13
  An Act of Surrender   14
  Genesis   17
  Caveat Lector   20

Act 1. Origins   21
  An Inconvenient Truth   23
  Leaving Home   27

Act 2. Awakenings   33
  School Days   35
  A Writer's Journey   39
  Writing and Spirit   46
  "I Must Teach"   52

Act 3. Exodus   57
  Upheavals   59
  Driving Ambitions   63
  Atlantic Time   66

Act 4. Nova Scotia   71
  No Rules   73
  Birth of a Book   77
  Home, Sweet Homes   80
  Gay? No Way!   84
  Inside "The MoonQuest"   87

Act 5. Toronto Redux   91
  Farewell to Nova Scotia   93

    Sight and Scent   96
    Voicing the Past, Healing the Present   101
    Of Dogs and Delusions   104

Act 6. On Georgian Bay   107
    Rainbow Connection   109
    At Home in Penetanguishene   112
    "Dialogues with the Divine"   115
    Return of "The MoonQuest"   119

Act 7. Back to Toronto   123
    Toronto Calling   125
    The Reiki Portal   128
    The Perils of Pauline   133
    Destination Unknown   135

Act 8. On the Road   141
    O, Canada   143
    A New Country   148
    Channel Surfing   151
    Sedona Beckons   153

Act 9. Coming Out   157
    Being Different   159
    Gay and Jewish   163
    Mom and the Psychiatrist   165

Act 10. Sedona   167
    A New Beginning   169
    The Name Game   172
    How I Met My Wife   178
    Married...with Kids?   184
    Roxy   188

Act 11. Hawaii   191
    The Land of Aloha and Uē (Crying)   193
    Sweet Surrender   196

Act 12. Return to Sedona — 203
   The Right Place — 205
   Changing Channels — 210
   Yes...Minister? — 213
   The God That You Are — 215
   The Art of Surrender — 218

Act 13. Scenes from the End of a Marriage — 221
   Ringing Out the Old — 223
   Never Forever — 226
   Signs of Dissolution — 229

Act 14. On the Road...Again — 233
   Guinevere — 235
   Pennies from Heaven — 240
   America the Beautiful — 244
   The End of the Road — 249

Act 15. Canada — 253
   Stranger in a Familiar Land — 255
   Larger Than Life — 257
   Hometown Ghosts — 259

Act 16. The Writer I Am — 263
   The Story Knows Best — 265
   Cover Story — 269
   The Voice of My Muse — 271

Act 17. Albuquerque — 275
   Hello, Albuquerque — 277
   Goodbye, Albuquerque — 280
   Coming Out (Again) for Christmas — 282
   All That Matters Is That I'm Writing — 284

Act 18. LA Story — 289
   Trading Open Spaces — 291
   A Time of Signs — 295
   Leap of Faith — 298

The Heart of Desire	301
Birthday Presence	304
Sacrifice and Surrender	308

Act 19. Retracing My Steps — 311
Back to the Future	313
Passion's Legacy	317
Movie Magic	320
The Write Place	322

Coda — 323
The Next Surrender...	325
...And the Next	329

Appreciation — 333

OVERTURE

The sweetest sound in all the world is the music of what happens.
FRANK DELANEY

You don't choose the writer's life; the writer's life chooses you.
TOM GRIMES

About This New Edition

A MEMOIR IS LARGELY a journey into the past — a photograph in time written at a particular moment from a particular perspective and built on the foundation of a particular history. The original edition of *Acts of Surrender* was just such a memoir. However, the journey that it set out for readers didn't leave them in the past; it carried them up to the present, which wouldn't be a problem except that the first edition's present (late 2013) is not this one.

Given that, I wasn't certain how best to approach this new edition. Should I change nothing other than the cover and a few publishing details? Should I rewrite the entire book to reflect today's perspective? Or should leave the original content largely intact but throw in some sort of update to make my story current?

I chose the latter.

Apart from correcting a handful of typos and factual errors, I have altered nothing from the original edition. To catch you up, however, I have added a new final chapter that will speed you five years and a thousand miles to the present moment, which at this writing is April 2019 in Portland, Oregon. Enjoy the ride!

An Act of Surrender

It's May 6, 2012. I have just finished breakfast, and as I stare into my empty coffee cup, I contemplate my immediate future. It has been less than twenty-four hours since I completed a final draft of my novel *The SunQuest* and along with it an odyssey that has occupied nearly one-third of my life: Eighteen years ago I surrendered to the words that would become the first draft of *The MoonQuest*, a story I knew nothing about, a story that would launch a fantasy trilogy that I did not yet know existed. Now that I have written "The End," both to *The SunQuest* and the trilogy, what's next for me?

As I stare into that coffee cup, I am certain that another draft of this book, of *Acts of Surrender*, must follow *The Q'ntana Trilogy* on my creative agenda. How can it not when *The SunQuest* is, among other things, about Ben's coming to terms with *his* past? How can it not when Ben's story, like Q'nta's and Toshar's before him in *The StarQuest* and *The MoonQuest*, is also my story? Hardly a day went by while I worked on *The SunQuest* that I failed to notice a parallel between Ben's life and mine, between what he discovers through reliving his journey on the page and what I have already discovered through living mine on these pages.

At the same time I ask myself: Wouldn't it make sense to wait a month before starting a new draft of *Acts of Surrender*? Between the *Q'ntana* screenplays and novels and early drafts of this memoir, I have been writing nonstop for nearly two years. Maybe it's time for a break. Besides, I have a business trip coming up in a few weeks. Wouldn't it make sense to wait until I get back?

You would think that after writing three fantasies where conventional sense is an elusive commodity, not to mention penning two drafts of a memoir that exposes similar threads in my own life, I would have more sense than to ask questions about sense. Apparently, I don't.

The coffee cup is still empty and my mind wanders, away from my creative life and on to my life — not that it's altogether possible to separate the two. I have now been back in Albuquerque for eighteen months. A 2010 move from here to Los Angeles ended after ten weeks when I felt a call to return to New Mexico. Through this my third sojourn in Albuquerque, I have become aware how much my life here has come to resemble my 1994-95 time in rural Nova Scotia: a hermit-like existence where little occurs beyond my writing. In Nova Scotia my focus was on the first two drafts of *The MoonQuest*; once they were finished, I found myself back in Toronto, my monkish tendencies forgotten.

There is, however, one significant difference between these two periods in my life: In Nova Scotia I had no conscious desire ever to leave. I believed that I had rebirthed myself on the East Coast, and when the call came for me to return to the big city, I was initially startled and dismayed. Here in Albuquerque, I have never stopped longing to be back in LA, to resume a life that has felt on hold since I returned here.

Suddenly, the opening scene of *The MoonQuest* pushes my mental wanderings aside. In it the dreamwalker Na'an interrupts an elderly Toshar, who has long resisted writing his story.

"It is not for me to boast of my exploits," Toshar argues.

Na'an disagrees. "It is your story to tell," she insists. "It is for you to fix it in ink, to set the truth down for all to read."

I cannot move on to other realms and set off on other journeys until I have told my story, I hear myself speak out loud, paraphrasing Toshar's thoughts in *The MoonQuest*. The words catch in my throat, and I'm gripped by an emotion so powerful that I find myself close to tears.

I can't know what those other realms and journeys might be. I can't know whether, in another parallel to my time in Nova Scotia, they will mark the end of my creative retreat and launch me back into the world's bustle — this time to LA instead of Toronto. What I can do is recognize the charge I experienced and the truth that underlies it: Like Toshar, I must tell my story, *this* story, or I will not be free to move forward with my life.

I know one other thing: Whatever the "sense" of the matter, I cannot wait a month to begin. In the act of surrender that is this book, I must begin now...in that realm where all stories begin: Once upon a time...

Genesis

I BEGAN THIS BOOK in mid-2009, shortly after having finished a first draft of *The StarQuest*, the second novel in my *Q'ntana Trilogy*. I did not want to write a memoir, and as Toshar did with Na'an in *The MoonQuest*, I kept arguing about it with my ever-insistent Muse. Who, I asked repeatedly, would care about my personal stories? Perhaps, had I known back then that the title would be *Acts of Surrender*, I might have seen the cosmic joke and given in more gracefully. Perhaps, had I seen the parallel with *The MoonQuest* sooner, I might have been more pliant. Muses, though, are doggedly persistent, and in the end my resistance proved futile...as it always does.

Ironically, the challenge I faced when beginning *Acts of Surrender* was similar to the one I had encountered with *The MoonQuest*: I did not know the story. Oh, I knew my story or at least my version of it. What I didn't know was the book's shape or its theme. How could I begin to write without knowing these things? Without knowing these things, how would I be able to condense more than a half century's living into a compelling, manageably sized narrative?

An outline was out of the question. As I often confess in my talks and workshops, I have never managed the art of the outline. Even in high school, when I was required to submit one with an essay, I wrote the essay first and crafted the outline afterward. Without knowing it, I had already adopted a writing philosophy I would not consciously connect with for nearly two decades: Just start and let the story reveal itself to you in the writing.

Could I do that in a nonfiction memoir with the same success I had achieved in novel and screenplay? Could I trust that my memoir was its own entity separate from the story I had lived and that it knew more about itself than I did? Could I surrender to that superior wisdom? Perhaps the more appropriate question was, How could I not?

As you will read in these pages, much of my life has been about growing into a place of surrender. To be clear, I don't use the word "surrender" to describe a demeaning or submissive stance. Rather, I acknowledge the existence of an infinite mind whose wisdom transcends my conscious thoughts and I do my best to defer to it. This is not an energy that exists separate from me. It is not a white-bearded, white-robed gentleman peering down from on high. Whatever it is — and I don't pretend to have solved the theological/scientific question of the ages — it is something that is both within me and of which I am part. Whatever it is, it is definitely smarter than I am, and *that* is where my surrender is directed.

Of course, I would have to write a book of my stories in the same way I had lived them: from a place of surrender, trusting that the story of my memoir would reveal itself to me in the writing of it, just as the story of my life has revealed itself to me in the living of it. In other words, how could *Acts of Surrender* be anything but another act of surrender?

Writers often balk when I suggest that their stories are wiser, cannier and craftier than they could ever hope to be. Writers, like all human beings, prefer to believe that they can be in control and still create from a place of infinite possibility. Not even the God of Genesis is that arrogant. God doesn't "make" creation happen. God allows creation to occur. "Let there be light," He says. And light appears. Not because God forces His will on it. But because He allows light its natural form, shape and substance. What happens when each day's creation is done? He doesn't sit in judgment over it, deeming it worthy or unworthy. He recognizes that all creation has innate merit and declares it to be "good."

I spent more than half the years I have lived so far with my eyes closed and ears blocked to infinite mind, *my* infinite mind. Although we are all born with a direct link to that source of wisdom and as young children act from it, we are often shut down to it by a so-called "grown-up world" that lives in fearful denial of anything that cannot be accessed by our five physical senses. I don't know why or when I was shut down, or by whom. But, clearly, I was. It wasn't until a creative and spiritual awakening began to move through me in my early thirties that I began to tune in to the infinite possibilities of the invisible.

My life since then, as you will discover, has been rocky, on-the-edge and unconventional. It has been scary, disrupted and a distant remove from what most people still cling to as "security." It has also been creative, exhilarating, passion-filled, vibrant, exciting, adventurous and enriching. It has pushed me beyond the boundaries of what I believe and what I believe I want, and it has propelled me beyond the frontiers of the conventionally possible. In every moment, it steers me on a course that I could never consciously chart for myself. In every breath, it reminds me that the story knows best — the story I'm living as much as the story I'm writing.

I wouldn't have it any other way.

Caveat Lector

MEMORY IS A FUNNY thing. My sister and I have distinct and distinctly different memories of the same events, even though we grew up in the same house with the same parents. No doubt, my daughter and her mother also view the common events of our lives through different lenses than I do. My versions are no more or less correct than theirs.

In a world where objective reality does not exist, no memoirist can make a claim to absolute accuracy. Every story or history is told from a point of view. This one is mine. All I can guarantee is that what I have written in these pages is true to my experience, and that where details stray from verifiable fact, the energy of my impressions remains unalterably true. In the few instances where names have been changed, it is either to avoid needless embarrassment or because I can no longer trace the originals.

Speaking of names, several people in my life, myself included, have undergone at least one name change over the years. I have tried to minimize the inevitable confusion by calling people by whichever name is accurate at the time a particular story takes place. In this, as in so much of my life, little is straightforward!

Act I.
Origins

I come from the Dark where all things have their beginning.
P.L. Travers

*There is nothing in a caterpillar
that tells you it's going to be a butterfly.*
R. Buckminster Fuller

An Inconvenient Truth

THERE ARE THREE stories of how I came to be: the conventional one, the one close family and friends were told, and the truth — a truth that remained hidden for decades, like many others in the house of secrets in which I grew up.

A few months after my mother died, I went to visit her oldest friend, Sophie Katz. I arrived at Sophie's suburban Toronto home armed with a tape recorder and questions, determined to learn more about a woman who had rarely spoken about herself or her past. Animated even though she was reclining on her sofa, Sophie recounted story after story about their growing-up years in Montreal. My favorite, because it revealed a side of my mother that I had never witnessed, had the two of them, in their teens, strolling down Boulevard Saint-Laurent, then Jewish Montreal's Main Street. This would have been in the mid-1930s, at the height of the Depression. As Sophie described it, a vagrant sitting on the curb grabbed my mother's ankle. She shook it free and they continued on. After half a block, my mother stopped, spun around and marched back. Glaring at the vagrant, she kicked him hard, then returned to Sophie.

Strong-willed, an odd blend of fear and fearlessness: that was Edith Plotnick Gerson Ravinsky. Edith was the English version of her Yiddish name, Esther. Although I never knew her as Esther, it's as Esther that I like to imagine her: the biblical queen who risked everything to follow a higher imperative.

Like her namesake, this Esther took risks, but she mitigated hers by never speaking of them. This Esther looked only forward, either because the present was too painful or the past could harm her if disclosed. This Esther, according to Sophie, was so determined to have a second natural child that she would bypass my father, whose diabetes had likely rendered him impotent. When I asked another close friend of my mother's whether she could verify Sophie's story, she shared the version she and a handful of others had been told at the time: artificial insemination, donor unknown — a rare but viable practice in 1954.

Viable, but according to Sophie, not true. In the middle of our "interview," she stopped and sat halfway up. "Do you want to know everything?" she asked forebodingly.

"Of course." Why wouldn't I?

"Sydney was not your father."

I stared back, dumbstruck. Not for the first time in my life, and certainly not for the last, I realized that I was not who I thought I was.

"You know how sick he always was. I didn't want you to think that you carried any of that."

My father, Sydney, had been in and out of hospitals for as long as I could remember — all due to complications brought on by his diabetes. One of our basement playrooms had once been his architectural office, an office I don't remember him ever having occupied, although through my childhood it still held his drafting table, drafting tools and rolled-up sketches and blueprints. Deteriorating vision had ended any active practice long before his death at fifty-six, two months shy of my fourteenth birthday. By the time Sophie told me what Edith had confessed to her many years earlier, Sydney had been so absent from my life for so long, both emotionally and physically, that the news didn't leave me with any sense of loss. How could I lose a father I had never had?

"So who—?"

"George Wior was your father."

I knew George Wior. He had been a family friend when I was very young and our eye doctor for many years. Edith had worked briefly as his receptionist after Sydney died in 1968.

"George Wior? But— How?"

George was studying medicine in France when the Nazis invaded his native Poland. When it became clear that France would soon be equally dangerous for Jews, he and his wife fled to Canada. Their first stop: Ottawa, where Sophie and her husband then lived, as did my parents. I don't know how the Wiors met the Katzes and Gersons. All Sophie could tell me was that a spark passed between George and Edith in their first meeting, a spark that quickly exploded into an affair.

By late 1953, Edith began to long for another natural child. Her first, my older brother, Michael, had died in 1952 at age ten, two years after my sister, Susan, was adopted. Michael was another family secret: Born in 1942 with Down Syndrome, he was institutionalized at age five and never mentioned again.

Edith's affair with George had ended years earlier, but they were still in contact, if fifteen hundred miles apart: She and Sydney were back in Montreal and George now lived in Winnipeg on his own; his wife had returned to Poland. In early 1954, according to Sophie, Edith traveled secretly to Winnipeg to see him, and there I was conceived.

The closest Edith ever came to telling me her inconvenient truth was on a muggy August morning in 1979 — ironically, a day before the eleventh anniversary of Sydney's death. I was working at Montreal's Concordia University at the time, in the public relations office. My mother and I spoke regularly and it wasn't unusual for her to call me at work. What *was* unusual was the conversation… and what was left unsaid.

"George died," she announced with few preliminaries. "A car accident. Yesterday."

For the next five years, until Sophie's revelation, something about that conversation haunted me. Of course, I was sorry to hear that George was gone. Yet I hadn't seen him in several years and had never felt close to him. My mother, though, seemed more upset than would be normal at the death of a man who, to my knowledge, was no more than her current eye doctor and former employer. After all, it had been nearly two decades since he had been part of our family's social circle. Something felt off about that phone call, even if I couldn't then touch what it was. When Sophie revealed my paternity and told me about the affair, it struck me that Edith had been trying to communicate something that she didn't dare put into words.

Did Sydney know that I was George's son? Or was the artificial insemination story primarily for him? Regardless, he would have known that I wasn't his. Perhaps that, more than his illness, explained the emotional absence I always felt from him.

By August 1968, Sydney had been a full-time resident of Montreal's Grace Dart Convalescent Hospital for several years. Just about every Sunday through that time, Edith, Susan and I would make the ten-mile trek to Montreal's east end to visit him. With no car, it took us three city buses and nearly ninety minutes to get there. The Sunday that would turn out to be his last, I stubbornly refused to accompany them, a surprising stance, given my generally compliant nature. Instead, I announced that I would spend the afternoon with my best friend, Gary Friedman. There was an argument, but I would not be moved. Eventually, Susan and Edith left, and I walked the two blocks to Gary's house. A few hours later, a mysterious phone call to Gary's mother had me shuttled up the street to my cousin Stanley's house, where I shared an uncomfortably quiet dinner with him and his family. A few hours after that, Edith and Susan pulled up in a car, one of my uncles', their eyes puffy and red.

"Daddy died," my mother said and took me in her arms, grateful that I hadn't been present for his fatal heart attack.

For a long time, I felt guilty that I hadn't been there for him. It never occurred to me to question why I would need to be present for a man who had never been present for me. A few years after my visit with Sophie, I found a letter that my father had written to me when I was at summer camp. I would have been eleven or twelve at the time. Whether Sydney had distanced himself from me the day I was born or some time later, the man who signed that note was not the father a child longs for. It wasn't signed with "love," the way I signed cards to my daughter when she was that age. Rather, it ended with, "Kind regards, Daddy." I wept when I read his shaky scrawl all those years later, not for the father I missed, but for the father I missed having.

That was the father Sophie took away from me that spring afternoon in 1984. In that moment, a moment when it seemed as though there was nothing to feel, I felt nothing.

Leaving Home

IN 1983 I WAS A freelance writer and editor, most of my income derived from my Quebec-correspondent post with *The Chronicle of Higher Education*, a Washington-based trade weekly. I had no awakened spirituality then, yet some powerful inner force urged me to leave Montreal and move to Toronto. There was some logic to the call. As an English-language freelancer in a largely French-speaking milieu, my prospects for professional advancement could only improve in English Canada's cultural and communications capital. At the same time, it seemed heartless to consider a move at that time. How could I leave when my mother had cancer and an uncertain prognosis?

Today, buttressed by two decades of surrender, I would trust the imperative and make the move, however emotionally torn I might feel. With today's awareness, I would also understand why I had to leave: Edith was such a dominant force in my life that I had to empower myself to separate from her before she left me by dying. At the time, though, all I could do was balance guilt and responsibility against a certainty that I neither understood nor dared communicate, while gathering whatever scraps of logic I could to support my case.

First, I called my editor at *The Chronicle* to ask whether I could stay on were I to be based in Toronto. His reply was more than I could have hoped for: "We now need someone to cover the whole country. Would you like to be our Canadian correspondent instead?" My monthly retainer would be increased accordingly.

So far, so good.

Next, I made a surreptitious visit to Edith's oncologist. "I know this isn't a fair question," I began awkwardly, "but how long does my mother have?" If he were to answer, "Oh, years," I could leave without guilt. If he were to reveal that her time was short, I could choose to wait Edith out and delay the move.

Dr. Frank's reply was, well, frank...and wise. However, it failed to offer me the guilt-free certainty I was seeking. "I can give you a statistic, but that wouldn't mean anything. Cancer patients in your mother's situation can live five weeks, five months or five years. Or longer." He paused and tented his fingers. "You have to do what's right for you. You have to live *your* life, not your mother's."

He was right. In the next days, I confirmed my move with *The Chronicle* and broke the news to my mother, who was sad but stoic. Two months later, excited to be embarking on my biggest adventure yet, I was gone.

I didn't stay gone for long. Soon after I had settled into my new apartment, I began regular pilgrimages back to Montreal, treks that increased in frequency once Edith started spending longer and longer periods in hospital. I loved my mother, but the stress of returning "home" to a dying parent did more than anything else could to transfer my feelings of home from Montreal to Toronto. My chest would tighten when I boarded the eastbound Rapido on Friday, relaxing only once the westbound train chugged out of Montreal's Central Station a few days later.

Generally on those visits, I slept in my old room — itself a peculiar experience in historical revisionism. You know how in the movies, the returning offspring always comes back to a childhood bedroom that has been preserved with museum-like authenticity, complete with trophies, pennants and other adolescent kitsch? Not in my case. A redecorating spree not long after I moved out stripped my room of all memory-triggering nostalgia. It was now Edith's den, filled with her books and pictures. Like so many other occasions in my life, my past had been erased from view.

It was now March 1984. I was packing for another trip to Montreal when my sister called. "You know," she said with disturbing prescience, "maybe it would be smart to pack your suit and anything else you might need for the funeral. Just to keep in Montreal. That way if anything happens on a weekend you're here..." She left the sentence unfinished.

I folded the only suit I had ever owned into my suitcase. I would leave it in Montreal for the inevitable moment that I hoped would never come.

The moment came sooner than either of us could have expected.

Four days later, I stepped into Edith's room at the Jewish General Hospital. She was pale and drawn, her scalp visible through a delicate web of white. I was shocked at how little of her seemed to be left. How could this be the tough, tenacious woman who had borne, raised and protected me? This wraith could have been flattened by the early spring breeze fluttering outside her window. When her brother Henry came by after lunch, he was shaken by what he saw. He didn't say, "She's going to die today." He might as well have. Those were the words I heard.

"No," I argued silently. "Tomorrow. Not today."

I had brought a stack of books to help me pass the time, but I couldn't focus enough to read. All I could do was sit and stare at this ghost of my mother and repeat under my breath, "Tomorrow. Not today."

Edith spoke few words that day. She spent most of it with her eyes closed, sleeping or resting, possibly unaware of my nervous babbling...or of my presence. When I was talked out, I watched her in silence. After a while, I took her hand, leaned in and, with surprising strength, said, "I just want you to know that you have been the best mother anyone ever could have and I love you very much."

I don't know whether she heard me. I hope she did, because Edith did not consider her mothering to have been much more successful than other parts of her life.

A year earlier, before my Toronto move, I had been to the house for our usual routine of dinner and Scrabble. Afterward, we sat quietly on the floor in the darkened living room, waiting for my stepfather, Jack, to get home so he could drive me to the nearest Metro station. By then chemotherapy had thinned Edith's thick hair into baby silk, now its natural white. Her wig, which matched the dark brown coloring she had been applying since the first strands of gray began to show up years earlier, sat pinned to its stand in her bedroom. She no longer wore it around the house. Her pride in her appearance had weakened. Or perhaps she had grudgingly surrendered to the fact that she could no longer control her appearance...or anything else. A sickly yellow light filtered in through the venetian blinds from the street lamp next to our driveway. I can't remember now whether she looked at me or away as she spoke into the silence.

"I've made a lot of poor choices in my life," she said softly. It felt then as though she was referring to both her marriages. Each had been convenient; neither ever seemed to bring her much joy. With stereotypical Jewish-mother guilt, she may also have been holding herself responsible for my homosexuality, Susan's teen rebelliousness and all other perceived deficiencies in our lives — past, present and future.

I don't know when Edith stopped fighting for her life, but it was long before this March day at the Jewish General. It could have been the sudden death of one of her closest friends a few months earlier. It could have been before that, when I left her for Toronto...or earlier still, when, consciously or not, she might have welcomed cancer as a release from those poor choices. That afternoon, death was not something she had any interest in postponing. Soon after Henry and his brother, Isidore, left, Edith began to wheeze and struggle for breath. Nurses and inhalation therapists rushed in with oxygen. Weakened though she was, Edith clawed at the oxygen mask, her eyes wide and pleading. She wanted the mask off.

"It's just to make you comfortable," I managed to say and squeezed her hand. She squeezed back weakly and closed her eyes.

The afternoon passed. First Jack came in, then Susan arrived, anxious and tired, from work. Susan spent a few minutes in the room with Edith, then she and I took the elevator down to the hospital cafeteria for a quick dinner. Thirty minutes and a tepidly mediocre meal later, Susan and I stepped back onto Edith's floor.

Something had changed.

Jack stood outside Edith's room, pale and stooped. The corridor seemed darker, though looking back, it can't have been. I wouldn't have known how to describe energy and vibration back then, but the air itself seemed different — at the same time both somber and peaceful. I know that someone must have told me and Susan that our mother had died moments after we left for the cafeteria. And I know that Susan must have rushed into Edith's room with me. But my only memory has me sitting in the same vigil chair I had occupied all weekend, holding Edith's still warm hand and sobbing. I can't have sat there long, but it seemed like forever.

If Edith's soul had already vacated her body, I am certain now that it had not yet left the room. I didn't believe in souls and spirits in those days, but in revisiting that scene as I write this, I *know* that the limp hand I held was somehow also holding mine, that the Esther she had once more become was waiting to be sure that Susan and I were all right before moving on. She had waited, too, to die — choosing her moment with the same care and precision she had applied to so much of her life. Edith could have died at any time. Instead, she waited until I was in Montreal and on that day, waited until she had seen her daughter. Then she waited until both her children had left the room, either so that we would be spared the trauma of seeing her die or she would be spared the trauma of leaving us.

By that time, I had experienced more death than the average twenty-nine-year-old Canadian: first my paternal grandmother, then my father and, finally, my paternal grandfather. But I had never seen a dead body. Open caskets are rare in the Jewish tradition. The one thing that struck me through my tears was how peaceful she looked. If my father's death had stripped away the strains and anxieties of her twenty-seven-year marriage, leaving her looking younger and more vibrant, her own death dissolved the strains and anxieties of a lifetime. Her physical body was still wraith-like, but for the first time in my memory, it looked free and untroubled.

My mother rarely pressured me to be or do anything other than what I chose to be or do. Yet as courageous as I had allowed myself to be while she was alive — to come out as a gay man, for example, or to quit a secure job for the risks of freelancing or to leave my hometown — all my choices and actions had been colored by how I thought she might respond and had been filtered through her world view. With her gone, all her hopes, fears and expectations for me were gone too. Suddenly, without being conscious of it or of what it meant, I was free. It would take a few more years before I could begin to grow into that freedom, before I could let it unalterably transform me and my world.

Act 2.
Awakenings

To be what you must, you must give up what you are.
YUSUF (CAT STEVENS)

The state of becoming is always a state of change.
FRANK LLOYD WRIGHT

School Days

Given how passionate I am about writing, you might think that I always wanted to be a writer. Nothing could be further from the truth. Thanks to my mother, I grew up loving to read, and books were always an important part of my life. But I hated writing. English was among my least favorite subjects in school (only gym class was worse), and through my first thirty years, I did everything possible to avoid creative pursuits.

Whatever happened in my early childhood to so turn me against self-expression is long forgotten. Looking back, though, I can see that I was destined to be a writer. I can see, too, that my Muse began her cunning, undercover campaign decades before I succumbed to what some have called the "incurable disease of writing." Was my fate already sealed in Grade 1 when my composition "The Monster Snowplow" won such kudos from my teacher that the gold-starred foolscap half-sheet bearing my childish scrawl remained pinned to my playroom wall for months? Or was that just a teaser for a more potent symbol? I doubt that my fourteen-year-old self linked the Hermes nameplate on his first typewriter to the eponymous winged-heeled messenger god. Now, however, it's easy to see the hand of my Muse in that. I even see her hand in whatever it was that crippled my creativity. Without the journey from total shutdown to unconditional surrender, there could have been no *MoonQuest* and no *Voice of the Muse*, and one of the overarching themes of my work would never have been.

Writing wasn't the only area of my life where self-expression was stifled. Shy and introverted, I grew up with few friends and kept largely to myself. By the start of Grade 10 (junior year in the Quebec school system), Gary Friedman, to whose home I had escaped the day my father died, was still my only friend of any consequence.

Then Greg Peterson burst into my life. I didn't know Greg, but I was certainly aware of him. The most charismatic kid in the school, Greg was known to most everyone at Mount Royal High. Those who didn't soon would. In a small school with no history of theatrical productions, Greg charmed the principal into letting him mount a production of the musical comedy *Mame*. And in one of those milestone moments that changes everything, someone convinced me to join the *Mame* chorus and work on publicity for the production.

It's inconceivable to the Mark David I am today that the Mark I was then could have agreed to either, let alone to both. Sing in public? Even as part of a group? I had refused to join Glee Club because I believed I couldn't sing. And publicity? If being in the chorus meant turning my introverted self inside-out, being a public face of the production was in some ways worse. For one thing, I would have to write, even it was only formulaic press releases.

Mame was a sellout success, playing to three nights of standing ovations in March 1970. It was also a personal triumph: For the first time in my life, I was part of an in-crowd and was friends with the most popular boy in school. Even more significant for my Muse, I had dissolved the first bricks in the giant wall that had always blocked my creativity.

My Muse was far from done with me. Nor was Greg. With the school still buzzing from *Mame*, Greg began preparations for the following year's even more ambitious *Hello, Dolly!* This time, I was in charge of the publicity team and my chorus role included a line of dialogue in the biggest production number of the show. Even more surprising, I mustered the courage to audition, unsuccessfully, for one of the male leads.

Hello, Dolly!'s success eclipsed *Mame*'s, with the added drama of a week's postponement when a brutal storm dropped more than two feet of snow on the morning of opening night, shutting much of Montreal through the weekend.

I would be involved in four more of Greg's theater productions over the next few years, mostly as publicist, a role I also assumed for two college musicals and, as a paid freelancer, for a small professional theater company. I had fallen in love with theater and left my insular world behind. And I was writing...sort of.

My high school graduation in 1971 coincided with a radical change in Quebec's education system. Instead of four years of high school leading directly into university, the provincial government had established an intermediate, two-year junior college system, free of tuition. Those whose families could afford it, like Greg and most of my high school clique, went to McGill University's college-equivalent program, which was not free. Only two friends joined me at Vanier, the nearest public college, where stultifying loneliness replaced my exciting, socially active times with *Mame* and *Hello, Dolly!*

The next act of my theater involvement wouldn't play out until after I graduated from Vanier. Meantime, with no idea what I might want to do or be for the rest of my life, I switched majors multiple times during my four Vanier semesters. I also sat through batteries of vocational aptitude tests. One test urged me to become a funeral director; another insisted that my ideal career would be in accounting. No test suggested anything creative. None offered any solutions to my career confusion. In the end, I opted for the business program at Montreal's Sir George Williams University. Not because of any aptitude test; it just seemed the most sensible option for a sensible guy.

I hated it. I hated the narrowly focused program that forbade electives outside the faculty until final year. I hated the drearily shabby Norris Building where most business classes were held. And aptitude tests notwithstanding, I hated accounting. I also hated the Accounting Department, where exams were designed to ensure a high proportion of failures and where failures were posted weeks before the grades themselves went up. I had always loved math, mostly because there was only ever one right answer and, unlike creative writing, there were no dangerous shades of gray that could invite judgment and open me to ridicule. But accounting was different from the math courses I had enjoyed. Or maybe I was different.

A year of the Sir George Faculty of Commerce was all I could stomach. At the end of my second semester, I transferred my academic credits five miles west to Loyola College, where business administration carried a more liberal-arts spin. It was also where Greg, bunches of new artsy friends and my Muse were waiting for me. Freed from the Sir George restriction on electives, I indulged my real interests with courses in English drama, stage design and stage lighting, and I began to consider marrying my business and theater pursuits with a career in theater administration — the perfect way to satisfy my artistic inclinations without forcing me to be artistic.

My Muse had other ideas. Anything that might sideline rather than foster my creativity would itself have to be sidelined. Instead of transferring to Toronto's Ryerson Polytechnical Institute, then home to the only undergraduate arts administration program in the country, I completed my business degree and graduated — not from Sir George and not from Loyola but in a sense from both: from Concordia University, the fruit of an awkward, government-mandated merger between the two institutions.

Writing was still on the agenda, as were Concordia and Toronto, even if I didn't yet know it.

A Writer's Journey

IN 1975 TOMMY Schnurmacher was an ambitious promoter then operating at the fringes of Montreal's English-language entertainment scene. I must have met him during one of my theater-publicity gigs and I must have impressed him, because a few months before I graduated from Concordia, he offered me a job in his just-launched entertainment-oriented PR firm, Momentum Media. Not much of a corporate type despite my business education, I leapt at the opportunity to avoid the suit-and-tie crowd and to mingle instead with the artistic set.

The nineteenth-century walk-up on Rue de la Montagne that housed Tommy's funky, top-floor office suite stood near the edge of what had, one hundred years earlier, been known as Montreal's Golden Square Mile, home to the Scots robber barons who had then formed the city's wealthy elite. By the seventies, the stately sandstone homes on that downtown stretch of de la Montagne had become one of Montreal's restaurant rows. It was an unfashionable office at a fashionable address.

To the delight of my Muse, I spent most of my time at Momentum Media writing, even if it was only press material for a client list of small-time performers and artists, most of whom faded into obscurity long ago. Not so Tommy, who became a top-rated Montreal radio personality. Although I was laid off after less than a year when Momentum Media failed to muster the momentum to support my salary, three events still stand out for me from that brief period. The first, a personal thrill, was meeting cabaret singer Jane Olivor, booked into a client's Avenue du Parc nightclub as part of her debut-album tour. The second was befriending office receptionist Tammy Silny; eighteen years later, Tammy would play a pivotal role in my unexpected move to Nova Scotia. The third, undoubtedly orchestrated by my Muse, was the noncredit news-writing course I took at Concordia.

Why would someone with no interest in a writing career sign up for a journalism class? I must have seen it as a potential boost to my PR aspirations and, at the same time, no threat to my still-active phobia around creativity. It helped that instructor George Mitchell, the insightful, southern-drawling managing editor of *The Montreal Star*, presented news-writing as a formula only slightly more complex than the one I had easily mastered for press releases. From my Muse's perspective, the personable Mitchell was also an influential contact. His reference would help me secure my next job, one that would involve even more writing. And his position at what was then Montreal's premier English-language daily would help launch my freelance writing career.

It took five months of unemployment before George Mitchell's reference had its intended effect. Meantime, against a backdrop of Montreal's Olympic summer, my only writing involved job applications and my only sport revolved around pinching pennies in order to be able to survive on unemployment insurance.

Although I had never been much of a sport-spectator and although the years of municipal politicking leading up to the opening ceremonies were as thrillingly dramatic as any Olympic match, it was still depressing to miss Montreal's biggest party since the Expo '67 world's fair. More depressing still was my daily walk past The Word. Fewer than a hundred steps from the front door of my 1920s apartment building, the year-old second-hand bookstore was already a fixture in McGill University's student-ghetto neighborhood. It was certainly a fixture for me. From the moment I realized that it wasn't a Christian bookstore, I was in there daily — buying, buying, buying...until bookcases became my primary furnishings and Adrian King-Edwards, The Word's rumpled, long-bearded owner, became my willing accomplice and enabler. Putting my book addiction on hold for five months was among the biggest challenges of unemployment.

The biggest challenge, of course, was lack of work. Although I mailed scores of unsolicited applications to public relations directors across the city, most ignored me. One of the rare replies came from Stirling Dorrance, advancement director at my alma mater. "Nothing right now," he wrote. "Stay in touch."

I did. Multiple times. And one October afternoon, when leaves throughout the city had already turned gold and scarlet, Dorrance dispatched me to Bishop Court, the turn-of-the-century luxury apartment building that had been renovated to house Concordia's top administrators. Joel McCormick, the university's iconoclastic information director, barely glanced at my resume when I walked into his office. Instead, he perused Mitchell's letter and promptly assigned me three test articles for the school's independent-minded *F.Y.I.* house organ. With the recent, unexpected resignation of Loyola's sole information officer, Concordia's messy merger politics demanded an immediate replacement. If my articles passed muster, I might have a job.

Without even knowing what *F.Y.I.* stood for, I called the relevant faculty members, wheedled my way into instant interviews and thanks to Mitchell's course, produced all three pieces in time to meet Joel's impossible deadline. Joel read them through, grunted grumpily, made some scratches on the page, passed them to *F.Y.I.*'s editor, grunted again and hired me. Suddenly, I was a staff writer and information assistant. Housed in an elegant Loyola office with my boss five miles away at Sir George, I had more autonomy than anyone else in the department.

With the experience gained on *F.Y.I.* and its *Thursday Report* successor, I felt confident enough to offer my first freelance article to *The Montreal Star*. I had already converted my passion for local history into a vast personal library of histories, pictorials, architectural companions and nineteenth-century guidebooks, thanks to Adrian at The Word. Drawing on those sources, I wrote a short piece on a little-known Golden Square Mile park, which *The Star* published in its weekly *Scene* magazine. To friends and family, Percy Walters Park became "Mark's Park," and I was officially a freelance writer.

My Muse was pleased. I wrote several more historical pieces for *Montreal Scene* and even pitched a related book idea to a local publisher. My proposal languished on an editor's desk, then died. Soon after, *The Star* also perished, victim of a bitter pressmen's strike.

If *The Montreal Star* launched my freelance career, it was my first feature for *Performing Arts in Canada* magazine that revolutionized my self-image as a writer.

Back at Mount Royal High School, Faith Silver had been my freshman English, history and homeroom teacher. A spritely, red-headed presence with a passion for her students, she and I developed an early bond when we discovered that her cousin was my dentist. The bond deepened when she was named staff advisor for our *Mame* and *Hello, Dolly!* productions. It matured into a friendship after I graduated. When a year later she moved to Ottawa, I would occasionally take a day trip up to see her. On this particular visit, I stepped off the Voyageur bus clutching the copy of *Performing Arts* that contained my inaugural feature, a piece on Montreal's historic La Poudrière playhouse that blended my two passions: theater and local history.

"I always knew you were a good writer," Faith said a short while later when she handed me back the magazine. I had arrived in time for lunch and she read my article while we were waiting to be served.

Even as I smiled and thanked her, a silent voice shrieked: "Why did you never tell me that when you were my English teacher?" Maybe Faith had told me and I had blocked it out. Maybe she hadn't. Regardless, a decade later I could finally accept that I was a writer. A *good* writer.

Not a creative writer, of course. I wasn't ready for that. Not yet.

With the success of my first article, I became a regular *Performing Arts* contributor and, ultimately, a contributing editor. Of the dozen or so pieces that I wrote, one still stands out above the rest — not only for its subject but because the way I approached it offered the first hint that I might be expanding into more expressive kinds of writing.

Norma Springford was the diminutive dynamo who had not only founded the Sir George Williams University theater department but had been a major presence in Montreal's English-language theater community in the 1940s and 1950s. Strong-willed, determined and with little patience for fools, Norma welcomed me into her world when I claimed Concordia's theater program as my own, at least as far as the public relations office was concerned.

Neither she nor my *Performing Arts* editor was enthusiastic when I proposed a Springford profile. But I finally wore them both down and the result was, I believe, my finest writing of that period. While I may have been a good writer back then, what I really was was a good reporter, allowing little more than facts, color and, in the case of my book and theater reviews, dispassionate opinion into my articles. With this piece, however, I allowed myself to inject my real affection for Norma and some measure of our personal relationship into my writing. It would take several years before I could fully free my soul into my writing and my heart onto the page. With my Springford profile, I took a tentative step in that direction.

By the end of 1978, Concordia had a new public relations director, David Allnutt. Only six years older than me, the handsome, curly-haired wunderkind had already served as executive assistant to the previous Quebec premier and chief of staff to three of his senior cabinet ministers. He arrived with a mandate to professionalize our reactive information office into a proactive PR department that would capitalize on his government connections. It wasn't long before Allnutt consolidated his new operation by transferring me from Loyola to the main downtown office. Soon after, he promoted me to editor of *The Thursday Report* and, later, to assistant public relations director.

Like many of my pursuits over the years, including writing, I launched into my editing career with minimal knowledge and no training. I knew nothing about editing, layout or design. I even suggested to David that he look elsewhere. He ignored my reservations, urging me to jump in and learn along the way — a valuable lesson that I have turned to many times since.

Today, as I key this into my laptop, it's hard to remember those precomputer days. We typed (and retyped) our articles on IBM Selectrics. The typesetting shop produced strips of copy, which I proofed, hot-waxed and tediously and meticulously laid out on flats according to my rough paper-and-pencil design. From there, the printer created photo plates, and twelve hours later a truck delivered bundles of *Thursday Report*s to campus.

Editing a weekly for one of Canada's largest universities was like being in charge of the newspaper for a small town, with all its dimension, diversity and ego...and with its long hours and poor pay. What made it fun was that *The Thursday Report* was then a house organ like no other. In some strange holdover from the sixties, we had a level of editorial freedom that my colleagues at other colleges envied. For example, when I refused to write an article supporting the university's controversial desire to tear down a historic building, David didn't argue. Instead, he asked me to cover an open meeting on the subject — honestly and objectively.

While I loved the job, it also introduced me to what my mother called my "nervous stomach." There were few nights when I didn't bring work home with me...and didn't wash it down with a Maalox cocktail. Still, job pressures didn't spark my resignation. My success, coupled with David's plans for me and the office, did.

It was a fall afternoon in 1980. Mount Royal's oaks and maples had already burst into fiery display and a chill had begun to cut into Montreal's balmy Indian summer. Gripping his ever-present cup of coffee, David motioned me to follow him into his office. Bishop Court had already begun to empty out.

"Close the door," he said furtively.

David's windowless burrow crackled with electricity, as though its heavy wooden beams anticipated the great revelation that was about to unfold. David didn't smile as he sat me down and settled in behind his desk. But his eyes were bright with excitement.

"I have a plan," he announced, "and you're part of it." He grinned. "A big part."

I edged forward. My jaw tensed. I fidgeted.

"I want to expand this office from a public relations department to a public *affairs* department that would encompass PR, government relations...and much more." David leaned forward, an aura of empire-building surrounding him. "I want you to take over as PR director. You would still report to me, but you would be in charge of all this." He indicated the warren of offices and alcoves that was now his realm alone. "I have it all worked out, but I want you on board before I present it to the Rector."

David continued talking — about the intricacies of his plan and his strategy for getting it approved. I heard only the occasional word. My deafness wasn't daydreaming excitement. It was anxious foreboding. My nervous stomach pinched, and I wondered if I had any Maalox in my desk drawer.

I had no insightful inner life in those days. Whatever guidance system operated within me kept a low profile. A few years later, it would urge me to move to Toronto. This October day, it flashed an alarming array of warning lights at me. I knew I should have been excited. This was an unparalleled opportunity for advancement. Sure, the university was struggling against a regime of funding cuts that had inflated workloads and deflated salary expectations. That was just an argument in favor of David's ideas. Montreal's second-string English-language university needed better relations with a French-language government committed to pulling Quebec out of Canada, a government that was the source of most of the institution's budget. Allnutt, with his influential contacts in the provincial capital, was well-placed to spearhead that transformation.

And yet...

And yet without knowing why, I knew this was the last thing I wanted.

As the days passed, I tried to be as equivocal with David as I could be. Meantime, I edged closer and closer to resigning. The only way I could describe it to friends was that I felt as though my career was being hijacked, as though it was pulling me in a wrong direction. It felt illogical, ridiculous...even stupid, especially as I couldn't identify a "right" direction. At the same time, I was unable to shake the feeling that accepting David's offer would be worst mistake of my life.

A few weeks later I quit. I would freelance until I could figure out my next step. Meantime, I convinced David to let me edit *The Thursday Report* on contract for the rest of the academic year and I became Quebec correspondent for *The Chronicle of Higher Education*. My Muse had turned me into a full-time writer.

Writing and Spirit

CAREN PUMMELL was the soft-spoken, auburn-haired associate editor of *Ontario Living*, a monthly lifestyles magazine housed in an undistinguished tower in Toronto's uptown Yonge-Eglinton neighborhood. I had been working at the magazine several months as an almost-full-time freelance editor when Caren pulled me aside one day.

"I've just taken this amazing creative writing workshop at the University of Toronto," she gushed. Caren didn't gush. "You've *got* to take it." Caren *never* pushed.

This time she did. More than likely, she was unknowingly channeling my Muse.

"Let me explain about me and creative writing classes," I said edgily. "I don't take them." I avoided them because my caricatured view was that after you wrote, you rose to read what you wrote, everyone ripped you and your work to shreds, and you slunk back into your seat in humiliation.

"No," Caren insisted. "Personal Creativity and Writing isn't at all like that."

I was skeptical, but Caren would not let up. At every opportunity through the day she insisted that PC&W was beyond amazing and that its instructor, Carole Leckner, would change my life.

She would soon be proven right. On both counts.

The Saturday morning of the workshop, I woke tense and irritable. The fifteen-minute walk to the university campus did nothing to ease my anxiety, nor did the stark, utilitarian classroom. Two decades later, I remember only my fear. I remember none of the other participants, and what little I recall of the workshop itself is only because a few years afterward I would be teaching one identical to it.

Although most of my writing to that point consisted of magazine articles, government documents and corporate brochures, I had attempted one short story a few years earlier, based on the dramatic details of my birth. The result was dry and emotionless. I failed, I would later realize, because I hadn't written from the heart of the story; I hadn't written from *my* heart. I hadn't because I couldn't. As I waited uneasily for the workshop to start, the shutters on my emotional and creative life were still bolted shut and my willingness to open them, even a crack, tentative.

Carole was warm and nurturing, with an infectious smile that could melt any heart, even mine…although it would take more than a day's exposure to do it. As Caren predicted, her workshop was the antithesis of all my fears. It was safe, encouraging and inspiring, and it became the foundation for my creative process, as well as for all I would ultimately teach about writing.

Our day began with "clustering," Gabrielle Rico's brilliant brainstorming technique for getting past linear thought. As someone who had been living in his head for so many years, I found clustering frighteningly freeing, a disturbing initiation into a world beyond the mind-centered. Clustering forced my logical, intellectual self to take a back seat to the weirdly inexplicable. Clustering opened me to new thoughts and new associations. Clustering began to pry open my emotional and creative shutters.

Clustering turned me into a poet.

I doubt that I was a much of a poet. But for someone strapped for so long in the straitjacket of structure, poetry freed me to fly, if haltingly, into a place of imagery and metaphor, a place where words exploded onto the page in whatever order they chose, a place so foreign to my writer-editor mind that it could find no way to intervene.

If clustering ignited the process of getting out of my head and into my heart, so key to everything I have lived and taught since, Carole cultivated and supported it — always lovingly, always intuitively, always ready to challenge me on my bullshit.

I had my first experience of all three in our second exercise, a visualization to guide us into writing about an early childhood experience. I wish I could report that I responded to the exercise from the same place of unconditional surrender that I now teach. I wish I could report that I experienced the instant transformation that in future years my students would demonstrate. I can't. My resistance was massive; my fear, nearly insurmountable. My mind rebelled. Surrender was denied. And as I flailed around for something, *anything*, to write, my grade-school "Monster Snowplow" composition popped into my head. I hurriedly scribbled a rehash of it — with all the depth you would expect from a six-year-old. Carole unhesitatingly called me on it. But she did it in a half-joking way that dulled the impact and freed me to say yes when, at the end of the day, she invited us to an ongoing series of follow-up classes.

The classes were sporadic, spread over a year, and took place in Carole's over-cluttered, overheated apartment in a Raglan Avenue high-rise. Through the months, I slowly began to open to the world of my imagination. The poetry continued, and I wrote "Good Jewish Girls Don't," an almost-published short story based on an imagined event in the Rue Saint-Urbain childhood shared by my mother and Sophie. Almost published, because it reached an enthusiastic editor a week after he had shut down his literary magazine.

Early in our work together, Carole and I discovered one of those peculiar, synchronistic links that suggests larger, unseen forces at work. Not only was she also a transplanted Montrealer, but the one time she had called Concordia's PR office, about a student-writing anthology she was producing, I had taken the call. I couldn't then have anticipated the profound impact Carole would one day have on my life.

Some months after our final writing class, Carole called.

"I'm teaching a meditation course next month," she said. "Would you be interested?"

For all the creative openings I had experienced, mostly under Carole's tutelage, I still only trusted what I could see and touch. Meditation was not part of that worldview.

"Uh," I equivocated, searching for a polite way to say no. "Can I think about it and call you back?"

I thought about it lot over the next days...more than I expected to. I didn't want to take a meditation class. I *really* didn't want to. Yet I couldn't bring myself to say no. The same mysterious inner voice that had urged me to quit my job and move to Toronto, that had pushed me into taking Carole's writing workshop, now nudged me to say yes. When I still resisted, the voice crooned a reason my mind could accept: "You know you've been feeling stressed. Take the class. It will help you relax. You need to relax..."

Had I suspected what else the meditation class would open me up to, I might have hurled the phone out the window. But as has happened so often in my life, I was tricked into doing the right thing.

Who did the tricking? I could call it my Muse or God or divine intelligence or higher self. I could call it Spirit or the Universe. I could call it Frank or George or Veronica. The name doesn't matter. Whatever I might call it would be but a manmade label for a spirit and energy that lies beyond my mind's still-limited capacity to encompass. It's an infinite indwelling presence that is simultaneously my wisest aspect and the ineffable universality that is the sum of all that is. Today, in recognizing it to be wiser than I am, I do my best to surrender to it. Unconditionally, if imperfectly. Back then, I was an agnostic leaning toward the atheistic. The only deity I knew was the theoretical Old Testament God of my culturally Jewish but religiously spare upbringing. If my Jewishness had always been important to me, that importance showed up only in historical or ritualistic ways. I lit the Hanukkah candles, for example, and back in Montreal had helped devise a Friday evening *oneg shabbat* service for the gay Jewish group I belonged to. And when a few years before my first class with Carole I had visited the seventeenth-century ghetto synagogues of Venice, I was profoundly moved. Not by God or religion. It was 250 years of continuity and shared culture that had affected me: In those second-story sanctuaries, generations of men had recited the same prayers I had studied and learned for my bar mitzvah.

Reassured that no part of my outlook would be threatened by a course that was all about relaxation, I finally found the courage to call Carole back. I would take her class.

"I'm postponing," she said in what for me was something of an anticlimax. "I'll call you when I reschedule."

I hung up, not a little relieved. Some part of me already knew that this course would be about more than relaxation, and I was happy to delay the profound life changes that I didn't dare acknowledge were awaiting me.

If Carole's writing classes nudged open the door on my creativity, her meditation classes, finally offered a few months later, yanked it open on my spirituality. I didn't surrender any more easily into the meditative process than I had to the creative process. But once I did, I began to experience depths within myself that I hadn't imagined could exist. My meditations were rich with inspired vision, imagery and insight. Dreams took on new significance as I remembered more of them and delighted in their meaning and symbolism. Still a voracious reader, I devoured book after book on spirituality, Jung and metaphysics. Suddenly, I was experiencing the numinous, trusting the ineffable and awakening to an inner life that threatened to overwhelm my outer one.

On the final evening of the class, Carole pulled me aside as the others were leaving. "How's your writing going?" she asked, already, I suspect, knowing the answer.

"It's not." Apart from "Good Jewish Girls Don't," I had written nothing that wasn't a freelance assignment. My creativity, nudged awake during her writing classes, had fallen back asleep.

For the next year, I worked with Carole one-on-one, often weekly, sometimes multiple times a week. The fiction was that she was my creativity coach. The reality was that she was guiding me into a whole new way of living and being. She was my spiritual mentor, awakening me to parts of myself that had long been waiting to be acknowledged. Once acknowledged, they bulldozed through my life, leaving nothing unexamined and little unchanged.

I journaled. I meditated. I journaled. I clustered and wrote poetry. I journaled some more. I researched George Wior and his life, sharing what I learned with Sophie Katz. My dreams were vivid and evocative, and I recorded and explored each one. Carole and I talked about it all: my mother, my fathers, my sister, my dreams, my writing.

Toward the end of that year, my interest in dreams prompted me to seek out a Jungian therapist. There were several in Toronto, and when I had narrowed my choice down to two, a true Jungian solution presented itself: a dream. In the dream, I'm wandering through a basement corridor with my dog. When I come to a nameplate bearing the initials B.B., I know that I have found the right door and I step inside.

One of the two therapists on my list was Bruce Barnes.

"I Must Teach"

"Would you like to teach a section of Personal Creativity and Writing?" Carole Leckner asked me that question three times during that first year I worked with her. She had already trained two instructors to teach alongside her and was certain that I would make a great third. The first time she asked, I said no. The second time she asked, I said no. The third time, I also wanted to say no. Instead, I asked for time to think about it. Then I had a dream so powerful that I knew I would have to say yes.

The dream takes place during World War I and features a married couple: Beth and her overprotective husband, George. Beth is injured when the jeep they're driving hits a land mine. Now, George sits at her hospital bedside, trying to discourage her from teaching, a pursuit he considers too dangerous.

"I *must* teach," Beth proclaims with incontrovertible certainty and passion.

As the dream fades, I hear the Hebrew synagogue prayer that is sung every Saturday morning when the Torah scroll is held up for the congregation to see before it is returned to the ark. It translates as, "This is the law that Moses placed before the children of Israel: from the mouth of God to the hand of Moses."

I didn't know what it would mean to say yes. I knew only that even though the protective George aspect of me was concerned for my safety, I had no choice. As the Beth part of me put it: I *had to* teach.

If the coaching I had experienced with Carole to that point had been in-depth and intense, what followed was even more so. PC&W was more than a ten-week writing course. It was a profound exercise in letting go control and freeing up creativity and spirituality. It was not only a new way of writing, it was a new way of being. I couldn't just teach the course. I had to grow into some version of its precepts and philosophy. I had to let go of who I had long thought myself to be.

The first of two nightmares of the period spoke to the inner revolution I was undergoing. In it, I'm clinging to the roof-ledge of an early skyscraper, my feet dangling from the high-rise structure. "Let go," a voice repeats over and over, gently but insistently. I peer down at the street far below and grip more tightly still. The voice continues to urge me to let go. I can't do it.

I woke from the dream sweat-soaked and terrified, even as I recognized its significance. I meditated daily back then, sometimes multiple times a day. Carole had not taught us any particular orthodoxy, which I appreciated. Rather, it was all about stillness, breath and allowing ourselves to travel to a deep place within, where we might be greeted by visions, guidance or silence. She also never forced us to sit with our backs unsupported if we preferred a more agreeable stance. After trying out various places and postures, I settled cross-leggedly into the wing chair in my living room. It was comfortable, its forest green color was calming, it supported my back and its "wings" offered the illusion of a womb-like enclosure. It was to the meditative safety of that chair that I brought the scene from my nightmare later that day.

"Let go," the same voice repeated.

Again, I held on, my fingers cramped and in pain.

I repeated the experience twice more in the next days, each time with similar results. The me who was hanging on to this old structure lacked the courage to let go, to trust that in releasing my grip from this old paradigm, I wouldn't plummet to the ground and die. Finally, when I conjured up the scene a third time a few days later, I let go. Had I grown more courageous in the intervening days? No. I let go because the pain of holding on had become unbearable. I fully expected to slam into the pavement. Instead, I floated feather-like into what I could only describe at the time as the arms of God.

Was I ready to release the old and move forward? Not entirely, as my second dream would demonstrate. In it I'm walking out of a multistory parking structure when the uniformed attendant steps out of his booth and bars my way, refusing to let me pass. I shout. He shouts. I shove. He shoves. Once again, I woke up drenched in perspiration. This time, I was more angry than frightened. This time, it took only a single session in the wing chair to reach resolution.

"Why won't you let me pass," I ask the guard, politely this time.

"I'm afraid that if I do, I'll be out of a job," he replies.

"I still need you," I offer reassuringly. "But I need you to act more as a filter than as a gate. I need you to protect me more discerningly."

"I don't know how."

"Are you willing to learn?"

He pauses in thought for a moment then stands aside to let me pass from the dank dark of this structure — this place of parking, of storage, of non-motion — but not before we've shaken hands and hugged.

More than a decade later, I would write an essay taking issue with those who were calling for the "death of the ego." Killing off that parking attendant, that ego-aspect of me that seemed so intent on preventing my forward motion, was my preferred option in the nightmare, and it didn't work. It didn't work because my life's journey is one of integration not disintegration. It's about bringing into community and communion all parts of myself, including the ones that misbehave out of fear. It's about reassuring, retraining and loving even those parts of me that have outgrown the tasks I created for them. It's about moving forward in wholeness. It's about eschewing self-directed violence and embracing all I am, in love. While I couldn't have articulated any of that after I left that parking garage, I felt it deeply.

PC&W's focus might have been on intuitive free-flow, but I was still too controlling to trust my inaugural teaching experience to anything so whimsical. I demanded a script. My Muse would have none of it. I had barely begun plotting my presentation on my laptop when my hands cramped up so painfully that I couldn't type. I laughed grimly at my predicament as I recognized that, just like in my dream, I would have to let go. I would have to trust that when I faced those strangers in that classroom, Carole's training and my inner resources would guide me…perfectly. Intellectually, I had no argument. Emotionally? The twenty-minute walk to the University of Toronto's Larkin Building the September evening of my first class felt like a death march. Success would be as big a death as failure, the death once again of who I had believed myself to be.

I dodged the rush hour traffic on Queen's Park, crossed behind the Faculty of Law and paused on its rear terrace. My heart thumped. My breath raced. Eyes closed, I gripped the stone balustrade and attempted a fast-forward rehearsal of the class. My brain refused to cooperate, broadcasting instead a cacophony of crazed static.

"Breathe," I heard myself say softly through the din. "Slowly."

I slowed my breathe as much as I could, which wasn't a lot, and found that if I stopped trying to anticipate the class, the static would stop. As it did, a trio of encouraging faces formed in my mind's eye: my mother and Sydney and George, my two fathers. All the disharmony of their complicated relationships dissolved in that instant of unconditional support. I would not have to face those students alone. I would make it through the evening. I would do more than that. I would make it through all that teaching this class would open up for me.

I experienced a similar terror some years later, when I was to give an impromptu inspirational talk. That day, no vision of my smiling parents showed up to reassure me. Instead, as I breathed into my panic, I realized that the part of me that was feeling fear would not be the part speaking. It was a revolutionary *aha*, one that freed me to surrender to the all-knowing, eloquent side of me that I trusted to be in tune with my audience. It worked: That evening I gave one of the most powerful, heartfelt and inspiring talks I had ever presented.

The ten weeks of that first PC&W course raced by in a blur of creative flow — mine and my students'. By the final night, I was hooked. How could I have refused to teach? If I had, I would not have witnessed the miraculous transformations that unfolded week after week in front of me. I heard it not only in my students' writing over those ten classes, I saw it in their faces, now softer, and in their body language, now more relaxed. I would also have refused the gift of *my* transformations, equally radical. If tension and an overpowering need to control had crippled my hands while preparing for my first class, by week ten I had relaxed into the same intuitive free-flow I was teaching. It was liberating, exhilarating and a little bit scary. As in my meditative response to my nightmare, I had let go an old, familiar structure. I hadn't hurtled to a painful death. I had floated effortlessly into the arms of my own God-self.

Encouraged by my experiences and by my students' enthusiastic response, I signed up to teach not one but two sections of Carole's class the following semester, spring 1994. I was also scheduled to teach PC&W again in the fall term. I never did. Once again my Muse had other plans.

Act 3. Exodus

One does not discover new lands without first and for an extended time losing sight of all shorelines.
ANDRÉ GIDE

Hebrew Scripture is full of old men in long beards saying to God, "You want me to do what?"
MADELEINE L'ENGLE

Upheavals

IN SPRING 1983, once I knew I would be leaving Montreal, I made several house-hunting forays into Toronto. My focus was downtown's Church Street corridor, which had not yet exploded into today's pulsing Gay Village. Rather, Church was then a semi-quiet, semi-commercial thoroughfare with only a modest gay presence, one block east of the retail bustle of the city's legendary Yonge Street. Many of the streets linking Church and Yonge were narrow and tree-lined, packed with a century's eclectic array of housing styles. I settled into a bright, one-bedroom apartment on one of them. And I do mean "settled." By the time my first PC&W class was over, I had been living at 60 Gloucester Street for over a decade, and an insistent inner voice was urging me to move.

I didn't want to move. I was comfortable in my tenth-floor aerie with its skyline views and with its twenty-foot balcony that I had carpeted and furnished with potted houseplants, potted tomatoes and a full-size kitchen table and chairs. From late spring until early fall, I lived, ate and worked out there. Its location, too, was ideal. I could walk nearly anywhere in the central city and bicycle well beyond. If my destination was too far or involved strenuous hills, the Wellesley subway station was only a few minutes away.

Yet something within me had changed. For a decade, I had thrived on my neighborhood's blend of buzz and community and had coveted my easy access to much of Toronto's vitality. Now that my inner world was expanding, I couldn't bear the outer noise and had less and less patience for the crowds, traffic and grit. Even as I heard the call to move away and recognized it as right, I argued against it. Resistance, however, only delays the inevitable. Soon after, my building's owner slipped a note under my door: All balconies were being reconstructed, which meant that all balconies had to be cleared, indefinitely, while work proceeded. Within days, my compact living room had been transformed into a jumbled jungle and my sanctuary-home had turned into a horror. By the time work was complete, I had surrendered. A few weeks later, swallowing my anxiety over the steep rent increase, I signed a year's lease on the spacious ground-floor unit of a quiet west-end triplex ten minutes from High Park, Toronto's largest green space.

I had lived in my Montreal walk-up for eight years and my downtown Toronto apartment for nearly eleven. Expecting to stay in my new Rowland Street home for at least four, I hired a friend to paint it, installed new blinds throughout and in March 1994 moved in. I couldn't have predicted that within seven months, I would have divested myself of nearly everything I had just moved, would have bought my first car and would have relocated to Nova Scotia, a province that I had never even visited. For the moment, I began to unpack my old life into the new one and, almost immediately, wrenched my back. Badly. So badly, I that could barely walk.

Like my nervous stomach, my lower back has always been a weak link in my physical makeup, occasionally kicking out when I'm under stress. In Eastern traditions, the two chakras, or energy centers, that govern the lower back are the root chakra and the sacral chakra. The root relates to issues of self-identity and basic physical and emotional security. In psychologist Abraham Maslow's hierarchy, it lies at the base of the pyramid, dealing with physiological and safety needs. The sacral chakra governs sexuality, fertility and creativity. An unsettling array of issues represented by both chakras would soon flare up to turn my already-upside-down life inside-out.

Once settled into the tranquil solitude of Rowland Street, I began to view it as a step toward an even quieter life — away from the city and up to the rolling Caledon highlands northwest of Toronto. My objective: country living in five years.

I was sharing this goal with Tammy Silny over the phone one April morning, when she interrupted me. "You're going to think this is crazy," she began in her characteristically self-deprecating way, "but I can actually *see* you living in the country. East of here, somewhere. Near the water. It could be on Lake Ontario... No, it seems more like Maine. Or Nova Scotia."

Tammy would never have described herself as psychic or intuitive, but for the next twenty minutes, she painted a picture, stunning in its detail, of how she saw my life unfolding. More stunning still was how accurate it all seemed. Not in its precision but in its feeling.

Thirty minutes later I was on my bicycle, pedaling west along Annette Street toward the Humber River trail. "Yarmouth," a voice whispered to me on the breeze. "Yarmouth," it repeated through my afternoon ride along a river route not yet awakened to spring greenery. All I knew about Yarmouth was that it was in Nova Scotia.

When I got home I pulled out my atlas and found it: the largest town in southwest Nova Scotia, across the Bay of Fundy from Maine. *Nova Scotia? Maine? Maybe Tammy really is on to something.* "Yarmouth is as good a rural destination as any," I said aloud, shutting my Rand McNally. "Anyhow, I don't have to decide anything yet. It's five years away."

So I thought...

As the weeks passed and I surrendered more and more fully to the idea of moving to Nova Scotia at some future date, I could feel my planned timeline collapsing in on itself. Five years became three years, then two. I didn't hear voices; it was more an intuitive feeling sense, one that often bubbled up into my conscious awareness during my long, meditative walks in High Park.

One May morning, as I ambled along the park's Grenadier Pond watching the ducks and geese stir up the still water, my Nova Scotia departure date shrank again — from eighteen months away to twelve. I collapsed onto the nearest rock, pulled my journal from my backpack and scribbled furiously. What would it be like to leave Toronto? What would it be like to move somewhere I had never been, to someplace more rural and remote than I had ever considered living? My life to that point had been controlled and largely free of risk. Yes, I had moved to Toronto. But I had visited often enough that I knew my way around, and my *Chronicle* opportunity guaranteed me a basic income. But Nova Scotia? In a *year?*

The first thing I would have to do was fly out for a visit. Before I could do that, I would need to learn how to drive. Again.

Driving Ambitions

ALTHOUGH I LEARNED to drive at seventeen and had always renewed my license, I had been behind the wheel of a car only once in the twenty-two years since passing my driving test. High school friends practiced on and ultimately drove their parents' cars. The only car in our household was my stepfather's forest green Chevrolet, and my mother refused to let me ask Jack if I could drive it. So when Maxim Mazumdar tossed me his car keys one day in 1973 and asked me to pick up something for Phoenix Theatre from a downtown supplier, my only driving experience had been a dozen instructional hours and a thirty-minute test.

Mazumdar was the handsome powerhouse whose charisma was even more magnetic than Greg Peterson's, his partner in the fledgling theater company. I should have said no. I didn't, both because I was embarrassed to admit my deficiency and because no one said no to Max. Not because he was pushy and arrogant, though he was, but because his charm, however manipulative, was irresistible, especially to someone as insecure as I was.

The drive downtown in his aging, powder-blue Valiant was uneventful. I parked, picked up the package and, on the way back, found myself crawling along the curb lane of densely trafficked Boulevard Saint-Laurent. A few yards ahead, a parked sedan blocked my forward progress. Too timid to force my way into the next lane, where Montreal's hyper-aggressive drivers jockeyed with alarming intensity, I gently tapped on the brake. I would remain in place until some Moses-like act parted the cars to let me in. Rather, I *intended* to gently tap the brake. Instead, I gently tapped on the gas pedal and accelerated...right into the rear fender of the parked car ahead.

Shit!

Meekly, I squeezed out of the car, trying to save myself and Max's door from being propelled into the next block by the traffic stream. Had I damaged one of the cars? Both of them?

The door of the parked car swung open fearlessly.

Shit!

A stocky, black-haired man in his late thirties exploded onto the street, his mood as dark as his hair.

"What the fuck do you think you're doing?" he shouted over the passing cars. He glared at me, then leaned down to inspect the damage. It was minimal, but I was terrified. I was uninsured. I didn't know where Max kept his registration. I didn't know the status of his insurance. I didn't want this reported.

"It-it's not my car," I stammered.

He leaned into my face and stabbed a finger at his rear fender. "Look at what you've done to my car. Are you crazy?" Then he spun around, searching for a pay phone or, better still, a passing police car.

I stepped back. "Can we— I mean, I'll pay for the damage. But can we—"

"Fucking right you will. Gimme your insurance info."

"Th-that's what I'm trying to tell you. It's not my car. It's a friend's. I don't know where he keeps his stuff." I looked at him pleadingly. "Can we leave insurance out of this? Can I just pay you the cost of fixing it?"

Like a greedy cartoon character who blinks dollar signs, he leered at me piggishly then jotted down my driver's license information. Instead of my home number — I didn't want anyone to know what had happened — I gave him the Student Services number at Loyola. He used it. Frequently. Every few days, he would update me on the rising cost of the repair. Every day, I dreaded stepping into the Student Services office, a home away from home for me and the rest of the campus musical theater crowd. It took me months to pay him off, and by the time he was out of my life, I was so traumatized that I never drove again.

As the years passed, I claimed that cars were irrelevant to my life. Why would I need to drive when I had access to one of the finest public transit systems on the continent? With Atlantic Canada now beckoning, I had no choice but to confront my terror. There would be no public transit in rural Nova Scotia, where walking and cycling would be of limited value. Although I still had a driver's license, I didn't dare use it without a serious refresher course. Shakily, I scanned the Yellow Pages for a school that specialized in adults. I felt too humiliated at thirty-nine to want to be surrounded by teenagers.

My stomach churned as I walked to the High Park subway station a few days later. It continued churning through the train's three miles of clackety rocking to Islington station. From there, on legs that didn't want to walk, I somehow made it the few hundred yards to the school, into the classroom and into my seat. The only face I now remember belonged to an East Indian woman, an immigrant, who looked as terrified as I felt. I don't know why she was scared, but my deeper fear had nothing to do with cars. I feared for my life — for the life that lay ahead and the life I would have to give up to live it. I feared the freedom I yearned for. I feared all the still-unknown and unknowable ways my life would unfold *because* I was free to drive. That freedom to drive would play an unimaginably pivotal role in my life in the years ahead. For now, I made it through the classroom and road instruction, and after a few weekends' practice in a rental car, I was ready to fly to Nova Scotia.

Atlantic Time

As I stepped off my Air Canada jet and into the airport terminal on a late-July afternoon, all I knew was that after a few nights in Halifax, I would drive south to Yarmouth County. Beyond that, all I could do was hope that my two-week Nova Scotia tour would somehow confirm my call to move east.

It did. Unequivocally.

The first sign occurred my second night in Halifax. Down the street from my B&B, a shabby second-run cinema was showing Kenneth Branagh's *Henry V*. Having missed the film when it first played five years earlier and with nothing else to do, I bought a ticket. Toward the end of the movie, when against all odds Henry and his ragtag army defeat the French on St. Crispin's Day, I burst into tears. The scene reminded me that with faith nothing is impossible. Still, to staunch any wavering doubts, I returned the following night. Two viewings convinced me that like Henry's army, I would leave the battlefield of my own fears singing *"non nobis domine,"* and all would be well.

My first stop after Halifax was to be the tiny village of West Pubnico, its Acadian roots still present in a largely French-speaking population. Twenty-five miles southeast of Yarmouth, West Pubnico is one of a collection of Pubnicos clustered around Pubnico Harbour, a small inlet of the Gulf of Maine. I had discovered the area through Dorothy Gilman's memoir, *A New Kind of Country*. Best known for her Mrs. Pollifax mysteries, Gilman had spent several years in the eighties living in East Pubnico. Reading her story convinced me to make Pubnico my destination as well.

Another sign occurred in the parking lot of the West Pubnico Pharmasave on the final Sunday of my trip. I had spent the afternoon thirty miles away, wading through the shallow Atlantic waters of Cape Sable beach, and had so sunburnt the tops of my feet that I could barely stand wearing shoes. I needed some sort of salve...and lots of it. There was only one place in all the Pubnicos to get it: the Pharmasave, open on Sundays for a single hour, from six to seven in the evening.

At 5:45 I pulled into the parking lot and switched on the car radio while I waited for the pharmacy to open. On the air was *Cross Country Checkup*, the Canadian Broadcasting Corporation's national weekly call-in show. The topic? "Giving Everything Up to Follow Your Dream." The featured guest moments after I tuned in? The editor of a local newspaper, who had recently quit her corporate job in Montreal to follow her dream of returning to her Acadian roots in southwest Nova Scotia.

The following morning I drove to the newspaper office, introduced myself to the editor and shared my story. Her Second Street office would be my first shaky stop eleven weeks later when I passed through Yarmouth on my way to my new Pubnico home.

When I returned to Toronto, my anticipated move date was still eleven *months* not weeks away. I couldn't see myself leaving any sooner. After all, I was scheduled to teach a ten-week PC&W class in September. Besides, an upheaval of this magnitude would take time to organize.

Once again, my Muse had other ideas: While the other two sections of the ever-popular class were nearly full, no one had signed up for mine. This was unprecedented. In all the years the university's Continuing Studies department had offered the course, rarely had a scheduled section failed to exceed its minimum registration. Never had it attracted *no* students. What was going on? My first thought was to let the course's fate determine mine: If my section were canceled, I would advance my departure. By next morning, I had changed my mind. I realized that I had spent too much of my life letting external circumstances rule my decisions. This time I would act differently.

What's keeping me in Toronto? Is it just the class? Or is there some other reason to stay in town until spring? If it's just the class, is that reason enough?

By the end of the day, I had canceled my teaching plans and launched my exodus plan. It was simpler than I had expected: Whatever couldn't fit into my new sea-blue Dodge Caravan wasn't coming. And as I would not be returning (I naively saw Nova Scotia as my new permanent home), there would be no Toronto storage unit. In the first of what would be six divestments over the next sixteen years, I sold or gave away most everything I owned, including the forty boxes of books I had moved from Gloucester to Rowland Street. I did it without ever holding a garage sale. Somehow, by telling friends, colleagues, neighbors, students and several used-book dealers that I was selling everything, everything went — so quickly that I had to push my departure date forward by a month or spend all October in an empty flat. My revised plan had me leaving on September 30. Three nights on the road would land me in Nova Scotia on October 3, the morning of my fortieth birthday.

I remember nothing of my childhood birthdays. I don't remember parties, though there must have been some. I don't remember presents, though I know I received them. You would think that I would remember my eighteenth birthday — a landmark in any journey to adulthood. It's a blank. My twenty-first stands out only because that's when I moved into my first apartment. But I don't recall any celebration surrounding it.

The only early birthday it would be impossible for any Jewish boy to forget was my thirteenth — not the day itself, but my bar mitzvah, six weeks later on November 11; ironically, Remembrance Day in Canada. Apart from the blur of wobbly knees and congratulatory hugs from people I barely knew, my clearest memory is of my father watching me intently from his wheelchair, a white-clad orderly at his side. By then, nine months to the day before his death, he was already a full-time resident of the Grace Dart Hospital and this was a rare day away for him.

Perhaps the most significant aspect of that birthday event was the week's Torah portion, the one I had spent months learning in a bearded rabbi's dark study: *Lech L'cha*, the third Sabbath reading of the Jewish year. In it God commands Abram (not yet renamed

Abraham) to *"lech l'cha,"* to "go forth" to a strange land: "The Lord said to Abram, Go forth from your native land and from your father's house to the land that I will show you." At seventy-five, accompanied by his wife, Sara, and nephew Lot, Abraham left all that he knew and followed that higher imperative into unknown territory. I couldn't know at thirteen how fully that call would play out in my life...and on future birthdays, beginning with my fortieth.

After weeks of nonstop, panic-free activity — shedding my possessions and shutting down life as I knew it — I woke up in my New Brunswick bed and breakfast on October 3 to a queasy stomach. Anne Fawcett, whose *Comforts of Home* B&B guide had been my Nova Scotia travel bible during my summer visit and who was now hosting me in her own B&B on my final night's journey, had prepared a generous hot breakfast for this chilly Maritime morning. I barely touched it. I couldn't. Instead, I shoved my overnight things back into my overstuffed Caravan and hit the road. I barely noticed the fiery fall colors along one of New Brunswick's most scenic river drives. I was beyond stressed. I was numb.

I remained numb all the way to the Saint John ferry terminal and halfway across the Bay of Fundy. For the other half of the three-hour sailing, I was mildly nauseous. I wasn't seasick. I was terrified. I sat in the cabin and stared glassy-eyed at the ocean, unwilling to give my fearful mind any space. My fearful mind fought back. Within moments of driving off the *Princess of Acadia* ferry at Digby, I had pulled into a Shore Road picnic area, windows rolled up to keep anyone from hearing my soul-shaking sobs.

What have I done? I've moved a thousand miles from a comfortable home to a place where I know no one. What will I do here? What will I be here? Who will I be here? WHY am I here? WHAT HAVE I DONE?

For fifteen minutes, questions like these fired through me with staccato urgency as, white-knuckled, I gripped the steering wheel. Then, depleted by my tears and with no answers, I started the car and turned onto Highway 101 toward Yarmouth and the Pubnicos.

Whatever it meant, I was home.

Act 4.
Nova Scotia

Lose your mind and come to your senses.
Libra Horoscope, Halifax Chronicle-Herald

Sail away from the safe harbor. Catch the trade winds in your sails.
Explore. Dream. Discover.
Mark Twain

No Rules

It was a blustery November afternoon, barely six weeks after I had settled into my quirky Middle East Pubnico rental. I was thirty-five miles from home, taking a meditative walk along the rocky spit at the tip of the Wedgeport peninsula, open to whatever intuitive guidance might arise. It was a favorite spot, always wild with angry ocean. That afternoon, however, the ocean couldn't match my fury. As I walked, I sensed with increasing clarity and alarm that despite all the synchronicity that had lured me here, isolated Yarmouth County was to be little more than a way station on a road that would ultimately return me to Toronto. In the meantime, I could expect another move within Nova Scotia: to the Wolfville area, 175 miles to the northeast and one-third of the way across the province. I stomped back to my car and raged home, so upset that, compulsive journal-writer though I had become, I refused to chronicle this new awareness.

In a life largely devoid of diversions, journaling was how I spent much of my time in those early weeks. The owner of the well-worn, two-story clapboard house that I rented had moved to a seniors' facility, leaving behind most of her furniture, linens, dishes and pots and pans, but taking with her the television, stereo and radio. I had brought no music or music player from Toronto, only a broken-down clock-radio whose clock had long ago ceased to function and whose sole signal beamed in a single AM station. The owner had left me her upright piano, but it was so badly out of tune that I could never tell whether I hit the right notes or the wrong ones when plonking out a melody.

It was a life lived in retreat. When I wasn't scribbling in my journal, I read, meditated or, trailed by my surly neighbor's skittish white terrier, hiked the old railway right-of-way that hugged Pubnico Harbour. Once a week, I drove into Yarmouth for groceries, paling at Sobeys' winter prices for the vegetables that my then-vegan diet demanded and treating myself to lunch at the only sandwich shop with a vegetarian option. Now and again, I would take a random drive to explore the area. For the most part, I stayed close to home.

One exception occurred soon after I arrived, when I noticed a tiny event listing in the *Yarmouth Vanguard*: Nova Nada, a monastic community of Carmelite hermits in the Nova Scotia interior, was holding an open house. I saw no logical reason to go, especially given its location. If North Kemptville, the nearest town to the monastery, was itself over an hour away on back roads, Nova Nada was farther inland still. In keeping with its hermetic purpose, it was tucked away in a converted hunting lodge, accessed through miles of single-lane, boulder-strewn dirt road.

As always, logic was irrelevant. Some inner imperative kept returning me to the newspaper notice, and early the following Sunday, I car-trekked out to the cluster of wooden cabins that comprised the hermitage. There, I discovered a warm, welcoming community of deeply spiritual monks — both male and female. After Mass, I caught up with Father Tom and told him of the journey that had brought me to Nova Scotia.

"You should come out here for a retreat," he said.

"A retreat?" I retorted silently. "I'm *living* a retreat!"

For the rest of Open Sunday and through the long ride home, I couldn't get Father Tom's voice out of my head. By the time I reached Pubnico, I realized that he was right, even as what he had suggested made no sense. I resisted for a few days, then finally called Sister Susan, the retreats manager, to make inquiries.

"We have no openings until the end of November," she said. "Is that okay?"

I had no plans for that or any other time, and on November 24, having no idea what to expect, I drove back to Nova Nada — only to discover that with Father Tom away for the week, I would be bunking in his cabin.

As an order of hermits, the Nova Nada monks spent most of their week in solitude and personal retreat. They prepared and ate most meals alone in their individual cabins, sharing only two dinners each week in community — a rule that was expanded to three during my stay to accommodate US Thanksgiving. Most of the monks were American and had come to Nova Scotia from Nada, the Spiritual Life Institute's original hermitage in Crestone, Colorado. One full day every week was also passed in silence, with verbal interaction restricted to emergencies. Even Mass had an isolationist aspect to it, in keeping with both the order's purpose and one of the first lessons this retreat was to teach me.

For the Mass on Open Sunday, we visitors had experienced traditional church seating. That was not what I faced when Brother Brendan, my spiritual advisor for the retreat, guided me to my assigned, front-row pew in the rustic chapel. Retreatants, like our monk hosts, worshiped from individual, self-contained seats with high backs and blindered sides to ensure direct communion with God and to eliminate all human distraction. For anyone raised Catholic, that posed no problem. As a Jew with minimal Mass experience, I had been counting on visual cues to show me when to stand, sit and kneel. Here, I would have to make my own rules and find my own way, regardless of established convention.

I had spent much of my life trying to fit in, determined to melt into the crowd. That I had rarely succeeded never diluted my desire to avoid notice. Even in the midst of the uniformity of that *Hello, Dolly!* chorus two decades earlier, I had managed to call attention to myself: During one night's performance, while all my fellow Harmonia Gardens cooks and waiters knelt in tribute to Dolly, I mistakenly leapt to my feet. It would be several years after Nova Nada before I would formulate my first "rule" of living and writing, the one I would offer up at all my writing workshops and would include in *The Voice of the Muse: Answering the Call to Write*. But it had its genesis at Nova Nada — "There are no rules: There is no right way. There is no wrong way. There is only your way."

If my experience with Mass offered me a powerful lesson in following my own inner guidance, my first night in Father Tom's cabin offered me a more mundane challenge. The cabins were all heated by wood stove, an effective method for half the night. Then the cabin would grow increasingly frigid in approaching winter's subzero temperatures, unless I climbed down from the loft to rekindle the fire. Those same temperatures made middle-of-the-night pit stops less than comfortable: Father Tom's cabin had no indoor toilet, just an outhouse fifty yards from the front door. I quickly discovered that if I kept the fire alive, the cabin would remain warm enough to keep my bladder happy, which meant that I could stay inside for most of the night.

My days at Nova Nada were not much different from my days in Pubnico, at least on the surface. I prepared simple vegetarian meals in my cabin, went for long walks on the property, meditated frequently, journaled often and read voraciously, discovering May Sarton and Henri Nouwen and rediscovering Madeleine L'Engle and J.R.R. Tolkien in the monastery library. If no dramatic insights rocked my consciousness, this intensifying of my retreat was working furiously at deeper levels.

It snowed early on December 1, the morning I left Nova Nada. It was the first snow of the season and a sprinkling that made the drive out even more treacherous than the drive in had been. I had not wanted to leave and asked what might be involved in joining the order as a monk. I had felt safer at Nova Nada than I had ever felt, cocooned from the very world that I knew would soon urge me back to Toronto. Even as Brother Brendan and I discussed my options that final morning, I knew that I couldn't stay. If I did, I would be running away — from the world, from a passion I couldn't yet articulate and from a destiny I could not yet touch. When I pulled back into my driveway a few hours later, I knew I that I would never go back.

Birth of a Book

MUCH OF MY JOURNALING over the years has been a stream-of-consciousness free-flow, similar to the Muse Stream technique I encourage in *The Voice of the Muse* and in my writing workshops. Rather than a diary-like reflection on the day's events, it has been a way to get past the limiting thoughts of my mind and enter into that inner place of infinite wisdom where powerful stories and unexpected insights arise. One of those insights showed up in my journal within days of my return from Nova Nada as I found myself writing, "It's time to stop journaling."

Time to stop journaling?

My journal had been my best and only friend through my first two months in Nova Scotia. The thought of letting it go terrified me. I may not have been using the word "surrender" yet, but I was committed to the concept. I would do my best to follow my highest inspiration, however inscrutable. That day, I set my journal aside. I would record no emotions, experiences, dreams or meditations. Nor would I seek guidance from the blank page. Instead, bundled up against the wintry bluster off Pubnico Harbour, I walked and walked and walked. When I wasn't walking, I curled up in a chair and read or meditated. I was bored and with no writing outlet, tense.

Nine months earlier, my moving boxes still stacked against the walls of my Rowland Street flat, I had hosted a writing workshop in my living room. Present were the six PC&W students who had asked to continue with me in a series of private classes. That morning, I had devised an exercise based on Courtney Davis's *Celtic Tarot*. The deck had so seduced me a few days earlier in Toronto's Omega Centre bookstore that I couldn't not buy it, even as I failed to understand the impulse. Now I did. I would have each student draw, closed-eyed, one of the major arcana cards. Then with their eyes open to the chosen card, I would lead them through a guided visualization into writing.

I rarely write during a workshop that I'm facilitating. Instead, I watch the participants, hold space for them and remain available to them. This March 28 class would be different. Once the six women were engrossed in their writing, some inner imperative insisted that I also pick a card. I reached into the deck and pulled the Chariot. Without full awareness of what I was doing, I then picked up my pen, pulled my yellow-paged notepad toward me and began to write. What emerged, after a rambling preamble, was the tale of an odd-looking man in an odd-looking coach. Pulling the coach were horses as oddly colored as those on the tarot card. That scene would become the opening of the first draft of a novel I knew nothing about.

Next morning I picked up the story where I had left off, and most mornings for the next few months, I continued writing. It was a challenge to my controlling self, who bridled at the journey into the unknown that each word represented. So stressful was the process that after a few days I forced myself to write in bed before getting up. I figured that if writing was the first thing I did, I wouldn't spend the rest of my day trying to avoid it. I also wrote longhand. It wasn't that I believed handwriting to be superior. Rather, years of freelance writing — crafting other people's stories to other people's deadlines — had forged an uneasy association with desks and keyboards. It was easier for me to be creative as far as possible from my computer. My penmanship being as poor as it was, though, I resolved to type up each day's output as I went along.

By the time I left for my exploratory trip to Nova Scotia, I had written a hundred pages of this still-untitled fantasy tale. When I returned to Toronto two weeks later, my focus had shifted from the story I was writing to the story I was living and to the upheaval being stirred up by my accelerating cross-country move.

It was now mid-December. I had not opened my journal for a week, and although I went to bed earlier and earlier, my days felt endlessly long. One afternoon after I returned from my walk, I had a sudden urge to dig out my fantasy manuscript, buried as deeply in a box as it had been from my thoughts. I dusted it off and placed it on a corner of my kitchen table. I didn't dare open it. It sat next to me through a dinner, a breakfast and a lunch. It sat there, both seductively and accusingly, daring me to pick it up and read it. A dozen times through those twenty-four hours, I reached for the stack of pages then pulled my hand back. I was afraid to touch it, afraid that the manuscript wasn't any good, afraid that I had outgrown it and would have to abandon it.

After lunch that second day, I gingerly carried it into the living room. Although I was certain it would be unreadable, I set a pen and notepad next to me...just in case it wasn't. Two hours later, barely aware of what I was doing, I picked up pad and pen and began to write, continuing as effortlessly as though I had stopped for five minutes not five months. What I realized as I dove back into the story was that I hadn't outgrown it. Rather, it had been so far ahead of me that I had needed those five months of life experience in order to be able to catch up with it and carry on. Three months and three hundred additional pages later, the first draft was finished — a year to the day after the Toronto class that had birthed it. And it finally had a title: *The MoonQuest*.

Home, Sweet Homes

NOT LONG AFTER I returned to *The MoonQuest* on that wintry Pubnico afternoon, I knew with the same inner knowingness that had guided me to Nova Scotia that it was time to move on. Not to Toronto, or even to Wolfville. Not yet. What was clear was that I needed to stay in southwest Nova Scotia for the present. What was also clear was that my next rental needed to be unfurnished.

Unfurnished? How?

I had no furniture...no household goods at all beyond the few I had picked up at the Yarmouth Zeller's to fill in the odd gaps in my kitchen. Nor could I furnish a house from scratch. I had resigned from *The Chronicle of Higher Education* before moving to Rowland Street and had given up my lucrative contract work for the Ontario government when I left Toronto. I had no income, only savings.

"Don't worry," my inner voice replied, in a refrain that would repeat, unaltered, over the years.

I did worry, but I began house-hunting anyhow. I quickly narrowed my search to Tusket, some twenty miles nearer to Yarmouth, only because when a friend mentioned the village, something about it felt right. What didn't feel right was the first area house I inquired about: a two-story, three-bedroom cottage in nearby Amirault's Hill. The house was electrically heated, a deal-breaker as far as I was concerned.

"The house has a Kemac stove," the owner offered, trying to reassure me.

Not knowing what a Kemac stove was, I wasn't reassured. Instead, I determined that it would be prohibitively expensive to heat a house that size through an Atlantic Canada winter and discarded the owner's information, along with the address of the rental.

Two days later my phone rang. "It's John in Tusket. From the house in Amirault's Hill. We spoke the other day. When do you want to come out to see it?" I had never given John my telephone number, only my name and town. He had found me in the phone book.

Nothing about the white clapboard house near the end of Chemin des Gasson appealed to me. It wasn't quaint. Its surroundings weren't picturesque. Unlike my Pubnico house overlooking sapphire Pubnico Harbour, it was inland, with neither ocean access nor views. The nearest water was an unscenic tidal marsh a short walk away. Even so, I knew it was the right house, not only because it had chased after me and not only because Gasson was similar to Gerson. I just knew it. I hated that it was the right house, but it was. I signed a three-month lease.

The only good news was the Kemac stove, which I discovered to be a wood-and-oil-burning cookstove that dominated the spacious kitchen and heated the only parts of the house I ultimately used: the kitchen and the living room, which I converted into an all-purpose space. I closed off the rest of the house.

As for furniture, I wouldn't need much but I would need some. I would also need kitchen basics. To my amazement, nearly all the essentials magically started showing up the moment I surrendered to the move. My handful of Yarmouth-area friends eagerly unloaded their excess household goods on me — on the understanding that I would *never* return them. George and Paul donated a massive slab table, a chair and a floor lamp. Margaret threw in a rickety kitchen table and an assortment of mismatched flatware, cookware and utensils. Potters Michael and Frances Morris contributed their unsellable crockery seconds.

But I still needed a bed.

A few days before move-in, I drove over to Yarmouth to look at mattresses. I tried a half dozen at Nelson's furniture store then, indecisive, walked back out onto John Street. I had taken only a few steps when I noticed a sign that I had never seen before: "Hans Bregmann, Naturopath."

Curious, I wandered in. Bregmann's waiting room was deserted, and Helga, his receptionist, was eager to chat. She was Hans's wife, she said, and they and their two young children had just moved to Yarmouth from West Germany. They also happened to have a single mattress they weren't using, she added when I told her the story of my impending move.

"Take it," she said, "for as long as you need."

The Bregmanns invited me to dinner that night and when I left, a single mattress strapped to my roof, I had a fully, if oddly furnished home.

By March, with my first draft of *The MoonQuest* nearly finished, it was time to start thinking about Wolfville. I set the manuscript aside and drove north for a visit.

Wolfville is a picturesque college town in the apple tree country of the eastern Annapolis Valley, about sixty miles northwest of Halifax. Although half the population of Yarmouth, its more central location, along with the dominating presence of Acadia University, has made it one of Nova Scotia's cultural capitals. Knowing no one in the area, I made Acadia's continuing education office one of my first stops. Maybe I could leverage my teaching experience at the University of Toronto into a writing workshop at Acadia.

"We would love to have you," Terry White exclaimed when I had shared my background and philosophy. "Send me a proposal and I'll make sure it gets approved." We chatted some more. "Do you have a place to live here yet?"

I shook my head.

Terry scribbled a name and phone number onto a scrap of paper. "Ron MacInnis," she said. "Call him."

An hour later, I was driving the twelve scenic miles north to Pereau to meet her former landlord.

A few inches shorter than my five-foot-eleven and a few pounds heavier than my one hundred and forty, Ron wore a worn tweedy jacket and sported a graying beard and mustache. He grinned warmly and offered me a tour of the renovated farmhouse he shared with his wife Carol and their two sons.

"There's no front-door key," Ron said as he ushered me in. "Actually, there are no house keys at all. We lost them a long time ago and never bothered replacing them." He also confided that the key to his station wagon never left the ignition. "That way, I always know where it is."

Our final stop was a spacious one-room apartment on the second floor. The moment I saw the wood stove, stepped out onto the tiny balcony overlooking acres of farm- and woodland and felt the embracing energy of the place, I fell in love with it.

"I'll take it!"

Ron smiled apologetically. "I think it's already rented."

My heart sank.

"If anything changes, I'll let you know. Okay?"

"Oh. Okay."

I got back into my car, pulled onto the tree-lined gravel of Hubbard Mountain Road and, downhearted, returned to Amirault's Hill.

A week passed. I woke to a chill, late-March morning, lit the Kemac and cooked myself a pot of oatmeal. Breakfast done, I unplugged my phone, pulled out my *MoonQuest* manuscript and sat, feet up, as close to the stove as possible. Then, Toshar-like, I began to write — not with quill and parchment but with blank paper and pen. Three hours later, I dropped the final period onto the final page of the book's first draft. It was March 28, exactly a year since *The Celtic Tarot*'s Chariot card had launched the story. I sat motionless, stunned by the synchronicity. A few moments later, I rose, threw another log into the stove and plugged the phone back in.

It was already ringing. It was Ron. "Shannon changed her mind. The apartment is yours if you want it."

I arrived at the MacInnis house on a sunny May 1 afternoon, the final stop on a scenic, two-week road trip that had taken me from Nova Scotia's southwest tip up through its rocky Cape Breton highlands — the first of many journeys of transition I would experience in the years ahead. I pulled into the deserted drive, opened the unlocked front door and climbed the worn wooden stairs to my new apartment. It was empty. Ron had promised furniture. There was none, and I had none. I had left all my Tusket hand-me-downs behind. Close to tears, I sat on the front stoop and, not for the first time on this odyssey, wondered what brand of insanity had brought me here.

Gay? No Way!

A FEW WEEKS LATER, the MacInnis clan took off for the weekend, leaving the house in care of Michael Bradley, a bearded eccentric of an author who seemed to spend every waking moment downing tumblers of red wine. By then, of course, Ron had filled my flat with all the comforts of home: kitchen necessaries, a queen mattress and linens, a rocking chair and side table, a dining table and chair, an eclectic collection of lamps, and wood for the stove. Bradley and I sat at the MacInnis kitchen table that Saturday evening and I told him how I had come to find myself under Ron and Carol's roof.

"You're not married?" he asked.

"I'm gay," I replied.

"No way," he slurred.

I didn't pursue it. We moved on to other subjects, but my mind raced back a year...

Early for my appointment with Bruce Barnes, the Jungian therapist, I had wandered around Sir Winston Churchill Park, across St. Clair Avenue West from his basement office. After a time, I found a park bench on the grassed-over reservoir and pulled out my journal. A dream of the time had my Gloucester Street apartment in deconstructive disarray as it underwent radical renovation. Dream symbolism often defines our home as an expression of self. My crosstown and cross-country moves had not yet emerged as possibilities, but I was already feeling the radical renovation of my life. I would feel it even more dramatically moments later, when I set pen to page.

"Everything in your life is now up for reevaluation. *Everything*. That doesn't mean that you have to let anything go. It does mean you have to be open to looking at everything."

"Okay," I agreed silently. "I can do that."

"...Including your sexual orientation."

What!!??

Coming out as a gay man at twenty had been unsettling enough. I was now being urged to reexamine an identity that had defined my adult life?

"I don't think so," I said aloud. I shoved the journal into my backpack, stood up and began to wander through the park.

It's not fair. I don't know how to be anything else, anyone else. How can I stop being gay?

It's not about stopping anything, other than your limited view of yourself and your world.

I've never been with a woman. I never wanted to be.

Are you being honest with yourself. Have you never been attracted to a woman?

I thought back. I'd had one girlfriend during my high school years. We met during *Mame* — we were both in the chorus — and Jill became a "placeholder," someone I liked who could both fill the role of girlfriend and be my prom date. But I never felt any adolescent sexual stirrings around her. What I felt most was confusion, along with gratitude that she seemed to expect nothing from me. Frankly, the locker room before and after gym class held more inchoate sexual interest for me than Jill did. A year or so after Jill and I broke up, I experienced a strange and awkward make-out session with a close woman friend. As with Elizabeth, who would be my only other girlfriend after Jill, that encounter was mostly about me trying to prove my heterosexuality to myself. With Elizabeth, I had also been trying to prove something to Greg Peterson.

It was fall 1973. The leaves on Concordia University's Loyola campus had begun to turn, and orange and crimson patches were spreading through the greenery. Greg and I strolled up West Broadway, the street that formed the campus's western boundary, discussing Phoenix Theatre business. Abruptly, he stopped and turned to me.

"I'm gay," he said.

My eyes widened.

"So are you," he added.

"You don't know what you're talking about," I retorted.

Sure, I knew a handful of gay men at Loyola and through my theater contacts. But I wasn't one of them. Despite a physical attraction to men that had manifested in my life at least as early as TV's *Tarzan* and an emotional attraction that long predated it, I could not see myself as gay. Why would Greg assume I was gay, I asked silently, unless it was to feel better about being gay himself? The part of me that was in denial of my own sexuality was offended. Within weeks, I was chastely dating Elizabeth, a high school girlfriend of Greg's. Greg and I continued to work together over the next year or so, but we were never close again.

"Are you being honest with yourself," my inner voice repeated.

Do you mean Cathy?

A recent editing colleague, Cathy always triggered in me a confusing and uncomfortable attraction every time we met, leading me to wonder, sometimes, just how fixed my orientation was. So there was a precedent, of sorts, for this inner questioning about my sexuality.

Can you be open to possibilities beyond those you can imagine?

That seems to be how I'm living my life. There is hardly anything about it right now that I could have imagined.

Can you be open to one more?

I didn't answer. I climbed the concrete steps to the reservoir and gazed up into the cloud-studded sky, so infinite in its reach.

I guess. Maybe.

As I headed back toward St. Clair and my therapy appointment, I arrived at an inner compromise: I'm attracted to guys, I said, but I'm open, in theory, to whatever other possibilities present themselves. Two years and fourteen hundred miles later, other possibilities would.

Inside "The MoonQuest"

IF I KNEW NOTHING of *The MoonQuest* story I was writing during those early weeks in Toronto, I knew little more once I picked it up again in Nova Scotia. Some days, I didn't know where the next scene would carry me, until it did. Some days, I didn't know where the next word would carry me. Each day's writing involved a constant struggle between mind and heart, between my perceived need to control and the story's insistence that it have its way with me. As stressful as it was, my writing process was also profoundly liberating, freeing me in ways that transcended *The MoonQuest*. Without that unconditional if grudging surrender, I doubt that I would have found the courage to launch many of my own versions of Toshar's journey in the years ahead.

I began my second draft soon after I moved into the MacInnis house. Most mornings, I would install myself in a white Adirondack chair on the front lawn, the typescript of my first draft on one broad arm and my notepad on the other. I wrote longhand, as I had done with the initial draft; composing in the morning, typing at night. This second draft was no less intuitive than the first, although in different ways. At last I knew the story. Unfortunately, I also knew that I would now have to retell it in the first person. And I knew why.

I had only recently returned to Amirault's Hill from Wolfville, my first *MoonQuest* draft not yet complete, when I realized that I would need to alter the book's point of view. The *aha* came in that morning's writing. Instead of the day-to-day continuing of the story that had been my routine since beginning the book, what emerged was an unexpected first-person account, narrated by Toshar as an old man. I knew in that moment that *The MoonQuest* was *my* story, conveniently masked in metaphor and a third-person telling. Convenient, because had I been aware of its autobiographical nature from the outset, I wonder whether I would have been able to write it. Now that I had released the complete narrative onto the page, I had no choice but to continue — now in the first person.

How? If I were to recraft *The MoonQuest* from Toshar's perspective, I would have to cut many scenes, add new ones and subject those that survived to wholesale revision. I had learned editing as an intellectual, left-brain activity far removed from the creative process, but I quickly jettisoned that paradigm. Instead of focusing on mechanics, I treated the story as its own sentient entity. Instead of trying to figure out which scenes to retain and which to cut, I allowed the story to tell me what worked and what didn't, what to fix and what to leave alone. The experience of my first draft had helped me trust in the wisdom of the story. Now I let myself trust that same wisdom to play out through my rewrite. More than a decade later, I would use the identical strategy to adapt *The MoonQuest* book into a screenplay.

Halfway through the summer, Ron rescued two orphaned baby raccoons. He set up a bed for them in a kitchen corner and bottle-fed them as conscientiously as any mother would. As they gained confidence and started to wander around the property, they would often jump up on my lap while I was sitting outside writing. Sometimes, they slept. Other times, they scooched up my arm, kneading and sucking on my skin while making contented nursing sounds. As they sucked and I wrote, the dog of my first *MoonQuest* draft became Nya the k'nrah of my second.

Other elements of my time in Pereau also found their way into the story. Ron's frequently uttered "Oh, my heavenly days" would become the perfect exclamation for the constantly — and comically — distraught Ferryman. And my emotional collapse in Blomidon Provincial Park would become Toshar's.

Blomidon Provincial Park is a stunning fusion of deep woods, frothy beach and crimson cliffs jutting into the Bay of Fundy, twelve miles northeast of Pereau. On my hike through its dense woodlands one summer afternoon, I experienced none of the bloodthirsty insects or malignant tree limbs that Toshar would encounter on his ill-fated forest trek. But I did fall into a sudden despair at least as profound as his. One moment, I was in awe of the park's natural beauty. The next, I didn't know how I could take another step — either on the hiking trail or on the journey that had brought me to Nova Scotia, a journey that would soon return me to Toronto. I stumbled back to the car and drove shakily back to Pereau. The following day, still feeling unsettled, I managed to ease some of my anxiety by transferring it to Toshar.

Act 5.
Toronto Redux

Your only obligation in any lifetime is to be true to yourself.
Richard Bach

I do not listen to the voice of reason; I dance to the song of possibility.
Amie Barnes

Farewell to Nova Scotia

As summer evenings cooled into fall and my second draft of *The MoonQuest* wrote itself to completion, I could feel my time in Nova Scotia drawing to an end. A year earlier, the thought of an ultimate return to Toronto had spiraled me into uncontrollable panic. Now, to my surprise, I welcomed the prospect, even as I didn't know when my exit visa would show up.

It didn't take long.

After my workshop success in June at Acadia, I facilitated two more writing classes in the Wolfville area, then spent late August and September traveling the region to offer three more: up to Cape Breton Island, over to Sackville, New Brunswick for a return visit to Mount Allison University, where I had given a tightly scripted public lecture a few years earlier, and back down to my old Yarmouth-area home.

I had met Jackie Schofield at one of her yoga classes early in my time in Amirault's Hill. Some twenty years my senior, she was more fit and limber than many thirty-year-olds. She was also an aspiring writer and we became fast friends. When, months later from my Pereau home, I mentioned to her that I would be offering writing classes again, she encouraged me to give one at Th'YARC, The Yarmouth Arts Regional Centre. With Jackie's help, the workshop filled up rapidly.

At the end of a creatively full afternoon, one of the women polled her fellow participants. "Would any of you be interested in starting a writing group so we can keep doing what we did here today, but on our own?" A half-dozen hands shot up. The result was Write Away, a group that, still with some of its original members, has grown into an active member of the Yarmouth area's cultural community.

It was October 3, the night of my forty-first birthday and a few weeks after I returned from Yarmouth from my last scheduled writing workshop. The MacInnis house, nearly always buzzing with family activity, was unusually quiet. Alone by choice in my candlelit apartment, I let my rocking chair lull me into a meditative trance. After a few moments, my eyes shot open. The moment had come. It was time to plan my return to the big city.

Birthdays for me have rarely been about crowds and parties. Rather, they have nearly always been about shift and transformation. Shortly before my twenty-first, I came out as a gay man; shortly after, I moved into my own apartment. Just before my thirtieth, I lost my mother's wedding band — a symbolic break from the past and from her influence. I had been wearing it as a memento since her death six months earlier; it slipped off my finger at Stonehenge. A few weeks before my forty-second birthday, I would launch a new life in Sedona; four weeks after my fiftieth, that life would abruptly come to an end.

I had arrived in Nova Scotia on my fortieth birthday. Now, a year later, I knew not only that it was time to leave but that I needed a Toronto roommate — not strictly for financial reasons but because I had never lived with anyone before, other than my family, and I sensed that it was time for that experience.

How would I find a roommate from a thousand miles away? Where would I find someone with similar sensibilities? Even had I not lost touch with most of my Toronto friends, I could think of none who would understand my spiritual journey of surrender.

"Write Dov," an inner voice urged.

Write Dov? Why? I hardly know him.

I had met Sander Dov Freedman a few years earlier at a Toronto gathering of North American gay Jewish groups when we found ourselves side-by-side at the same banquet table. While there was no instant chemistry, there was enough companionable connection for us to exchange addresses and phone numbers. I would run into him every now and again in the year leading up to my departure for Nova Scotia. We always promised to call each other. We never did.

The day I moved into Ron and Carol's, there was letter waiting for me. Originally mailed to my final Toronto address, it had followed four cascading mail-forwarding orders to find me in Pereau. It was from Dov, and it marked the start of a friendship that would grow and deepen in the succeeding years. By early October, though, we had exchanged only a few letters and had never spoken. Contacting Dov about roommates did not seem to make much sense. What about my life did?

"I'm moving back to Toronto," I wrote, "and I'm feeling as though I need to live with someone for the first time in my adult life. If you hear of anything, please call or write me."

Normally, mail between Toronto and rural Nova Scotia would have taken a week. Three days later my phone rang.

"Is this Mark?" a male voice asked.

"Yes."

"Hi, my name is Fred Henderson. I work with Dov. I hear you're looking for a roommate. Me too."

Six weeks and many phone conversations later, I pulled up in front of an anything-but-tony townhouse in Toronto's tony Forest Hill Village. I had given Fred carte blanche to find us a place. This was it.

Once again, I needed no furniture. Fred had a houseful, including a mattress I could use as a bed.

Sight and Scent

Fred had described the house on Thelma Avenue as "original." It was certainly that. Listing so dramatically to the west that it remained standing only by the grace of God (and with the support of its attached, next-door twin), our narrow sliver of a home rested on little but the earthen walls of the skunk-dug tunnels that criss-crossed its underside. We didn't know about the skunk colony when we moved in. It was already winter and although skunks don't hibernate, they are much less active during cold weather. By early spring, however, we came to realize how numerous they were, and where they lived: alarmingly close. I would soon discover just how close.

I was outside one morning, eyes closed, doing yoga stretches in our tiny backyard. Suddenly, I heard a low growl. It was the dog. I opened my eyes, but my glasses were in the house. All I saw, with myopic fuzziness, was a stand-off between Roxy and something black-and-white.

The addition of Roxy to our household a few months earlier had not pleased Fred's two cats, who regularly conspired to torment the naive cocker spaniel. One day, for example, Roxy let Mister Mister chase her up the narrow staircase that led to the second-floor bedrooms. Roxy thought it was a game. It was, but at her expense. Beauregard, the other cat, had tucked himself just out of sight at the upstairs landing. When Roxy reached the top step, Beau swiped at her with his paw, claws mercifully retracted.

Mister Mister was large and black, with white markings, so I assumed that he and Roxy were having it out again, this time in the backyard. Yet something was different about Roxy's stance and sound. I squinted for a better look. It wasn't Mister Mister. It was—

I leapt to my feet and lunged for Roxy. As I scooped her up, the skunk sprayed us both, full force.

A few hours and many skunk-shampoo showers later, I headed downtown for an appointment with my optometrist. It was a damp spring afternoon, one of those days where odors hang motionless in the moisture. They hung motionless on me too when I stepped onto the subway train for my ride to First Canadian Place. Everyone in the subway car smelled it. And in that strange blend of annoyance and curiosity often adopted by crowds, everyone's eyes darted around, seeking out the source of the skunk-stink. Looking to deflect attention from myself, I, of course, joined them.

That afternoon's eye exam carried its own significance on my journey of surrender. A month earlier, I had taken my first class with Elizabeth Abraham, a holistic vision educator who insists that physical vision can improve without surgery. Instead, she prescribes a combination of eye exercises, relaxation techniques and other natural methods. One of her earliest directives was that we remove our glasses, not only in class but through as much of our daily life as we could.

Take off my glasses!? I panicked. For as long as I could remember, reaching for my glasses had been my first act of the morning, and removing them my final ritual before sleep. If my eyes were open, my glasses were on. There were practical reasons for that. The vision in my right eye, my good eye, has been severely myopic since birth. My left eye, on the other hand, is so astigmatic that no prescription can help it. Until Elizabeth's class, I'd had no experience of seeing without glasses.

"Take your glasses off," Elizabeth said, "and focus not on what you can't see but on what you *can* see."

Nothing. I won't be able to see anything. I was wrong.

Next morning I left my glasses off and discovered that I could shave, prepare breakfast and read without benefit of "correction," a word that itself suggests something inherently incorrect about eyesight that isn't twenty/twenty. If going glasses-free within the safe predictability of my home was one thing, stepping outside was another. I felt naked and unprotected in the open-ended outdoors, a world that exaggerated my inability to see beyond the end of my nose. Emotionally, it felt as though I had lost control of my environment and with it my life.

Yet despite my discomfort, I *could* see — more and more as I left my glasses off for longer and longer periods. As I did, I discovered that my glasses, for all they clarified, also concealed much. My vision, for example, wasn't fixed; on some days I could see more clearly, and in some light I could see more clearly still. I learned, too, that my vision had as much to with brain function as with ocular function. In other words, my mind began to fill in many of the gaps in my physical vision, when I relaxed enough to let it. The most surprising revelation shouldn't have been surprising at all, as it matched a spiritual precept I already practiced: The more I focused on what I could see, the more I saw; the more I focused on my lack of vision, the less I saw.

This wasn't just any optometrist whose office I would be polluting with skunk. This was one of the rare Toronto optometrists who, like Elizabeth, believed that people like me were not doomed to a downward spiral of deteriorating vision. Rather, she believed in giving patients' eyes the space to improve, and she gladly wrote prescriptions weaker than twenty/twenty to help with the process. I left with a twenty/forty prescription, the legal minimum for driving.

I continued with Elizabeth's exercises over the next few years and found that with each successive optometric exam, my eyes *did* improve — not dramatically, but enough that I could continue to weaken my prescription with every visit. Then life got in the way. By 1999 I was only rarely doing my eye exercises. By early 2007, when I had my eyes checked for the first time in five years, I had long ago abandoned Elizabeth's vision-improvement recommendations.

"Your eye strain isn't because your glasses are too weak," my LA optometrist pronounced at the end of the exam. "It's because they're too strong."

My eyes had improved? How? Through the previous two years, I had meditated rarely, done little exercise, taken few supplements, eaten too many fast-food meals and spent most of my time either behind the wheel of a car or in front of a computer screen. How could my vision be better?

I sat in my car after the appointment and pondered the question as a rare Southern California rain splattered noisily on my windshield. Could it be that what I *am* trumps what I *do*? Could eye exercises and meditation matter less than the spirit and philosophy that underlies them? If that were true, could a life lived in surrender to the infinite wisdom of an infinite mind produce health benefits equal to more accepted methods? My own life suggested to me that it could: I hadn't been to a doctor in nearly a decade, nor had I suffered anything more than the occasional cold or mild flu. People even told me that I looked younger. I thought back to the "rules" for writing that I had crafted a few years earlier for an early ebook version of *The Voice of the Muse* and wondered whether I could apply them to life. I pulled out my computer, looked up the originals and realized that with minor modifications I could, easily. I adapted them on the spot.

- RULE #1. There are no rules: There is no right way. There is no wrong way. There is only your way...the way that works for you.

- RULE #2. What works today may not work tomorrow, so you might as well live in the present moment.

- RULE #3. Listen to your heart and trust it; it speaks with the voice of God (or whatever you call that divine intelligence or infinite mind we all carry).

- RULE #4. Be vulnerable: Share your pain and your passion. That's what makes you human.

- RULE #5. Treat yourself as you would your child or best friend: with love, compassion and respect.

- RULE #6. Don't live your life according to others' expectations... or according to your own preconceptions. Free yourself to follow the path that is uniquely yours, and surrender to its gifts and surprises.

- RULE #7. It's not how often you meditate, it's whether you live your life as a meditation.

- RULE #8. Giggle. Smile. Dance. Guffaw. Don't take life too seriously. Just as you don't censor your pain (see Rule #4), don't censor your joy.
- RULE #9. It's not how hard you push, it's how fully you surrender.
- RULE #10. Find your passion and embrace it. Passionately.
- RULE #11. It's not about being perfect, it's about being human.
- RULE #12. Empower yourself: This is your life. Don't let anyone else tell you how to live it (or not live it).
- RULE #12½. There are no rules. None. Never.

Was I living these perfectly? Of course not (see Rule #11). But to the best of my imperfect ability in each moment, I was living as authentically as I could, surrendering as unconditionally as I could to the truest path I could envision, honoring my passion with each choice and focusing, as I had done in my early days with Elizabeth Abraham, on what I had, not on what I lacked. If that was keeping me healthy and improving my vision, I was determined to keep at it. Would it continue to work as well for me in the years ahead? Only time would tell.

Voicing the Past, Healing the Present

I WAS ALREADY FEELING the transformative effects of my vision work with Elizabeth. Not only was my outer sight being strengthened, so too was my inner sight. Now with one sense being enhanced, why not work on another as well? That's what I thought when I saw an ad in *Now*, Toronto's alternative weekly, for voice classes. One of my closet desires had always been to be a singer, even though I was shy and self-conscious about my voice — which made my high school audition for a singing role in *Hello, Dolly!* that much more surprising. I would have been even more surprised had I foreseen the unique and unusual way that this aspiration would play out in the years ahead. Meantime, I called on the *Now* ad. That's when I discovered that it wasn't a singing class at all; it was a voice class for actors.

"Not interested," I was about to say. Something stopped me, and before I knew what I was doing or why, I was signing up for what would turn out to be a life-changing experience. I didn't know at the time that instructor David Smukler was one of Canada's top voice coaches. After three courses with him over the next few years, I would understand why.

As our final exercise in that first series, we were assigned a Shakespeare sonnet and asked to memorize and perform it for the class using a Method-like technique. In other words, we were to find our own life and experience in Shakespeare's words and speak it from that place.

Mine was Sonnet 43.
When most I wink, then do mine eyes best see,

For all the day they view things unrespected;
But when I sleep, in dreams they look on thee,
And darkly bright, are bright in dark directed.
Then thou, whose shadow shadows doth make bright,
How would thy shadow's form from happy show
To the clear day with thy much clearer light,
When to unseeing eyes thy shade shines so!
How would, I say, mine eyes be blessed made
By looking on thee in the living day,
When in dead night thy fair imperfect shade
Through heavy sleep on sightless eyes doth stay!
All days are nights to see till I see thee,
And nights bright days when dreams do show thee me.

As I read and reread those centuries-old words of yearning and absence, it did not take me take me long to connect them with my father, whose absence, as Shakespeare put it, had turned all my days into nights. There was only one place, the sonnet suggested, where I could now experience a fully present father: in my dreams, with my eyes closed (winked) to that which was "unrespected." Only there, could my nights once more brighten into days.

Method actors are trained to harvest their emotional life in ways that bring authenticity to their roles. They're also trained to not let that connection interfere with the acting job.

"Feel what you feel," David instructed us, "but those feelings are there to fuel you, not to take over your performance."

They took over mine. Even though my solo rehearsals were as on-the-mark as a non-actor could make them, the moment I opened my mouth in front of the class, the dam broke. It took all the control I could muster to make it through the fourteen lines, let alone speak them without sobbing.

For years, I had claimed emotional detachment from the circumstances surrounding my paternity. Why would I mourn a father I had never experienced? Yet, telling my story through Shakespeare's words brought me close to an emotional truth that until that moment I had never been able to touch. When I signed up for David's class, I hadn't known why I was doing it. It certainly wasn't to learn how to act. By the end of that class, I knew why I was there: to learn how to feel.

I have never been able to identify what shut me down emotionally and creatively as a child. If it was some long-ago word or act, I don't remember it. But what if it wasn't something said, but something left unsaid? Can the absence of a father's loving words be as numbing to a child as the presence of his harsh words? What if my father's absence was a presence so palpable that it absented me from myself? What if in feeling devalued, however unconsciously, by two fathers, I devalued myself so completely that I erased magic and memory from my being?

I didn't make that connection all those years ago in the Actor's Equity rehearsal space where David Smukler then held his Toronto classes. I didn't even make the connection when I began writing this chapter. But every day's writing about the past has brought with it more revelations about the present. And every day's surrender to these pages reminds me that what I'm writing about is now, not then.

Of Dogs and Delusions

As I navigated Toronto's congested streets and freeways for the first time in fourteen months, grateful to have left the blizzards of Atlantic Canada behind, I wondered what my new housemate would look like and how we would get on. All I knew was that, like me, Fred Henderson was a gay man on a spiritual path, that our phone conversations suggested some degree of compatibility and that he came highly recommended by Dov. To fill in the gaps, I fantasized that he would be heart-stoppingly handsome and that some sort of happily-ever-after scenario was about to unfold.

My week at Nova Nada had not been my only monastic experience. From the moment of my conscious spiritual awakening, men and sex had largely receded from my awareness. It wasn't just the repeated call to be open to broader definitions of my sexual orientation. It was that all interest in romantic and sexual expression had dissolved. I won't claim never to have let my eyes linger on an attractive man, but it was a rare occurrence unaccompanied by much in the way of desire. Now that I would be back in Canada's gayest city, a piece of my old gay self returned. I would be sharing a house with a spiritually aware gay man, an unusual combination in those days. Surely, Spirit had conspired to connect us at all levels. Hadn't it?

It hadn't. When Fred strode out from his Wildlands League office to meet me for the first time — solid, white-haired and dressed unconventionally in checked pants and a Peruvian shirt — the hoped-for attraction wasn't there. That didn't stop me. Even though Fred never offered the slightest suggestion that he viewed me as anything but friend and housemate, my fantasy persisted. It took a few months and an overnight guest in Fred's bed to shatter my illusion.

My fantasy symptoms may have disappeared, but my underlying delusion did not. A decade later, when I found myself on an open-ended road odyssey, I would land in every new town wondering whether this was where my endless-seeming journey would at last come to an end. Was this my new home? Was this where I would finally settle and begin a new life? My experience with men had never been much different. Whenever I imagined a glimmer of interest, I would immediately project a fairytale fantasy onto the situation. "Is he the one?" I would ask. Invariably, he wasn't. It would take five more years and a similar situation with another spiritually aware gay housemate before I could recognize and begin to exorcise the pattern.

Today, I can see how romantically mismatched Fred and I would have been. His chronic taciturnity amplified my low self-esteem, and I spent most of our ten months together feeling unappreciated, unnoticed and undervalued. So when I sensed that I was again ready to leave Toronto and move on, little about my time on Thelma tempted me to resist. The only question was, who would keep the dog?

One January evening over dinner, Fred asked, "What would you think about us getting a dog?"

Fred and I may not have been in an intimate relationship, but one of our commitments to each other when we became housemates was that we would act like a family. We not only shared household tasks and expenses, we also split all food costs and ate as many meals together as schedules permitted. He pulled out a notice from the pet supply store around the corner: "10-month-old cocker spaniel needs new home. We hate to give her up. Call Trudy." I agreed to go with him to check it out, even though sharing a dog seemed an odd development for romantically uninvolved housemates.

"When I was a stay-at-home mom, having Roxy here was great," Trudy explained when we got there. "I'm back at work now, and with the kids at school… Well, we just can't look after her properly anymore."

Fred and I stared at the dog. Roxy's stub of a tail throbbed excitedly.

"If you take her," Trudy continued, "there's one condition. Could the kids and I come and walk her now and again?"

Fred was ready to pay his share of Trudy's nominal asking price on the spot. I was hesitant...until Trudy revealed that Roxy's birthday was the same as Fred's. That synchronicity was too much for me to ignore. We bundled the golden ball of furry energy that was Roxy into the car and drove home.

With their common birthday, I expected Roxy to be Fred's dog more than mine. That's not how it worked out. Because Fred was away at work every day and I was largely at home, Roxy bonded more strongly with me. When, that fall, it came time for me to move on from Thelma Avenue, there was no discussion about custody: Fred and I both knew that Roxy would be leaving with me.

Act 6.
On Georgian Bay

The dark night of the soul is a great passage to other illuminations.
JUDY COLLINS

In the depth of winter, I finally learned that within me there lay an invincible summer.
ALBERT CAMUS

Rainbow Connection

It may have been time to for me and Roxy to move on, but where to? All I sensed was that my next location would again be rural. Beyond that I knew nothing. One afternoon, to help me answer the question, I pulled out my Rand McNally atlas, flipped to the Southern Ontario page and meditatively scanned it. What leapt out at me was Lefroy, a tiny, summer-cottagey village fifty miles north of Toronto on Lake Simcoe.

A few days later, I drove up to the area, planning to begin my explorations in Barrie, the region's largest city. As I headed up the 400, the main northbound freeway out of Toronto, the sky darkened and a flash storm struck. By the time I neared Exit 75, about fifteen miles south of Barrie, the rain had stopped and a brilliant rainbow arced across the sky to the northeast. Ignoring my plans, I left the freeway, pointed my car toward the rainbow and zigzagged through a checkerboard of side roads and concession roads until I reached Lake Simcoe. When I looked up to see where I was, I discovered that I had landed on Killarney Beach...in Lefroy.

That was my first sign that I was on the right track. The second came the following Sunday, when I drove back up to Lefroy. This time I brought my bicycle. As I cycled around the quiet streets with their modest homes and vacation cottages, my eyes locked on a simple, sand-brick house. There was nothing unique about it. Like every other house on the street, it had a small garden, a fence and a freestanding mailbox by the gate. Not every mailbox bore the name of its householder. This one did, with gold stick-on letters that spelled out "Gawson."

Often, when a major life change appears on my horizon, even if I don't see it looming, a piece of my history shows up at the same time to remind me where I have come from, what I need to leave behind, what I need to honor from my past, or some combination of the three. Sometimes, it's a pattern of behavior. Sometimes, it's a thing or a place. Sometimes, it's a person.

This time, it was a person. To be more accurate, it was a family.

I grew up at one end of Montreal's single-block Atherton Street, at number 8125. The Laine family lived at the other end, at 8285. I don't remember now how it happened or why, but the Laines became a second family to me — Selma and Barney, their daughters Barbara and Joanne, their hairy keeshond Kiki and their two Siamese cats. While Kiki and Lucky, my cocker-terrier mix, rumbled boisterously in the Laines' fenced-in yard, I just hung around — mostly with Barbara, who was a few years younger — consuming large quantities of sugar-laden tea and butter-soaked challah toast.

At 8285 Atherton, Selma was in charge; Barney was warm but never seemed entirely present. If Barbara and Joanne, a few years her senior, fought — with their parents or with each other — I never saw it. At 8125, with my father by then a permanent resident of the Grace Dart Hospital, my mother was also in charge. There the surface similarities to the Laine family ended. Susan and I had struggled, sometimes physically and violently, since our early years. If our relationship had mellowed somewhat by then, the volcanic intensity of Susan's with Edith more than made up for it. At twelve and thirteen, I probably viewed the Laine household as a healthier, less volatile version of my own. I spent as much time there as possible.

I stayed in touch with the Laines after Barney and Selma sold their business and moved to Toronto. That's how I knew that Joanne had married Mark Gawson. So when I saw "Gawson" on that cottage mailbox that afternoon in Lefroy, something propelled me to the front door. All I expected to do was ask whoever answered whether they were related to Mark and Joanne. I didn't expect Joanne to open the door.

"Oh, my God, it's Mark/Joanne," we exclaimed in unison.

We visited for an hour, reminiscing and catching up, all the while amazed at the coincidence (in Joanne's view) and synchronicity (in mine). It was pleasant and companionable, and it underscored more than much that I had experienced since those nascent awakenings in Carole Leckner's meditation class just how much my old life, perspectives and connections had been stripped of their relevance.

When I was in Ottawa the following month, I looked up Barbara. Joanne had called her from the cottage while I was there and Barbara and I shared a superficially exciting but profoundly disconnected conversation. The disconnect was even more dramatic during our brief Ottawa visit. As close as our lives had once been, they had grown mutually alien. We parted promising to stay in touch. We never did.

I would never judge my life and path as superior to anyone else's. We are all precisely who and where we need to be in each moment. That was as true for Barbara and Joanne as it was for me. Yet whatever had once bound us had come unraveled. And whatever had bound me to those years on Atherton was also falling away.

Lefroy would soon fall away too. A few weeks after my reunion with Joanne, I returned to Lefroy, this time with Dov Freedman. I wanted to look at an apartment I had seen advertised and he needed to visit a nearby landscape-design client. We made a day's outing of it. The Lefroy apartment was perfect: cute, affordable and close to the beach. But there was a no-pets policy, and I had Roxy. Disappointed, I drove Dov to his client's. While they discussed business in the garden, I sat in the living room and pondered my Lefroy experiences. I could continue searching in the area, but something told me that the town had served its purpose. I would need to look elsewhere. At one point, I glanced up and noticed a New Age CD on the mantelpiece. It was *Sedona Suite* and its cover featured a view of the town's signature red-rock cliffs. I hadn't heard of Sedona before that day. I would be living there in just over a year.

At Home in Penetanguishene

With Lefroy no longer an option, I began taking exploratory trips up north to find its replacement. One afternoon, in a postage stamp-size metaphysical bookstore in Penetanguishene, something clicked. I was home.

Penetanguishene (Penetang to locals) is a small community at the southeastern tip of Georgian Bay, a massive Lake Huron inlet that's nearly as large as all of Lake Ontario. Overshadowed by neighboring Midland, only a few miles away but nearly twice its size, Penetang's two landmarks are a historic naval base and a maximum-security mental health facility. I never made it to either, but there were days when I was certain that I was destined for the latter.

At the time, all I knew was that I was feeling called to live in the Penetang area — preferably somewhere rural. I told a local realtor that I was seeking a secluded back-country cottage, perhaps near the water but certainly well out of town...preferably with furniture as, once again, I had none. She sent me to rental after rental but, like Goldilocks exploring the three bears' house, nothing felt "just right." Without realizing it, I was trying to recreate my first Nova Scotia experience: a remote retreat, but on Georgian Bay instead of Pubnico Harbour.

"I have one more," the realtor said, "a granny flat on Champlain Road. It's not quite out-of-town. But it's not right in town either."

"This can't be it," I moaned as Roxy and I pulled into the driveway of a two-story, white-clapboard house fronted by a single-level flat that had once been a country grocery. How could it be? Hardly bucolic, it sat a few hundred yards back from a main road, where cars buzzed by at the ninety-kilometer-an-hour speed limit. Worse, it wasn't furnished.

"We'll find furniture for you," Angela Emery assured me as she showed me the one-bedroom flat. She knelt down to scratch Roxy's belly. "Roxy will love the woods behind the house, and Jeremy will love Roxy."

Jeremy?

Jeremy was Angela and Jim Emery's nine-year-old son, their only child, and not exactly a selling point. I never got along with nine-year-olds when I was one. Why would I get along with one at forty-one? Even as I repeated my silent "this can't be it," I knew that it was. I knew too that there was no point in driving away. Like the house in Amirault's Hill, this one would just chase after me until I relented.

"I'll take it," I sighed.

Roxy and I moved in on my forty-second birthday. The leaves, which had barely begun to turn in Toronto, were already golden this far north. And the air, though still warm, carried the chill promise of what would prove to be my snowiest winter since growing up in Montreal — and my final one in Canada. True to her word, Angela had furnished the flat, in the same spare cast-off style I had been living in since Amirault's Hill: a queen mattress on the floor and a mismatched assortment of tables, chairs, lamps and accessories.

I was barely unpacked when Jeremy knocked on my door. Bright, energetic and mature, he insisted on taking me and Roxy on a tour of the dense woodlands that rose up to a forested ridge behind the house, enthusiastically pointing out all his favorite landmarks. The next afternoon, Jeremy again knocked on my front door. He came by the next day and the day after that. And the day after that. Rare was the day that he didn't — to wrestle with Roxy, to play games on my new computer or to just hang out. Come Christmas, he convinced his father to buy me a small tree, my first, when they were shopping for theirs. He then scavenged ornaments from Angela and stayed to help me decorate.

I tried to resist Jeremy. What did I know about kids? What did I know about entertaining kids? I was the youngest in my immediate family and among the youngest in my extended family. I had never babysat. I had no interest in having kids of my own. I just wanted to be left alone. But Jeremy was relentless. He insinuated his way into my life and into my heart and when, five months later, it came time to leave, he was my most difficult goodbye. Less than a year later, when I had to face my fierce resistance to starting a family of my own, my time with Jeremy was part of what made my ultimate surrender possible.

"Dialogues with the Divine"

MY FIFTH NIGHT IN Penetang, barely asleep for two hours, I awoke to a drenching, dry-mouth sweat and vague dream-memories of violent, meaningless death, betrayal and illusion. The nightmare ended with me journeying through era after era, from Roman times to the civil rights movement of the sixties, while a single hand stabbed everyone around me to death. Through the time-traveling carnage, I kept repeating, mantra-like, "I just want to say something." That line, so emblematic of longstanding blocks to my self-expression, haunted me until I set it down on paper. What emerged from those six words was an "inner dialogue" of such stunning and transformative depth that I knew that I had to keep at it.

I had learned this meditative writing technique from Carole Leckner and had used it often in my journaling. But never before had the words cascaded out of me so passionately, frequently and consistently. Although I had not yet heard of Neale Donald Walsch's still-new *Conversations with God*, my manuscript — by then titled *Dialogues with the Divine* — was taking on a similar form and tone. Reluctant to expose the fear and anxiety that was pouring out of me in so raw a fashion, I didn't want to see it as a book. But the same voice that came through on the page so reassuringly and encouragingly also had its forceful side. It didn't demand that I turn these conversations into a book. It did, however, insist that I stop hiding.

"Walk the earth naked, clothed only in your truth," I wrote one day. "Book or no book is not the issue. Coming out is the issue. Being out in the world with your truth is the issue." This wasn't about coming out as a gay man. I had done that more than a decade earlier with minimal fallout. It was about coming out as frightened, vulnerable and imperfect. It was about coming out as human.

Through five months of dialogues, I uncovered one hidden demon after another. All found their uncensored way onto the page, ultimately distilled into their single essence: Fear. Fear of sexuality. Fear of judgment. Fear of my vision. Fear of my voice. Fear of my power. Fear of the emptiness from which all creation emerges.

Although I had never been overweight and was never a junk-food junkie, I started to grow increasingly conscious of the ways I was using food in unhealthy ways: to fill emotional and spiritual voids, to assuage fears and anxiety...to fill me up so I didn't have to feel. My behavior, I realized through that long Penetang winter, was addictive. With few distractions, a marginal social life and little to occupy myself but my own thoughts and feelings, meals and snacks began to take on obsessive significance.

One January afternoon just after New Year's, I sat down with a book, a pot of herbal tea and a slice of Angela Emery's Christmas stollen. One slice of the rich fruit-and-nut loaf rapidly became two, not savored but bolted down, followed by compulsive fistfuls of trail mix. Hardly a binge. But hardly a healthy response to whatever was festering beneath the surface of my emotional life. Tea, a small sweet and book: It was a ritual I had long treasured...a controlled ritual with unwritten rules — about how much I could eat and drink, about how big the portions and how small the forkfuls.

"I'm out of control," I thought, as I tried, unsuccessfully, to focus on my book. "More to the point, my obsessive-compulsive snacking is in control." Moments later, I set down my book and began to write. "I'm afraid...of the emptiness. I'm afraid it will devour me, destroy me, annihilate me. I'm afraid if I don't stay full, I'll die."

It was hard to trust the response — that the emptiness was a gift, that it was an opportunity to listen to my heart, which could speak only through the stillness that emptiness could offer. "Listen to your heart," I wrote. "Your heart's voice is your divinity. Your heart's voice is your power. Your heart's voice is your light and your healing."

I *had* listened. That listening had brought me powerful gifts... creative gifts...healing gifts. That listening had birthed *The MoonQuest*, had carried me to both Nova Scotia and Penetang.

Now, these dialogues were showing me that I could not move ahead without a deeper listening, one that my fear-based behavior was trying to block.

At first, I replaced my old food rules with new ones, until I realized that rules would always be a way for me to avoid the emptiness rather than surrender into it. Rules would remove moment-to-moment discernment and in so doing, disempower me. "No rules," I wrote. "Just be with the moment. Be in the moment. And trust."

My morning routine during my five months in Penetang was to take Roxy for a long hike in the woods before breakfast. When I was anxious about food, though, I would spend my forty-five minutes outdoors focusing not on the scenery but on what I would eat when I got back. Once I saw how my mind was hijacking what should have been a meditative experience, I developed an exercise to keep me present. Each time I noticed my mind wandering back to my fridge, I turned my attention to my senses. What was I hearing? What was I seeing? What was I smelling? "I hear the birds," I would say out loud. "I see the grain on the tree trunk. I smell the decay of rotting leaves." Or I would take off my glasses and as Elizabeth Abraham had taught, pay attention only to what I could see, and speak that aloud. Some days, the exercise immediately banished my breakfast anxiety. Other days, I had to continue my enforced mantra-mindfulness until I got home.

In the two years that followed, I would shed more and more of my dietary restrictions until one day I dropped the last, the one that had kept me vegan for more than a decade. I was married by then, living on the Big Island of Hawaii with my wife and infant daughter, and we were about to order lunch at the Parker Ranch Grill in Waimea. As I scanned the menu for something edibly vegetarian, an odd force drew my eyes to the *keiki* (kids') menu. As soon as I saw the *keiki* burger, I knew I had to have it. For the first time since the early nineties, not only did I want beef, I craved it. I joked to my wife that Parker Ranch, one of the largest cattle operations in the country, must spray the area around its Waimea headquarters with something that turns everyone into beef-aholics. Regardless, I listened to my body, ordered the kids' burger and with that first delectable bite, ended my vegan regime. I also ended decades of digestive disorders. For years, my unhealthy anxiety around food had produced chronic gas, bloating and heartburn, regardless of how healthy my meals had been. After I relaxed my diet with that *keiki* burger, my attitude toward food also began to relax as I replaced the hard discipline of rules with the soft discipline of discernment. Now, I would ask my body what it required in each moment, rather than making innately flawed blanket assumptions. Now, in yet another area of my life, I would abandon control and trust my inner wisdom to guide me.

Return of "The MoonQuest"

AFTER MY TWO Nova Scotia drafts of *The MoonQuest*, I completed a third while living with Fred in Toronto. Once in Penetang, I was ready to launch into a fourth, but I couldn't get going. It felt as though my Muse was on strike. The linear technique I had used previously — starting at the beginning and rewriting/revising my way through to the end — wasn't working. After weeks of frustration, I remembered a technique that I had taught in my writing workshops, one similar to the "dialogues" that were already writing themselves through me. It involved having a meditative conversation with a character. But who should I "talk" to? With the story now told from Toshar's perspective, I knew enough about him. In rereading the manuscript, though, I realized that Fynda, Yhoshi and Garan, his three companions, were not fully enough drawn. So I sat each one down in turn and asked them to tell me more about themselves.

I did not like what I heard. Fynda shared a dream of being raped repeatedly by her father. Yhoshi told me of the sadistic pillage of his family's village. Garan spoke of how fear had disfigured him. I was horrified, not by the content of these nightmares but by the fact that I — a man of gentle spirit — could be writing such graphic, gruesome, grueling brutality. If every character in *The MoonQuest* was an expression of me, then I was as much Fynda's father as Fynda, as much the marauding King's Men as the innocent villagers. I hated it, but I knew it to be true. Just because I was easygoing and nonviolent did not mean that I lacked a dark side. Far better to be open to it than to repress it. Far better to let it out onto the page than to act it out. Far better to share it than to hide it.

My first sharing would take place, very publicly, a few days later.

The Daily Perk was a downtown Midland cafe that serviced the shops and offices in the area. Most days, it closed in late afternoon. One night a week, however, it stayed open into the evening for an open mic night, an eclectic, unscripted blend of music, poetry and literary readings. On one of those evenings, I found myself standing at the microphone, reading my trio of nightmare scenes aloud. The normally attentive audience seemed even more hushed than usual through my reading. Or was it shock?

At the end of the evening, a young man came up to me. "That was powerful," he said, then hesitated. "But don't you think it was too—" He stopped again, struggling for words. "Relentless?"

Yes, I replied silently. Aloud, I told him that the story knew better than either of us what it was about, and that my only job was to trust it.

I would also have to trust it to tell me where to place not only those scenes but the handful of new parable-like stories that I had written for Toshar, as well as several narrative pieces. How would those disjointed scenes fit into a manuscript that already felt complete? I pondered that fruitlessly for a few days then sat down, once again, to read my Toronto draft, this time with printouts of the stray scenes on the table next to me. To my amazement, scene after scene found a home — with magical ease and minimal transition. It was as though I had unconsciously left space for pieces of the story that I had not yet been ready to write.

Even after they were seamlessly integrated into the manuscript, those nightmare scenes continued to haunt me, and I kept searching for ways to delete them. I thought I had succeeded, if not with the book then with the screenplay, when I left them out of my first draft of the script. I feared that the graphic violence would push the ultimate film's rating to an unacceptable R. By the screenplay's second draft, though, I had found a way to write them more subtly and the scenes were reinstated.

Deep down, I always knew that Fynda's, Garan's and Yhoshi's reluctant sharing of their nightmares was integral to the story. Yet it wasn't until a year after *The MoonQuest*'s release that I understood why. Actually, I had to be told why — by Michael Hice, who was teaching a class based on the book at Unity Santa Fe, which, ironically, nearly banned it from its bookstore because of those controversial scenes.

"*The MoonQuest* is a story about the power of storytelling," Michael explained patiently, as if to a halfwit who had never read the book, let alone written it. "It's a story about what is destroyed when we're prevented from telling our stories and about the healing that occurs when we break through the silence and share those stories with each other."

I didn't like those scenes any more after Michael's explanation. But I respected them, and never again did I try to run from them or delete them.

Act 7.
Back to Toronto

The problem with new experiences is that they are so rarely the ones you choose.
Calvin & Hobbes

Intuition is the voice of the spirit within you.
Morgan Llewelyn

Toronto Calling

By mid-January 1996, I knew that my time in Penetanguishene was drawing to an end. Whatever had pulled me here had served its purpose. Once again, it would soon be time to move on. Once again, Toronto beckoned. As with my previous return to Toronto, living alone was not an option. This time, though, I would not be seeking a single housemate. This time, I felt called to look for a communal experience.

I was wary. Before Fred, I had never shared my living space with anyone. If that experience had brought up control issues for me, and it had, what would it be like to be part of a larger household? How would my unconventional life, uncommon spirituality and vegan diet fit in? I had no answers. I knew only that my inner guidance had never pointed me in a wrong direction. Every time I traveled past my fear and followed the voice of my infinite mind — my friend Adam Bereki would call it "following my inspiration" — the payoff was bountiful. The journey wasn't always comfortable, but it was always exhilarating, and it always challenged me to more fully express my potential.

Without knowing what I was searching for, I began to scan the classifieds in *Now*. One ad quickly stood out from the others. It was as though it had been written for me: An existing communal household, complete with vegetarian kitchen and a commitment to sharing a certain number of meals during the week, was seeking a new resident. I called on it immediately. By the end of my conversation with one of the residents, I was nearly sold. I had only one final question, the most important: Would they be okay with Roxy?

"I don't know," Lisa replied. "Let me talk to the others."

The following evening she called back. "Come on down! We all want to meet you...and Roxy."

Two days later, Roxy and I made the two-hour drive into the city — to 28 Pauline Avenue in Toronto's Bloor-Dufferin neighborhood, a Portuguese Catholic area crammed with three-story homes set back from tree-lined streets. In mid-February, the trees were bare, the lawns had a thin covering of city-gray snow, and the covered porches, overflowing with family activity in the summer, brooded emptily.

Pauline Avenue would be my second Toronto stop that day. My first was High Park, where so much had unfolded for me in the months before I moved to Nova Scotia. Only a mile or so west of Pauline, it was an ideal spot for Roxy to burn off some of her excitability and take care of canine business and for me to walk off my anxiety. I was nervous that I would be rejected by the Pauline Avenue community; I was equally nervous that I wouldn't be. Had I known how the next months would play out, I might have kept walking — as far from Pauline as possible. Instead, I followed park pathways made less familiar by winter and centered myself as best I could.

I spent six hours visiting with Roger, Susan and Lisa, being as spiritually open about myself and my life as I could. Ray and Jeff, the other two residents were at work. After giving me and Roxy a complete tour of house and yard, Lisa asked how I felt about the available bedroom, the smallest and darkest in the building, apart from Jeff's basement grotto.

I was honest. "If I were given a choice, I would much rather have Roger's room," I replied, "or yours." Roger's, in keeping with his unofficial post as head of household, was the largest and most desirable: a sunlit, bay-windowed space overlooking the street, probably the original master bedroom. Lisa's was only a touch smaller. While not as bright, it still felt open and expansive. The vacant room, by contrast, was painted a deep, dark green and had a single, lightless window. Looking back, I would call it appropriately womb-like. Then, it felt stranglingly tight, almost claustrophobic. It was also one of the noisiest bedrooms in the house, a potential concern for a noise-sensitive, light sleeper. Yet, everything about the bedroom, the house and its residents — at least those I had met — felt right.

Having learned the lessons of Amirault's Hill and Penetanguishene, I was ready to say yes. "If you'll have us, we'd like to take it."

Twenty-four nail-biting hours later, the phone rang. It was Roger. I moved in thirteen days later. Two days after that, while wandering the Bloor West Village commercial strip near High Park, I came across a sleek storefront that looked in on a pristine, white-painted interior. The sign over the door read "Wholistic Health Centre." The sign on the door read "space for rent." By the end of the day, I had rented space for Pathlights, the transformational center I had been envisioning since Thelma Avenue, signed up for a level-one Reiki class and registered for an advanced version of the Actors Equity voice class I had taken with David Smukler the previous year. I was clearly on a fast track to something, even if I didn't yet know what.

The Reiki Portal

A FEW WEEKS BEFORE I left Penetang, I had a call from Lorraine Gane. Lorraine and I had first met briefly in the late 1980s when she interviewed me for a copyediting job at *Toronto Life* magazine. I wasn't hired and our paths didn't cross again until a few years later when the publisher of Air Canada's then-troubled inflight magazine named us joint interim editors. Working together, we discovered common spiritual and creative currency and became friends. "I'm signing up for an introductory Reiki class in Toronto," she said. "You'll be back in town by then. Do you want to come?"

All I then knew about Reiki was that it was an energy-healing modality. I had no conscious desire to be a Reiki practitioner, but Lorraine's call reminded me of a dream from a few nights earlier. In the dream, my hands tingle with the energy that I have been focusing into the body of a woman I'm working on. "You're hurting me," she cries, gripping her midriff. "It's like a knife is plunging into me." When I look, there is a knife — right where she says she feels it. I awoke from the dream both excited and alarmed. "I feel the power," I noted in my journal. "But I don't want to hurt anyone."

The full-day workshop took place — with me but, ironically, without Lorraine — on Good Friday at Laurie Ward's Reiki Store on the fringes of Toronto's chic Yorkville district. The street-level retail area was a crystal store, where I would quickly rediscover a forgotten childhood love of rocks and minerals. Downstairs in the carpeted workshop space, I listened politely to Laurie's explanation of Reiki, a healing technique that had found its twentieth-century form in Japan and gained popularity in the West with the advent of the New Age movement. The history and theory bored me, and I wondered why I was there.

Different Reiki teachers have different approaches. Laurie's more orthodox method included two sets of ten-minute one-on-one "attunements," or initiation rituals, over the course of the day. After the first, I had no doubt that, dull theory notwithstanding, I was in the right place. After the second, I knew that I needed to sign up for a level-two class, even though I still did not see myself opening a Reiki practice. Through each attunement, I experienced transcendent visions as powerful as any I had yet encountered. My first ended with my vision of a solid-gold eagle soaring up into the sky; my second, with fire and ocean merging together in my hands.

My only doubt revolved around what I *wasn't* experiencing. All through the day, everyone else in class got hot, tingly hands when practicing on each other. Unlike in my dream, I felt nothing. I sensed where my hands needed to go, but I had no physical confirmation. None. Was I doing something wrong?

We were an odd-numbered group, and when for the final practice session I was paired with Laurie, I panicked silently. *My hands won't tingle and I won't place them correctly on her. This is going to be embarrassing.* I conveniently overlooked the fact that Laurie had already told us where on the body to place our hands, on spots linked to the seven traditional chakras.

In the years before Carole Leckner helped midwife my initial spiritual opening, I was a logical, nuts-and-bolts kind of guy. Anything I couldn't see or touch didn't exist. Period. God, as I wrote earlier, was a cultural theory, not anything with practical implications in my life. As for fairies, angels, departed souls and other disembodied energies, nothing could convince me that they were anything other than make-believe.

In the years since, I have learned to acknowledge the invisible, awaken to the unknowable and surrender to the ineffable. I never see auras or anything else that isn't physically present. I rarely hear actual voices. My hands hardly ever tingle when doing energy work. Instead, I sense these things. Given my skeptical past, my path has been to learn to trust those sensings, not only despite a lack of evidence but because of it, and to let M'nor's words in my *Q'ntana* stories banish whatever doubt shows up: "You either trust or you do not. There is no halfway in between."

Once Laurie settled herself onto the treatment table, I began the session as I had been taught, starting at the top of her head and following the chakras down toward her feet. I was nervous at first, but a profound knowingness quickly dissolved my anxiety. Although I was following the prescribed trajectory, I wasn't doing it by rote. I found myself listening to my hands, listening to her body. As I touched her hips toward the end of the treatment, my hands kept wanting to move to her shins. I resisted at first. Laurie had not said anything about shins. But the tug was so strong that I finally surrendered. Nothing in me was hot. Nothing in me tingled. Nothing in what I had been taught told me to keep my hands in place. Yet I couldn't move them. When the practice session was over, Laurie confirmed my intuition: Something *was* going on with her shins, and she had been grateful when I focused so much attention on them. It was the first of many reminders that I would receive over the years to trust what I knew to be true, regardless of conventional evidence or wisdom.

I signed up for Reiki II at the end of the class, still not clear why the attraction was so powerful. It wouldn't be until I was attuned as a Reiki master that summer — more than two thousand miles away in Missoula, Montana — that I would finally understand. What I learned then was that Reiki itself didn't matter. Rather, each attunement had been an initiation for me into deeper levels of consciousness, adding vibrant new threads to my tapestry of trust and surrender. As well, the moment Vish, my hippyish Missoula Reiki master, showed me how to give an attunement of my own — a key component of mastery training — I saw my next step: Against all Reiki orthodoxy, I would offer attunements as healings. That's a more common practice today, but in 1997 attunements were strictly reserved for those attending a Reiki workshop. Any other use was unacceptable. Laurie would not likely have approved. Vish, on the other, would have cheered me on.

I was on the road then, on the three-month, full-time journey that would ultimately carry me from Toronto to Sedona. As I traveled, I offered Reiki attunements wherever I stopped — outdoors where possible, and often at no charge. Over time these attunements evolved and expanded, becoming less fixed and more intuitive, until one fall afternoon, having just completed one atop Sedona's Rachel's Knoll, I realized that I would have to find a new way to describe what I was doing. Clearly, it was no longer a Reiki attunement. Within weeks, I added the component around which all others would ultimately revolve: the sound of my voice. It wasn't the kind of singing that I had fantasized about or that I had been seeking when I answered David Smukler's ad. But it became the cornerstone of the energy-healing modality I would develop and practice for the next nine years.

Back in Toronto, Laurie's May Reiki II class was as profound as had been its predecessor, offering up visions even more extraordinary than those I had experienced on Good Friday. More significant still was the name change it sparked. Today, I call myself "Mark David." David, though, is my middle name and until that class I had always been "Mark." Well, that's not entirely true. When I was little, everyone — family, friends, neighbors — called me Marky, a name I despised.

"My name is Mark," I would repeat to anyone who would listen. Everyone listened. Nobody heard. To them, I was still Marky.

One day, stubborn and resolute as only a preschooler can be, I took action. I would no longer answer to Marky, only to Mark.

"Dinner, Marky!" my mother called.

I ignored her.

"Marky, come here. I want to show you something." My sister, this time.

I ignored her.

"Hi, Marky," Mr. Pervin four doors down called to me as I passed. Ignored.

(He would later complain to my mother that I had been rude.)

It took a few days for family members to come around and a few days more for the neighborhood to join in. Within a week, Marky had ceased to exist. At last, not yet five, I was grown up. At last, I was Mark.

When, during the Reiki II class, a fellow student inadvertently called me David, not knowing it was my middle name, something told me that it had been no accident. Over the next days, everywhere I looked I saw stars of David and everyone I met seemed to be named David. That the "mistake" had occurred during something as powerfully transformational as a Reiki workshop convinced me that it was time to change my name. I considered "Mark David" at the time but rejected it, choosing to go with "David."

David Gerson I would remain for the next twenty months, until New Year's Day 1998 when a more radical name-change would take effect.

If I considered my Reiki II visions to have been powerful, those paled next to what I experienced back at Laurie's Reiki Store the following morning, during my first-ever kundalini yoga class.

"*Guru guru Waheguru,*" I chanted during the meditation that closed the session. "*Guru ram dass guru.*" I repeated the two lines over and over, focusing as instructed on my third eye (the energy center above the bridge of the nose, between the physical eyes). "*Guru guru Waheguru. Guru ram dass guru.*"

Tears welled up behind my closed eyelids and I felt strangely overwhelmed. Then I saw him again: a man in a white robe who I had sensed in a vision earlier in the class. I hadn't seen his face then, nor could I immediately identify him now. Then he moved closer. I gasped. The tears now streamed down my cheeks. It was Jesus. As a Jewish man, however unreligious, I was not accustomed to seeing visions of Christian icons. But the emotion I felt as he approached was so profound that it was impossible to question it or push it away. All I could do was surrender to it. First, he anointed my hands, then my third eye. From there, his hands slid up to the top of my head in blessing. Finally, he placed his hands on my heart. Only my continued chanting prevented me from exploding into sobs.

The following weekend, I participated in White Tantric Yoga, a day-long meditation event offered by Toronto's Kundalini Yoga Center in a vast, vacant downtown office suite. Many months later, I would learn that it generally took participants forty days to fully integrate the White Tantric experience. Often, I was told, a significant life change would mark the end of that period. No one mentioned anything about that to me on the day of the event.

Precisely forty days later, I would once more shed my belongings and, for the final time, Toronto. Without knowing it, I would be heading toward a new country, a new name and a new life.

The Perils of Pauline

THOSE EARLY WEEKS on Pauline Avenue with Roger, Jeff, Ray, Susan and Lisa were collegial, congenial and fun. In an echo of my time with Fred, we shared a communally prepared weekly vegetarian meal over wine, conversation and laughter. All my anxieties about sharing space with five strangers quickly dissolved and life took on a comfortable rhythm. Once I had set up my new Pathlights office, I spent most days there. Classes, workshops and friends occupied many of my evenings and weekends.

Perhaps all that busyness explains why I failed to notice something malignant festering beneath the surface camaraderie. There had always been a simmering tension between Roger and Ray, but it had never expressed itself beyond an occasional sharp word or look...until one Tuesday during a residents' meeting. Ray interrupted normal business to declare that he was no longer interested in the communal and vegetarian aspects of life on Pauline. He wanted to remain in the house, but on his own terms. Roger insisted that things stay as they were. Ray would not be moved. Roger refused to compromise.

Jeff, Susan, Lisa and I watched in increasing discomfort as the dispute grew ugly, petty, personal and loud, an uncomfortable reminder for me of all the volatile arguments I had witnessed between my mother and my sister, then in the throes of rebellious adolescence. Somehow, I had always found myself in the middle, with both Susan and Edith seeking to ally me to their side. The confrontation I recall most vividly ended in the bathroom, Susan standing fully clothed in the bathtub, my mother as close to her as the tub wall would allow. I watched from the doorway with the same impotent horror you feel when you see a highway accident. Whatever sparked that particular confrontation, all that distinguished it from dozens of others was how it ended: with a slap. I don't remember my mother ever raising a hand to either of us, which made this moment doubly impactful.

Only voices were raised that night in our Pauline Avenue living room, but the memory of those family battles flooded back to me, along with emotions I hadn't let myself feel growing up. Once again, I felt helpless. Once again, I longed to shield myself from the carnage. This time, there could be no way to shut down. There was no way to escape.

One evening a week later, I returned home from voice class to find Susan and Lisa sitting on the porch steps, close to tears. The antipathy between Roger and Ray had finally exploded — into a fistfight. The police had been called. Our "community" had unraveled.

Jeff, Susan, Lisa and I called an emergency meeting and asked both Roger and Ray to move out. Both refused.

As a child I had felt powerless in the face of Susan's and Edith's battles. In reality, I wasn't impotent; my mother and sister were so enmeshed in their drama that no contribution of mine could ever have diffused it. I wouldn't have seen that at the time. The youngest and most vulnerable in the family, I would instead have feared the consequences of confronting either. Well trained, however unconsciously, by those experiences, I spent the subsequent decades doing all I could to avoid confrontations, especially with men. A childhood surrounded by dueling Amazons, devoid of healthy male role models and overflowing with the humiliating ridicule of other boys had left me insecure about my masculinity. The idea of facing first Roger then Ray and telling each directly and unequivocally that I wanted him to leave filled me with dread. Somehow, I did it. Roger, finally conciliatory, agreed to go. Ray, overtly hostile, adamantly refused.

I, too, wanted to leave. I had been ready to go since Ray's open revolt. The fistfight had only escalated my eagerness. Now, in the barely disguised rancor that shrouded the house, I couldn't wait to give my notice. Yet every time I sought inner guidance, the answer was, "Wait." A few weeks later, having moved past my childhood impotence by facing at least some of my demons, I was free to go. With relief, I announced to my housemates that I would be out in a month, by the beginning of June.

Destination Unknown

As the end of both May and my days on Pauline Avenue drew nearer, I still had no place to move to. I had sensed strongly that I was not to seek out a new rental and assumed from that that a new home would turn up, as if by magic. It didn't. Not fully trusting my intuition, I responded to two housing ads during that period. I was turned down for one — or, rather, Roxy was. I rejected the other.

I spent the Victoria Day holiday weekend at Fred's summer cottage in Coe Hill, three hours northeast of Toronto. Fred and Dov drove back to the city on the holiday Monday but I stayed on, hoping that solitude would serve up some inspiration about my next step. What I received instead was a self-inflicted initiation. I was chopping wood with a small hatchet when, freakishly, the back of the hatchet head hit me on my third eye, drawing blood.

"That's how the Mayans opened an initiate's third eye," Bonnie, an Ottawa friend, explained over the phone later that night. Not with a hatchet of course, but through some process, no doubt much nastier, that also drew blood.

Had I opened my inner vision in a way that would show me what to do next? Possibly. The next morning, I felt inspired to drive to Ottawa, one hundred and fifty miles away, and then to continue on to Montreal. Without realizing it, I was planning a farewell visit to my hometown. I wouldn't return to Montreal for another nine years.

As move-out day approached, I still had no post-Pauline plans. *Maybe I'm wrong. Maybe I need to stay after all.*

"You can't," Lisa countered when I suggested that I might remain. My room had already been rented, to a young woman named Tracy.

"What about Roger's room?" It was still vacant.

Lisa shook her head. "Tracy is horribly allergic to cats and dogs.

She took your room on the condition there would be no animals in the house. Sorry."

If I couldn't stay and had no place to go, what was I to do?

The only thing I could think of, with only a handful of days remaining before I had to vacate, was to pack up my few belongings, store them in my Pathlights office and take off for a week's camping at MacGregor Point Provincial Park on Lake Huron, a hundred miles west of my old Penetanguishene home.

As I first conceived it, Pathlights was to be a soul-awakening center where I would use what I was learning on my spiritual journey to help others on theirs. I tagged it a "center for creative transformation" because in some inchoate way, I saw creative expression as a cornerstone of its approach. Its first year, when I was still living with Fred, I set up a booth at Toronto's Gay Pride Day. Not surprisingly, I attracted little attention and no clients. It didn't matter. The experience was more about my spiritual coming-out than it was about marketing Pathlights. A year later, Pathlights had graduated to its tiny, one-room office in the Wholistic Health Centre. Still, with few clients, I spent most of my days there working on revisions to *The MoonQuest* and *Dialogues with the Divine*. The office's greatest value, in the end, would prove to be as a storage facility during my soon-to-be two weeks of homelessness.

Although the only camping I had done as a child — in summer camp — had left me feeling inadequate, I decided while still living with Fred, that it was time to give camping a second chance. It was certainly time to get over my feelings of not-good-enough around outdoor pursuits. Although I belonged to a gay outdoors club at the time, the only activities I participated in were outdoors-light: day hikes, zoo trips, cottage weekends, barbecues and potluck dinners. When I saw a notice in the Out & Out newsletter for an introductory camping weekend, I immediately signed up and outfitted myself. But a few days before the event, a friend from Nova Scotia called to tell me that Carol MacInnis had leukemia. Without thinking, I canceled my Out & Out reservation, threw Roxy and my gear into the car and tented my way back to Pereau.

The camping gods must have determined that if I could survive my first night, I could survive anything. I did. Barely. When I pulled into the private campground near Trois-Rivières, Quebec, it was pouring. Relentlessly. With no sign of a letup. I found a campsite, pitched my tent, dug a ditch around it to avoid being flooded and huddled inside with Roxy — cold, wet, hungry and miserable. I wasn't sure that I would make it to a second night but I did, at New Brunswick's Woolastook Provincial Park near Fredericton. With that second night, near the water and under a diadem-like sky, I was hooked — so much so that when I got to the MacInnises', I pitched my tent in the yard rather than sleep in the house.

When I had lived in Pereau, I initially bonded more with Ron. Carol taught full-time at Acadia's School of Education, while Ron was largely home. However, the dynamic between me and Carol shifted a month before I left Nova Scotia, when she attended one of my workshops and experienced such a profound catharsis that all distance between us vanished. My return visit was a sweet reunion, and when it came time to return to Toronto, it was hard to leave.

Before I could leave Pauline Avenue, I had a wedding to attend. Although most of my Gerson relatives then still lived in Montreal, my younger cousin Howard had moved to Toronto a few years earlier to study law. His June 1 wedding, my first full Gerson gathering in many years, would be a posh hotel affair.

But who would I go as? If Fred Henderson's unconventional wardrobe had turned me off when I first met him, my antipathy soon morphed into an unconventional wardrobe of my own. My longstanding uniform of jeans, t-shirts and sweatshirts gave way to light-cotton pants and tunic tops from Toronto's little India, multicolored vests and Mexican wedding shirts from South American import shops, and my first pair of Birkenstock sandals. Ties, dress shirts, dress pants and a sports coat still hung in my closet, even though I hadn't worn them or my wingtip shoes since long before my exodus to Nova Scotia. Would I go the conventional route and wear those? Or would I go as I who I felt myself to be and risk raised eyebrows?

I knew what I wanted to do. I knew, too, what I was "supposed" to do. I was scared to do the former, yet knew I couldn't do the latter — especially once I tried on my old dress clothes. The tie choked me. The belted pants cut off deep breathing. The wingtips hurt my feet. Those clothes represented the Mark I had been, not the David I had become. When I put together my preferred outfit — black Indian kurta pants, an eggshell wedding shirt, my vest-of-many-colors and my now-ubiquitous Birks — I felt free, flowing, unrestricted and alive. That was who I now was. That was who I would have to be.

Growing up, I had never experienced the extended Gerson family as particularly warm and intimate. The families of my twin uncles Danny and Saul were close to each other, not so close to us. My other uncle, Gerry, married a woman who alienated all the other Gersons. Until her death, we rarely saw them or their kids. As for our branch of the family, Sydney was ill then gone and Edith worked full-time, an anomaly in those days. As well, unlike the other Gersons, we didn't live in the Jewish enclave of Côte-Saint-Luc. Did that sense of separation explain why I had always felt alien around my relatives? Was it because I was gay? Was it because I was unconventional? Or was it because I had always let my insecurities set me apart? Perhaps I would find answers at the wedding.

Though nervous, I felt true to my unorthodox self when I walked into the formalwear-filled Sutton Place banquet hall. No heads turned, and if anyone was judging me because of my outfit, they were too polite to show it. As for me, I had never before felt so comfortable around my extended family. I danced, laughed and carried on as though we were close. For the first time since I was too young to know any better, I felt no need to apologize for who I was. I just was.

I spent my week at MacGregor Point editing *Dialogues with the Divine* and waiting for the intuitive *aha* that would tell me what to do next. Yet when I returned to Toronto and my now-cluttered Pathlights office, I still knew nothing. That afternoon, and every afternoon for the next several days, I closed my eyes, went within and asked where I should spend the night. That first night I camped again — in the Glen Rouge campground on Toronto's eastern fringe. Instead of Lake Huron's cicadas lulling me to sleep and its loons singing me into a new day, I slept and woke to the rumbling thrum of traffic on the 401, one of the country's busiest freeways. Another day in the Pathlights office led me to the Town Inn, a hotel just steps from the Gloucester Street apartment I had occupied for over a decade. It felt odd wandering around my old neighborhood, now even more entrenched as Toronto's Gay Village. It felt foreign. It felt like a farewell.

The next afternoon, once again in my office, I wondered what to do.

"Richmond Hill," an inner voice whispered.

Richmond Hill? What could I possibly find in this largely sterile bedroom community north of the city? Despite my doubts, I followed the flow of commuter traffic out of Toronto and found a motel just off the town's old main street.

"Sorry," the desk clerk said. "No dogs."

Next motel, same rejection.

I cursed silently. "If the next motel won't take us," I grumbled to Roxy, "we're going back to the Town Inn. I don't care what the guidance is." To make sure that was even possible, I called the Town Inn. My room was still available.

I put Roxy back in the car and drove farther up the road. A few blocks up was another motel, clean but nondescript.

"A dog?" The clerk peered over his glasses at me, then glanced down at Roxy.

I clenched my teeth, waiting for the inevitable rebuff. *Town Inn, here I come.*

"How many nights?"

"Just the one."

He looked back down at Roxy.

"Well," he said, and paused. "Just one night, you say?"

I nodded.

He pulled a key from the rack.

"Come with me." He marched across the parking lot. "Just for one night," he called back over his shoulder.

I was grateful but angry. And scared. How many more nights

could I live like this? How many more days could I put off Souk, the owner of the Wholistic Health Centre? She complained daily that I was using my office as a storage locker, that it made her center look bad.

Before checking out of the motel the next morning, I took Roxy for a walk. A night's sleep had not calmed me. If anything, I was even more anxious with a new day ahead of me and no idea what to do with it. As we approached the edge of the property, I discovered that the motel was perched at the edge of a ravine. A wooded trail led down into an undeveloped basin. I slipped off my Birkenstocks, let Roxy off her leash and started down. As we reached the bottom, it was as though a lightbulb switched on over my head, just like I used to see in comic strips as a kid. In that moment of absolute clarity, I knew what I had to do. I would find a hotel for the next days and use that time to once again close down my Toronto life. When that was done, Roxy and I would get in the car with whatever was left and head west.

Perhaps I was so grateful for *any* answer that I surrendered willingly, even though I didn't know where I was going. Or perhaps it just felt so right that I didn't question it. But on June 19, having once more shed most my belongings, I hit the road...this time for parts unknown.

The next phase of my journey had begun.

Act 8.
On the Road

Nothing is lost. Everything is transformed.
Michael Ende

Do not go where the path may lead.
Go instead where there is no path and leave a trail.
Ralph Waldo Emerson

O, Canada

I DIDN'T KNOW where I was going or why when I drove out of Toronto on the morning of June 19, 1997. All I knew was that I would spent my first night eighty miles north in Washago with Trish Patterson, a teacher and musician I had met while living in Penetanguishene. Beyond that, the road ahead was unclear. I felt that open-endedness even more fully when I pulled out of Trish's driveway the following morning and continued north on Route 11, the two-lane highway that would carry me up to the Trans-Canada Highway, around the Great Lakes and west to...wherever.

I didn't get far that first day. Little over an hour after setting out, I saw an exit for Burk's Falls. Without thinking, I turned off. Not for the first time on this journey, it felt as though my car was deciding the route for me and I was just along for the ride. Even when I saw "Circling Hawks" on a sign above an Ontario Street storefront, I wasn't sure that that's what had brought me here. Still, I parked and went in, intrigued by the blend of Indian and metaphysical artifacts in the window. I browsed silently at first, too shy to strike up a conversation with the woman behind the counter. Eventually, I shared with her the story of my just-launched road odyssey.

"If you need a place to stay tonight," Lynette Brooker said, "stay with us. You can camp in the restored barn we use for events. In fact, we're having a summer solstice gathering there tomorrow night. Stay for that too, if you want."

Awed by the synchronicity that had brought me to Lynette's store, I readily agreed, though I wasn't certain about the second night. I assumed that I needed to keep moving, an odd attitude given that I had no known itinerary or destination. In the end, I stayed for the solstice gathering, which served up even more magical connections, including Reiki master John Lueck and his wife Ellen. I would spend my next night up the highway in Powassan at the Luecks', where John and I gave Ellen a powerful Reiki treatment. In gratitude, Ellen gifted me with an exquisite Indian feather fan that would travel nearly two thousand miles with me over the next weeks until I reached Medicine Wheel National Historic Landmark high in Wyoming's Bighorn Mountains.

Considered integral to Native American spiritual practice, the medicine wheel is a rock circle laid flush to the ground. Stone spokes connect this outer ring with a center-point, also of stone. Generally, four thicker spokes mark the four cardinal directions: east, west, north and south. According to archaeologists, the Bighorn wheel, with its twenty-eight spokes and eighty-foot width, is the largest ancient medicine wheel still intact. It was mid-July when I climbed from the parking lot to the medicine-wheel site, deep snowbanks still bordering the path at this ten-thousand-foot elevation. Even before I reached the wheel itself, I felt its magnetic pull. When I did reach it, I was overcome with emotion. All I wanted to do, as I meditated at each of the four directions, was cry, without knowing why. Back in the car, the engine already running, I saw Ellen's feather fan lodged in the passenger-side sun visor. It belonged here. I was certain of it. I switched off the car, climbed back up to the summit, circled the wheel three more times, then wedged the fan in the chain-link fence that protected the site, one of scores of offerings left by visitors.

The other gift of that solstice celebration was Claire Gibb, another Reiki master, who gave the two dozen of us gathered in Lynette's barn a group attunement. The moment Claire walked into the room, I knew I had to speak to her. As soon as I did, I knew we were family.

"Make sure you look me up if you pass through Sudbury," she said as she was leaving. Six days later, I did.

In the William Rand School, there are four levels of Reiki, not the more traditional three. The third level, which Rand calls Advanced Reiki Training, or ART, is a prerequisite for mastery. Claire had been trained in the Rand School. In exchange for an afternoon's private writing workshop, she offered me the ART attunement. It was that head start that would make my Reiki mastery so easy to attain a month later in Missoula.

Sioux Narrows Provincial Park sits on one of the thousands of picturesque inlets that comprise Lake of the Woods, a vast lake system that straddles the Ontario-Minnesota border west of Thunder Bay. In the summer its shores are lushly green, and haunting loon calls from mid-lake usher in its otherwise-silent dewy mornings.

That's what I woke to on the morning of July 9, 1997 — unknowingly, my last as a Canadian resident. As I had been doing most nights on the road when someone hadn't offered to put me up, I had been camping. I don't remember what drew me to this tiny park off the main road. It was about forty miles south of Route 17, the Trans-Canada Highway that had carried me west over Lake Huron and Lake Superior, the same highway I expected to travel into Manitoba. But here I was. After scribbling a few postcards, I broke camp and drove a few miles south into town to mail the cards. My plan was to return to westbound 17 and the Winnipeg Folk Festival, which was to open a few days later. Once again my car had its own plan. Without fully realizing what I was doing, I turned right instead of left out of the parking lot. My new direction was south — toward Minnesota, the United States and, unbeknownst to me, my new country.

"Where are you going?" the US border guard asked me at the crossing at Baudette. His demeanor was all business, but his eyes were kind.

"Camping trip," I replied nervously. It didn't matter how innocent I was, I was uneasy around authority figures.

He looked me over, taking in my Indian cottons and longish hair. He looked into the back of the minivan, packed with all I owned. He looked at Roxy, perched attentively on the passenger seat.

"Canadian citizen?"

I nodded.

He peered into the van again, then pointed to a parking lot alongside the customs building.

"Pull in over there," he said, almost apologetically. His name, I would learn later, was, like mine, David.

My first panicked thought was that I was in trouble. *He sees all my stuff and thinks I'm trying to move into the country illegally.* Nervously, I did as I was told. A stocky, Marine-like customs official met me in the parking lot. Unsmilingly, he asked me to take Roxy and get out of the car. His eyes were not kind.

One of my travel companions in those days was a Swiss Army knife that fit snugly inside a small, black leather pouch. When my Marine found it in the glove compartment, he removed the knife and peered into the pouch. He wiggled his pinky inside. Then he tipped the pouch over and tapped it from the top. In that moment, I realized the reason for the intense scrutiny, which had included a call to the Sudbury Travelodge to confirm that I had really stayed there. It had nothing to do with why I was entering the US. It was about drugs. Not surprisingly, he found nothing. I had never done drugs. Even when, in my twenties, friends had passed a joint around, I had declined. Not from prudishness. Whatever else drugs were about, they were about loss of control. And until my spirituality and the first draft of *The MoonQuest* forced me to abandon such long-standing rigidities, "always in control" had been my motto.

At the start of the search, I was anxious. *What if they send me back?* I watched nervously as the Marine pulled everything out of the car and set it on the pavement. When the stress grew too intense, I clipped Roxy's leash to her collar and walked her as far away from the inspection as I could. Finally calm, I answered my own question: *Then I'll go back.*

Baudette wasn't a busy crossing, and after a while, David and I began chatting — about metaphysics and spirituality, which he was opening to, and about his job, which he hated. And when the Marine clumsily replaced the wooden wine crate filled with crystals that served as my makeshift traveling altar, David reproached him.

"That's fragile stuff," he exclaimed.

Even after I crossed into the US, I considered this a temporary detour. America was a great place to visit, but why would I choose to stay? Even if I wanted to stay, it would not be legally possible. Better to keep to my folk-festival plans and find my way back up to Winnipeg.

Just as I had long been unaware of my deeply held desire to be a writer, I was also unaware that I harbored a similarly powerful call to settle in the United States. The nice thing about living in surrender is that as I remain open to the wisdom and guidance of my infinite mind — as I listen to my heart — my passions naturally find their way to the surface. On this particular journey, as had already occurred multiple times in the three weeks since I left Toronto, my car was often the key.

Before leaving Baudette, I consulted my road atlas and found a series of back roads west of town that would loop me back into Canada within a few hours. Soon, though, I found myself driving under a dense canopy of trees along a right-angled maze of Forest Service dirt roads, roads not mapped out in my Rand McNally. Ninety minutes later, to my surprise, I wasn't ninety minutes west of Baudette. I was back in Baudette, without knowing how I got there. In that moment, I knew that there would be no folk festival for me. I let the car pull me toward southbound I-71 and deeper into the US.

The pull must have been stronger than I knew. Within moments, a Minnesota state trooper had pulled me over for speeding. When he saw my Ontario plates and driver's license, he grinned and issued me nothing but a warning. His hometown, he said, was Kapuskasing, in northeastern Ontario.

Whether at home or in the car, the Canadian Broadcasting Corporation had long been my favorite radio companion. And with Baudette so close to the border, the CBC signal was still powerful. That morning, as most mornings, I was tuned to Peter Gzowski's *Morningside* program, a three-hour, magazine-style celebration of things Canadian. The signal started strong. But as I continued southwest toward Bemidji, *Morningside* grew weaker and weaker. Finally, Gzowski's voice stuttered into solid static.

Canada was gone.

In that moment, I knew that I was too — for good.

A New Country

THE NEXT WEEKS were a blur of driving, camping...and listening — to my inner voices and for the external signs that were also guiding me. In Bemidji the owner of Deep Lake Rocks directed me to Lake Itasca State Park, where the Mississippi launches its twenty-five-hundred-mile meander to the Gulf of Mexico. I spent my first night in my new country there, unofficially launching the US leg of my own meandering. From there I crossed into North Dakota at Fargo, where I witnessed the destruction that precedes creation: When the Red River had crested at fifty-four feet in a historic spring flood, even mature trees had been swept away by rushing waters that surged three miles beyond their natural shoreline. The muddy riverside park I walked through that morning was a tangle of dead tree limbs and stripped earth.

Ninety-five miles west in Jamestown, North Dakota, I stood in awe of my first white buffalo, its power evident even from my side of the fence at the National Buffalo Museum. And camping that night on the grounds of the Assumption Abbey in Richardton, North Dakota, I experienced another powerful sight: the fireworks-like lightning display of a far-distant thunderstorm. I had learned about the abbey's hospitality at a bookstore in nearby Dickinson and when I knocked on the door, yet another David, Father David Wolf, invited me to stay. I set up my tent in a vast open field — because of Roxy, I couldn't sleep inside — and took my meals with the abbey's Benedictine monks.

Power was everywhere in those landscapes, and I climbed, hiked and camped everywhere I could: Bear Butte, South Dakota, where for the second time in a week, a stray stone smashed into my windshield, forcing me to replace it; Badlands National Park, with its stark, primal rock formations and stark, primitive campground; the Black Hills, their unaltered granite cliffs as face-like as Mount Rushmore's; Devil's Tower National Monument, where I was as struck by the Native American legends linking it to the Pleiades as I was by the giant bear-claw-like striations that give the monolith its Lakota name of Bear Lodge; and the Bighorn Mountains, where I not only left my offering at Medicine Wheel, but experienced a moment out of time like no other.

From Buffalo, Wyoming, US-16 climbs through and past the pine, spruce, fir and aspen of Bighorn National Forest to a barren, scraggly 9,666 feet at Powder River Pass. There, a rugged rock formation juts up one hundred more feet to pierce what for me that July day was a cloudless, sapphire sky. I had no plans to stop, but something pulled me into the small parking area. I let Roxy out and she scampered up the rocks; I followed behind. After a few moments, I felt as though I was being whisked back in time...to the beginning of time itself, to a time of dragons, to a time before time. I stood still, the summer wind eddying around me, and I knew I had been here before — at the very timeless time I was sensing — even though it made no sense to my mind. I knew the dragons whose presence I felt. I knew too that I was experiencing a form of genesis — both the world's and my own.

In August 2006, on a similar if longer and Roxy-less road odyssey, I would find myself again in the Bighorn Mountains. I had not forgotten my Powder River Pass experience, but I had forgotten where it had occurred and had no clear memory of the rock formation. Suddenly, the road curved to the summit and there it was. There I was — almost nine years later, to the day. Once more, the rocks called me to them as, once more, I found myself in a time of personal transformation, a time of dragons, a time of genesis.

Wyoming carried me and Roxy into Montana and my first experience, near Helena, of a National Forest with no trees. Missoula, of course, brought me my Reiki mastery and, perhaps as a symbol of all the pieces of my past I continued to shed on this Exodus-like journey, the most spectacular sunset I had ever witnessed: a breathtaking symphony of crimsons, scarlets and wines, ambers, apricots and titians, and myriad shades of gray that burned against the dark, storm-pregnant sky and reflected up at me from the Clark Fork River.

From Missoula I followed the forests, hot springs and burbling waters of the Salmon River Valley into Idaho and Boise. There, as a special treat, I checked into the Boise DoubleTree. I had been spending more nights in motels as my travels continued, but this was my biggest hotel splurge to date.

Although I was still only a few years into this new world of spirituality and metaphysics, I had already had a few experiences of channeling — at a spiritualist church in Nova Scotia, at an event in Midland while I was living in Penetang, and at a Unity Church in suburban Toronto — but always as an observer. As I sat in my Boise hotel room, I knew it was time for me to give it a try. I knew it but I didn't like it. For all my commitment to surrender, I still have my moments of fear-based doubt and resistance. In a sense, there is no need for surrender where fear is absent, just as there is no need for courage. When I am fearless, I just do it, whatever the "it" happens to be. I don't analyze it. I don't judge it. I don't think about it. In fact, I don't even think. Action becomes as autonomic as breathing and the highest choice is never in doubt. It's never in doubt because it's not even a choice. It just is.

I surrendered to the call to channel that evening, but not without a fight. Not because I considered channeling too "out there." I was already pretty out there and I was getting more so every day. My resistance bubbled up from that same scared place from which I had struggled against *The MoonQuest* and, in my twenties, had passed up the pass-around joints: control. I didn't want to give any more up. In the end, I gave in. I always do. And if I don't remember what happened after I drew the curtains and closed my eyes, it's because the following night's channeling experience far overpowered this one in potency.

Channel Surfing

INSPIRED BY MY experience at Circling Hawks, one of the first things I now always did when arriving in a new town was to flip through the local Yellow Pages in search of health food stores, bookstores, and metaphysical shops and services. It proved an often-successful way for me to connect with like-spirited people on my travels. That's how I had found Deep Lake Rocks in Bemidji, the bookstore in Dickinson and Missoula's EarthSpirit Books, where I had been directed to Reiki master Vish. The Yellow Pages was also how I found downtown Boise's metaphysical emporium, which I drove out to the following morning on what I thought was my way out of town.

When I walked into the bright, spacious store, a voice greeted me from on high — not the disembodied spirit I had channeled the previous night, but Bodie Dugger, a slim young man with tousled blond hair and a face in that unclassifiable place between chiseled and cherubic. He was perched atop a stepladder rearranging merchandise.

"Where are you from?" he asked a few preliminaries later.

"Toronto," I replied.

He laughed. "No. What planet or star system? I'm from Arcturus."

Not a single customer wandered in during the hour-plus of our conversation, freeing us to chat nonstop about all things metaphysical. By the time I left, I knew I would stay the week so I could attend Bodie's full-moon gathering in seven days.

That afternoon, Roxy and I checked into the Shilo Inn, into a room right on the Boise River. That evening, I changed into my bathing suit and settled into the white-tiled steam room that's a fixture in many of the chain's properties. I had no plans other than to shut my eyes and relax into the steam. But after a few minutes, I felt another presence in the room. I opened my eyes and peered through the clouds of steam. I saw no one.

"Hello?"

No answer. I shut my eyes again.

Immediately, I sensed a white-robed man staring at me from across the room. He was tall, dark-haired, with a trim beard and mustache and a muscular build. A gold coronet rested on his head.

"Who are you?" I asked silently.

"My name is Arctur," I sensed rather than heard.

Right. My mind is still focused on Bodie and his Arcturian stories. It's playing tricks on me.

"This is no trick. I am Arctur," he repeated.

Once again, I was channeling. I don't know how long we conversed. Time had no meaning among the mystical swirls of steam.

"If Bodie's from Arcturus," I challenged, "where am I from?"

"Not that it matters," he replied, "but you're from Sirius...and stop being so serious."

I was too serious, too much of the time.

"There is someone here who wants to speak with you," Arctur said a few moments later.

I waited.

"Because this is so close to the anniversary of your father's death..." Suddenly I sensed my father's presence, Sydney's presence. My heart started to race.

"I'm sorry I couldn't be the father you wanted me to be," my father said. "I'm sorry I couldn't be there for you in all the ways you deserved."

I began to sob.

"But I loved you and I still love you," he continued. "And I'm so proud of what you're doing and what you're becoming. I couldn't be a role model for you, but you're now a role model for me. I'm watching you. I'm with you. I'm learning from you. Thank you."

Moments later, I sensed that Sydney and Arctur had left. I was alone, still crying. I opened my eyes. The steam room was empty. I wiped my face, collected myself and returned to my room.

How close to the anniversary is it? I fired up my laptop and opened my file of significant dates.

As close as it could be. My father had died twenty-nine years earlier — on that day.

Sedona Beckons

From Boise, I slipped into Oregon and discovered Bend, in the central part of the state. With high desert to the east, more than a dozen Cascade peaks to the west and the Deschutes River winding through it, it's a small city of infinite beauty and charm. I checked into a downtown motel, scanned the Yellow Pages and found a metaphysical store a few blocks away. One of the first things I noticed, in a wall rack by the front door, was a Mayan calendar created locally by a woman named Holly Davison.

Although Mayan-related material wasn't as prevalent in 1997 as it came to be during the approach to 2012, I had some familiarity with the subject. Still, it was less the calendar's theme than some ineffable urge that led me to call Holly on the store phone as soon as I saw her number on the back cover. Twenty minutes later, she and I met on a nearby bridge. The electricity was instant. It was as if we had known each other all our life...all our lives, perhaps. When I met her partner, Will Robertson, the following day, I felt the same about him. Roxy and I stayed with Holly and Will for four nights, and we were inseparable. It was also impossible to shut us up. We talked and talked and talked...through the day and into the night. On the fifth day, I woke knowing that if I didn't leave that morning, I never would be able to. It took many hugs and heartfelt promises to stay in touch before Roxy and I pulled out of their drive and headed for the mountains.

Holly and Will were not the only profound connections I made during those three months. Bodie Dugger, of course, was another. As was Carrie Shinners, who I met at Bodie's full-moon gathering. Owner of a small metaphysical store in nearby Nampa, Idaho, Carrie immediately felt like a long-lost sister. I spent my first night out of

Boise sleeping in her camper after giving her husband a Reiki attunement and talking long into the night with her about energy work, past lives and my travels. As I drove off next morning, I began to wonder whether the sole purpose of this journey was to reconnect with scattered members of a spiritual family I didn't even know I had.

From Bend, I wound through mountains and lava fields to Eugene. It was clean, green, progressive and artistic, and I should have loved it. Yet it was one of the few cities on my journey that I didn't care for. When I returned from a metaphysical store that to me felt remote and unfriendly, I packed the car and drove into the night toward the ocean. I woke next morning in Florence and immediately fell in love with the deserted beaches and rocky outcroppings of the Oregon coast.

I had driven as far west as I could. But my journey was not over. From the Oregon coast, I slipped down into California, where I camped among its northern redwoods before looping back into Oregon to check out Ashland. Ashland did not want to be checked out. At least not by me. It was the Friday afternoon of Labor Day weekend, the start of an annual Shakespeare Festival, when I drove into town. Of the eight states I had passed through, Oregon was the toughest when it came to pet-friendly motels. Ashland proved to be no exception. Between no-pets policies and the Shakespeare Festival, I could find only one available room; it reeked of cigarette smoke. Instead, I found I-5 and pointed the car south, back toward California.

I arrived in Mount Shasta City after dark and pulled into the KOA campground on the outskirts of town. It was Friday, August 30, the evening before Princess Diana's death. Although I generally paid little attention to the news of the world as I was traveling, I couldn't help but be startled by the sobering headline in the campground's newspaper box the following morning. Her death still imprinted on my psyche, Diana would appear to me in a vision a few weeks later in Sedona, during a powerful and transformational sound-healing session.

That day, my first full one in Mount Shasta, I explored the town. I visited its many metaphysical bookstores and gave a Reiki attunement at the headwaters of the Sacramento River, located in a city park. I also made my first foray up Mount Shasta. For generations, this solitary volcanic peak at the southern end of the Cascades and the town at its base have attracted artists, poets and spiritual seekers. Some have even come hoping to catch a glimpse of the Telosians, fabled residents of a Lemurian city said to be buried deep beneath the mountain. Legends dating back to the mid-nineteenth century describe Lemuria as an Eden-like continent in the Pacific Ocean; an earlier, more peaceable version of Atlantis. In fact, it was an article about Telos in an Oregon metaphysical newspaper that had sparked my curiosity enough to get me here. While I saw no tall, bearded men in flowing robes emerge from the woods during my stay, I awoke my second morning, camped high above town, from a dream so vivid that I was convinced that not only was Telos real, but that I had spent the night there.

Telos-seekers are not the only people attracted to Mount Shasta. Spiritual teachers of all stripes either live there or travel there to facilitate workshops. It was just such a workshop, advertised in a Santa Rosa, California newspaper, that would draw me back to the area ten days later.

From that first Mount Shasta visit, I twisted and spiraled west through the mountains and back toward the California coast. An early stop was Ferndale, a quaint Victorian village a few miles off US-101. Unusually that evening, I postponed looking for a place to stay, treating myself first to a sidewalk-cafe dinner and a local production of *Godspell*. Once the curtain came down, I was out of luck. I couldn't find a room. Using a combination of my instincts and the vague directions I had been given earlier in the evening, I followed a dark, curving, rural road toward the ocean. When I finally stumbled onto a beach, I tied Roxy up, pulled out my sleeping bag and called it a night. Next morning, I opened my eyes to a platoon of army cadets surveying me curiously as they prepared maneuvers a few hundred yards away.

I arrived back on the mountain on a Thursday, a few days before the September 14 workshop, and checked in at the McBride Springs campground. I hadn't even pitched my tent when I ran into a spritely blonde woman in her thirties who spoke with a French Canadian accent. I never learned her name, but I did learn that like me she was a Reiki master. We dined together at her campsite, and although we talked for hours, all I remember was a brief conversation about vision. My vision. I mentioned the natural vision work I had been doing. She spoke to me of inner vision. My inner vision.

When I returned to my campsite, Roxy snuggled into my sleeping bag at my feet and I threw an extra blanket over us for warmth. Although it was barely mid-September, the nights were already chilly at forty-nine hundred feet. It wasn't much warmer when I awoke the following morning, but the moment I opened my eyes I knew what I had to do — with a certainty that was staggering in its clarity of inner vision: I was to skip the workshop that had brought me here and depart immediately for Sedona. Why Sedona? I didn't know. Why the urgency? I didn't know that either. The only thing I knew was to pack the car. I walked to my nameless friend's tent to share my news. Her campsite was deserted. Moments later, mine was too.

The quickest, most direct route to northern Arizona would have been south along I-5 and west along I-40, a sixteen-hour drive. But I had moved through this odyssey largely on secondary roads, and despite the apparent urgency of Sedona's call, it did not feel appropriate to make an exception for this thousand-mile leg of it. Instead, I left Mount Shasta the back way, through Lassen Volcanic National Park, and spent four days driving through northeastern California, central Nevada, southern Utah and northern Arizona before pulling into a Route 66 Travelodge in Flagstaff, totally confused about the time. I didn't know then that Arizona stayed on Standard Time year-round, and my watch didn't match the announcer's on KNAU, the local NPR station.

The following morning, I skipped the hotel breakfast, found Oak Creek Canyon and began the winding journey down to Sedona. It was September 16, the morning of the harvest moon. What I was about to harvest — a new life and identity that would include marriage, parenthood, divorce and a road trip ten times the length of this one — was beyond anything I could have then imagined.

Act 9.
Coming Out

Good for the world in coming out.
When we come out, it's good for the world.
HOLLY NEAR

Be yourself; everyone else is already taken.
OSCAR WILDE

Being Different

I WAS TWENTY WHEN I came out to my straight friends and family as a gay man, thirty-nine when I reluctantly dropped the "gay" label, forty-three when I married a woman and came out as no-longer-gay to my gay friends, fifty when I lost the "married" label, and fifty-four when I came out all over again as a gay man. As with much else on my journey, the story of my sexual orientation is not straightforward.

Like many gay men of my generation, I grew up feeling as though I didn't fit in. In several tangible ways I didn't: I was Jewish and English-speaking in largely Catholic and French-speaking Quebec, and I was often singled out by my peers as less than masculine for my indifference to all sports, both participatory and spectator. That I cared nothing for hockey or for its local celebrity team, the legendary Canadiens, was a particular cause for contempt.

My neighborhood friends growing up were all girls. Together, we played house, rode kiddie cars, played hide-and-seek and watched *I Love Lucy* reruns. The boys on my street, all older, played street hockey, softball or football and taunted me for my sissyish ways. One girl's father even scolded me one afternoon because I was engrossed in cutout dolls with my trio of girl-friends when, in his view, I should have been tossing a ball with the boys.

I didn't fare much better through four often humiliating summers at Camp Wooden Acres. I never learned to swim; I was so tense in the water that even dead man's float couldn't hold me up. I never understood football; my survival strategy was to keep as far from the other players as possible. Baseball I understood perfectly: I understood that I could neither throw the ball with any strength nor catch it, so I always headed for the farthest outfield, where I prayed that no ball would ever find me. In camp as in school, I was always among the last chosen for any team. I was also less focused on what was going on in the game than on the bare chests of the shirtless team, a team I hated being part of because I was embarrassingly scrawny.

By August 1975, even though I couldn't acknowledge it, I had already experienced more boy crushes than opposite-sex dating. Greg Peterson had not been my first unconscious crush. Simon, an early Wooden Acres counselor probably was. I have vague memories of intimate if nonsexual fantasies about him during that prepubescent summer of '65. Although I had gay theater acquaintances and knew Greg and Max, I never made a connection between my feelings, my experiences and them.

Until I did.

I can't say what sparked the shift, probably because it wasn't a single action or event. I remember, one summer afternoon, hurling myself into the family kitchen in a fear-filled rage. The trigger, even if I could recall it, is less relevant than the pained confusion lurking beneath the surface of my psyche. But in a moment of Oscar-worthy high melodrama, I grabbed the whiskey decanter, the only liquor in the house apart from a souvenir bottle of white Israeli Carmel left over from my bar mitzvah, slopped out a several-fingers-full serving and downed it in a single, mouth-burning gulp — to the open-jawed astonishment of my mother and sister. At some level during that summer, I felt the ground rumbling beneath my feet, shaking the very root of who I thought I was. On that day, I didn't suspect sexuality as the root of my disintegration. Soon, though, dawning glimmers of realization crept into my awareness.

My first halting step, a natural one for me, was a trip to the local public library. As I thumbed through the card catalog then browsed the shelves, I purposefully selected only books that put a positive spin on homosexuality — while anxiously peering over my shoulder. Through many summer jobs at the library, I knew most of the staff and many of the patrons. Somehow, I found the courage to check out my small stack of books, smuggle them into the house and hide them at the back of a dresser drawer. Reading them proved both reassuring and alarming. Reassuring, because there was a growing community and history to support me in those post-Stonewall days. Alarming, because I had no idea how to navigate through this new world so centered, to the best of my limited awareness, on bars, booze and bathhouses.

My first foray into that world took me to Le Rocambole, *the* gay nightspot in the Montreal of 1975. Ever the observer (of everyone back then but myself), I made my way to the bar, sat on a miraculously vacant stool and ordered a Labatt 50. Clutching my bottle, I scanned the disco-noisy, smoke-filled room, praying to see a familiar face…praying that if I saw one, he wouldn't see me. I wasn't ready to be outed just yet. Did I belong here? It was reassuring to see men dancing with each and showing affection. But I had never hung out in loud, smoky straight bars. Being in a gay bar filled with men didn't make it any more "me." Once again, I felt the outsider. Mercifully ignored by all, I chugged down my 50 and escaped back into the sultry Stanley Street night.

Was this smoky, sexual, late-night life the one I was choosing? Could I find a place for myself in this alien world? It felt neither possible nor desirable. I slunk home, shed my tobacco-stinking clothes and slipped into bed — no clearer, no wiser, no happier.

If bars were out, I wondered in the days that followed, what was left? My library research had told me that a gay political and social culture existed alongside the bars and bathhouses. Montreal wasn't New York or San Francisco. Could anything like that exist here? I was too insecure to ask my gay acquaintances, and after his failed attempt the previous fall to out me, I was too angry and embarrassed to approach Greg. Instead, I did what many confused men of the time did: I looked up "gay" in the phone book. There were two listings, Gay-Fresh Cleaners on Monkland Avenue and Gay Montreal on Rue Sainte-Famille, in the McGill University neighborhood that would soon be my home.

I pulled the phone into my room and shut the door, first making certain that my mother and stepfather were out of earshot. I dialed part of the number and hung up. I dialed again, hanging up when it began to ring. I dialed a third time, then hung up as soon as I heard the click of someone answering. I couldn't do it. Instead, after my college class a few nights later, I walked east from Sir George to Rue Sainte-Famille.

A prosperous neighborhood of gray limestone and red sandstone townhouses when it was developed in the late-nineteenth century, the McGill Ghetto was by the mid-seventies a soot-stained blend of rundown student apartments, rowdy fraternity houses and lower middle-class flats, punctuated here and there by the first signs of sandblasted gentrification. From the outside, in the golden waning daylight of a late summer evening, the unmarked house that, according to the phone book, housed Gay Montreal looked much like any other on the street. Given the low profile of gay life in those days, that reassured me...but not enough to get me up the half-dozen steps to its Victorian front door.

With no change in gait and my heart hammering, I continued past the building, turning my head only slightly to steal a glance into the front-room window. I saw nothing. I circled the block and on my second walk-past casually slowed my pace. I hoped it would look as though I was studying the building's architecture when what I was really doing was trying to read behind its facade. It refused to be read. Its blank, faded elegance revealed nothing but a stony face. At the least, I had hoped to catch a glimpse of gay men entering or leaving, but in the dozen times I ambled past, no one crossed its century-old threshold. I wasn't going to be the first.

It was after ten when I got home, defeated by another fear-filled exploration of Montreal's still-mysterious gay world.

Days of depression followed, during which I snapped and snarled at home and sleepwalked through my classes, reluctant to say anything of substance to anyone for fear of revealing too much. Suddenly, I no longer knew how to relate to anyone. I was still Mark. But who was Mark? What was he becoming?

This summer term at Concordia would be my final semester, as I completed a business degree I had never really wanted. Soon after my visit to Rue Sainte-Famille, I finished my last class and my formal education. But I wasn't done with my gay education, or with Gay Montreal. Not yet.

Gay and Jewish

ONE EVENING, WITH my mother and stepfather safely out and my bedroom door firmly shut, I again dialed the number for Gay Montreal. This time, I forced myself to stay on the line.

"Good evening, Gay Montreal," a pleasant male voice answered.

"I-I think I'm gay," I stammered after saying nothing for what seemed decades but was likely little more than a breath.

Charles was a pro, expertly navigating me through my fears, reassuring me that I wasn't alone and inviting me in for a counseling session.

"Thank you," I breathed out in relief. "That would be great. I even know where you are. You're on Sainte-Famille, right?"

"Oh, no," Charles replied. "We moved out of there months ago. We're on Peel Street now, above Sherbrooke, on the west side of the street."

My mouth went dry. My stomach churned. My mind flew back to my Ghetto prowling. I could have rung the bell on Sainte-Famille and asked for— I couldn't bear to think about it.

Next afternoon, freshly showered and looking my twenty-year-old best, I climbed past a different set of Victorian limestones, somewhat more confident than I had been during my previous outing. This time, at least, someone was waiting for me. And who knew? Maybe he would be cute and think I was... Maybe we would bond right away... Maybe it would be a lasting bond... At the very least, maybe he would introduce me to gay sex... By the time I walked in, I had us living in the 1975 equivalent of gay connubial bliss — in one of those yuppified McGill Ghetto renos.

Charles was dark, heavyset and in his late thirties, unkempt in blue jeans and a rumpled white sweatshirt, not at all my *PlayGirl* fantasy. But then, I wasn't his. Compassionate and to the point, he looked me up and down and asked, "Are you Jewish?"

Having been born into a generation of Jews with a contemporary knowledge of the Holocaust, family memories of Eastern European pogroms and firsthand experience of anti-Semitism, I couldn't help but react to Charles's question with a genetic spark of paranoia. "Is it good for the Jews?" my mother would always ask in response to most world and local events. For her, it generally wasn't.

Trying to wipe my upbringing from my mind, I nodded.

"Then you've got to meet Roy Salonin!" he exclaimed.

I raised my eyebrows.

"Roy Salonin. He runs a gay Jewish group. It's called Naches." He pronounced it *na-kess*. Charles scribbled a phone number on a scrap of paper and shoved it across the desk at me. "Call him," he insisted.

Next I knew I was back on Peel Street, Charles having already faded into some recess of my past. Cars pushed past me up the steep hill. Crushes of McGill students swallowed me up and spit me out as they rushed to class. I was oblivious to it all. A *gay* Jewish group? A gay *Jewish* group? Called Naches? Talk about chutzpah! *Naches* is a Yiddish word that expresses the joy a parent only gets from children. For a moment, I wondered how much *naches* I would bring my mother when I told her I was gay. Only for a moment. With my next breath, I felt calmer and more alive than I had felt in months. *A gay Jewish group!*

For the next eight years, Naches formed the cornerstone of my gay experience. I attended weekly meetings and became one of the group's organizers. I wrote and produced its newsletter. I demonstrated with fellow members to protest police raids on gay bars and bathhouses. I wrote provincial and national legislators on behalf of the group to press for equal rights. I manned the Naches booth at the city's early Gay Pride celebrations. I let my name be used in articles in the *Montreal Gazette* and *Canadian Jewish News*, then sifted through the resulting answering machine messages — all ugly or obscene.

The hateful comments didn't matter. For the first time in a long time, I felt like I belonged and was comfortable with who I was. No one was going to take that away from me.

Mom and the Psychiatrist

WE ALL CARRY AROUND a handful of scenes that remain forever as clear as the day they occurred. In my life, these include the moment my mother told me that my father had died, my mother's death, my wedding and the morning my daughter was born. Equally vivid is the evening I told my mother that I was gay.

For many gay men who came out in the 1960s and 1970s, their parents were among the last people to whom they revealed their sexual orientation. For me, my mother was the first. We had always been close, she had always known and welcomed my friends and, most important, I still lived at home and knew that any attempt to hide my activities would arouse suspicion and damage our relationship.

It was an evening in late August, probably around nine. My stepfather wasn't home and my mother was lying on her bed reading. I poked my head through the doorway.

"Can we talk?" I asked.

"Of course." She laid down her book.

I sat on the edge of the bed. "There's something I have to tell you." I could feel my heart pounding and was certain she could hear it too. I felt nauseous. Although I was fairly sure she wouldn't reject me, I couldn't be one hundred percent certain. I had read about a Jewish father who not only declared his gay son to be dead but had sat *shiva* for him, observing the seven-day mourning ritual that follows a Jewish funeral. My mother wasn't that ignorant, but...who knew?

She said nothing in the moment after I broke the news then, calling on the "weak/absent father, dominant mother" school of gay origins, guiltily declared herself totally responsible for how I had turned out.

"I want you to talk to Dr. Lundell," she said. Frederick Lundell, the father of one of my Mount Royal High schoolmates, was a psychiatrist who had counseled her through my sister's rebellious teen years.

I shook my head. "Being gay isn't an issue for me," I said from some previously untapped well of courage. I had read even more horror stories about intolerant psychiatrists than I had about rejecting parents, and my sense of self was still too fragile to risk it. "If it's an issue for you, then maybe you should go see Dr. Lundell."

To her credit, she went. And when after her visit she told me that Lundell wanted to see me, I reluctantly agreed to go.

I was almost as nervous walking into the downtown Medical Arts Building on the afternoon of my appointment as I had been prowling the streets around Rue Sainte-Famille. What would he say? Would he try to "convert" me?

Our session was brief. Lundell sat behind his desk in a cloud of pipe smoke and said little, jotting only a few cursory notes onto a lined pad as I recounted my story. After a few questions and a request that I produce two drawings for him — one of a woman, the other of a man — he declared me mentally fit.

"I'll be happy to work with your mother on this," he said as I left, "if that's what she wants."

She did. Whether she saw Lundell once or dozens of times, she soon seemed more relaxed about my sexuality. Within a few months she was meeting my friends and contributing baked goods to Naches holiday potlucks.

Despite her fears and concerns — first about my homosexuality and later about my decision to be politically public about it — Edith always supported my choices, even those she didn't understand. At the same time, she desperately feared judgment. That's why she tried to hide the story about my brother, Michael. That's why she never revealed that my father wasn't who I thought he was. That's why even though my increasingly public profile guaranteed that all friends, relatives and acquaintances must have known that I was gay, she never talked about that, either. She still viewed it as her "fault."

Act 10.
Sedona

We must be willing to let go of the life we have planned, so as to accept the life that is waiting for us.
Joseph Campbell

Take the first step in faith. You don't have to see the whole staircase; just take the first step.
Martin Luther King, Jr.

A New Beginning

THERE IS A REASON why cars drive so slowly down Oak Creek Canyon, and it's not the narrow switchbacks that accelerate the fifteen-hundred-foot drop between Flagstaff's elevation and Sedona's. Highway 89a through Oak Creek Canyon is one of the most arrestingly beautiful roads in America, second in Arizona only to the Grand Canyon in tourist appeal. Following the sparkling creek that gives the canyon its name, the two-lane route is hemmed in by stands of nearly black ponderosa pine and juniper and by towering cliffs that darken suddenly from pale gray to vermilion.

"I'll never be able to leave," I whispered through tears at my first sight of the red rocks. I had seen crimson cliffs before, in Utah, but these were inexplicably different. "I'll never be able to stay," I muttered soon after, when I exited the canyon into the hurly-burly of Uptown Sedona in prime tourist season.

Moments later, driving down a broad gully devoid of buildings, still on 89a, I thought I had left Sedona behind. I was half-relieved. Then, as the road climbed back up, I found myself in somewhat calmer and more local West Sedona. My breath evened. Still, I didn't stop...not until I reached the final strip mall in town, anchored at its north end by Desert Flour cafe. Suddenly aware of the Flagstaff breakfast I had skipped, I pulled in and ordered a carrot-zucchini muffin and a mug of Tazo Zen tea.

Sharing tables with strangers is common in Europe. In North America, it is often considered a violation of personal space. Somehow, though, I found myself sitting on the outside patio with Alison, an attractive brunette in her early twenties. Desert Flour, she told me, was her final Sedona stop after having spent six months in town. Before leaving, she offered to be my Sedona tour guide, and her calming presence helped me feel as though it might be possible to stay on in this energetically turbulent place.

That night as the full moon rose above me, Roxy and I slept in the car on Long Canyon Road just north of town. The only other night I slept in the front seat of my Dodge Caravan had been a few weeks earlier in Bodega Bay, near San Francisco. As in Ferndale, I had arrived in Bodega Bay too late to find a motel. Unlike with Ferndale, I had been reluctant to risk a night on the beach in this more populated area. In Sedona, I could easily have stayed in a hotel. But something in me demanded as direct an experience of that harvest moon as possible, and the pullout was too narrow to accommodate both me in a sleeping bag and the car. I slept restlessly in the driver's seat and kept waking up, each time aware of the moon's progress — first, up over the windshield and, later, through the rearview mirror.

I woke up at first light cold and cramped. All I wanted was a hot shower. Skipping another breakfast, I drove straight to New Earth Lodge, a cluster of semi-rustic, two-room cabins at the top of Sunset Drive. I had seen an ad for it the previous day in a local metaphysical newspaper.

"Can I help you?" Francene Shoop glanced up from the complex accommodation chart she had been studying. Computer programs to manage hotel reservations already existed in 1997, but not at New Earth Lodge.

If Alison was my first Sedona guide, Francene would become my second. Diminutive, maternal and with incisive insight, she had a grounded common-sense attitude unusual for sometimes-spacey Sedona. She booked me into Room 13 for a week, and I proceeded to explore both the town and its red-rock vortexes.

According to many in the metaphysical world, what makes Sedona such a potent center for spiritual healing are the spiraling eddies of subtle energy found in many of its rock formations. It is said that Sedona has more of these vortexes than any other area on the planet. Whether or not the vortexes are real, my time in Sedona would be among the most profoundly transformational of my life.

Not much happened during that first week, other than long hikes with Roxy and long talks with Francene and her front-desk colleague, Grace. When checkout time came, I packed the car, paid my bill and waited in the lobby for FedEx to bring me my mail, shipped from the Toronto mailbox store where I kept a mailing address.

Eleven o'clock, FedEx's delivery guarantee, came and went. I called Toronto and was assured that the package had shipped in time for delivery that morning. I called FedEx with the tracking number and was put on hold.

"Still checking," the phone agent said a while later. "Can we call you back?"

I gave her the front desk number and continued chatting with Grace.

An hour passed. I called FedEx again.

"Still checking."

Finally, another hour later, the phone rang.

"We found it," the agent said. "It's in Phoenix." That was the good news. "Just let us know where you'll be tomorrow and we'll get it to you." That was the bad news. I had no idea where I would be the next day...or the day after that. I was an itinerant, on an open-ended odyssey. Or had it ended without me noticing?

"I'll call you when I have an address," I told the phone agent. Then I hung up and said another goodbye to Grace. I gathered Roxy, got in the car, switched on the ignition and shifted into reverse.

"No," I said out loud, my foot still on the brake. I shifted back into park, switched off the ignition and returned to the lobby.

"Is my room available through the weekend?" I asked Grace.

She studied the chart and nodded. My weekend extension stretched into another week, then another, then many more. When I checked out for the final time to move into my own place in town, I had lived at New Earth Lodge for one hundred days, ten more than I had spent on the road — and I had generated at least as many stories.

The Name Game

OVER THE YEARS, I have been presented with many assaults on my sense of who I think I am. Coming out as a gay man was one. Leaving my gay identity behind, then rediscovering it a decade later were two more. Learning that my father wasn't my birth father was yet another. Through those years, the name I chose to use in the world changed multiple times, sometimes subtly, sometimes radically, always a further expression of a shift in my identity. From Marky, I became Mark. Thirty-seven years later, I adopted my middle name, David, because I believed it to best convey who I had become...or was becoming. And it was David who drove into Sedona in September 1997.

David Gerson would see out the year. He would not be around for 1998.

I had been in Sedona barely three months when, Diana, a sound-healer friend I met shortly after my arrival, began to talk to me about spiritual names. She called them vibrational names (some call them soul names), and she believed passionately that if you had one, you had a responsibility to use it out in the world. "It's who you really are," she argued, "and if it's who you really are, then that's who you should be every day to everyone."

She was convincing, even more so soon when she announced the new name she had adopted: Irlianna. It had a nice ring to it...a powerful ring. And, strangely, it seemed to fit her — so much that, within a few days, I could hardly remember what her name had been previously. Yet as compelling as Diana-Irlianna's arguments were, the issue was theoretical. The only name I knew to call myself was David.

A few days after Diana became Irlianna, I was feeling homesick and called KA'Ryna, a Toronto friend I had met shortly before leaving town. KA'Ryna was a channel, though I had never experienced her work. I soon would. We had barely begun chatting that evening when she interrupted me and said, "I'm getting a message for you. Do you want to hear it?"

"Sure," I said.

A few moments later, she was "in the zone."

"Do you know your vibrational name?" the group she was channeling asked through her.

"No," I replied, somewhat unnerved. I had never mentioned my conversations with Irlianna.

"Would you like to?"

"Okay..."

"Would you like it to come through KA'Ryna or directly to you?"

"Through me, please." I knew that whatever might come would be more empowering were I to experience it directly.

I sat in expectant silence. Nothing happened for a few moments. Then, it was as though I was feeling the name without physically hearing or seeing it. I didn't want to hear it. I didn't want to see it. Despite my resistance, I began to sense first one letter...

A...

Then another...

K...

Then another after that...

H...

Then two more...

N... E...

"Okay," I cried silently. "I surrender!"

It was Akhneton, the name of an Egyptian pharaoh. The audacity of it astounded me. How could a good Jewish boy take on that kind of name? Later, after further research, I would learn that Akhneton was a revolutionary monotheist who took on Egypt's powerful priestly class and decreed that the many gods of their Amenist tradition were now folded into a single god: Aten, the sun god. I would learn, too, that Egyptologists believe Akhneton to have been Nefertiti's husband and Tutankhamen's father, and that the more traditional spelling is Akhenaten, pronounced Ah-keh-NAH-tin. What I sensed that evening with KA'Ryna was slightly different: AHK-na-tawn. That's the pronunciation I would adopt.

The next morning, in that hypnogogic state between waking and sleeping, I heard this phrase: "I am Akhneton Yoseyva, way-shower."

Yoseyva? What's that?

Whatever else it was, it was just as bizarre as Akhneton. In the spirit of surrender, I decided that I could accept Akhneton Yoseyva as a spiritual name, but that no one else would need to know about it. I would not use it out in the world. I would not share it with Irlianna.

My resolve lasted barely two weeks. On New Year's Day 1998, I pulled into my friend Lee Graham's driveway for a potluck dinner, eager to meet a Canadian family he had told me about. My six-month legal stay in the US as Canadian visitor would soon expire, and I knew it was important for me to remain in the country. How would I manage it? Maybe the Hunters, who had just moved here from British Columbia, would have an answer.

Tall, handsome and with dark eyes and complexion, Calen was a striking presence in Lee's crowded living room. Lee had appointed himself Sedona's metaphysical networker-in-chief and his regular potlucks filled his Village of Oak Creek home with a motley blend of visitors, newcomers and long-time residents. I pushed through the crush and introduced myself to Calen.

"I'm a dual citizen," he explained, when I asked how he planned to stay in the country.

So much for immigration advice.

"Your name," I said. "It's unusual."

"It's my spiritual name."

He had my attention. I began peppering him with questions: How had he chosen it? Had he changed it legally? What did his family think? How did he feel giving up his birth name? Twenty minutes later we were finished. So was David Gerson. When it was time to leave, I knew that I would have to walk out of Lee's house and into the world as Akhneton Yoseyva.

Fear of judgment had always hung heavily on me. That's what

kept me creatively blocked for so many years. That's what held me back from acknowledging my sexual orientation. That's what initially prevented me from owning the name Akhneton. Now, I would have to swallow my fears and reintroduce myself to the world. While it was easier to do in a town where taking on an unusual name was almost a rite of passage, I still had anxious moments. Yet, everyone responded to me as I had responded to Irlianna: Within days, most had forgotten that I had ever been anyone other than Akhneton.

Five and a half months later, still Akhneton Yoseyva, I leaned into the counter at the Yavapai County clerk's office in nearby Camp Verde. Next to me stood Kentia Kazantzis, my wife-to-be. We were applying for a marriage license. When the clerk printed Mark David Gerson, my legal name, on the form, Kentia blanched. She shifted her gaze from the license to me to the clerk and back to the license. Then she pointed a finger at the offending line.

"Can you add something to that?" she asked the clerk. "Like a nickname?"

"Like Bubba?" the clerk asked, in all solemnity.

"No," we exclaimed in unison.

Once again, Kentia looked from the name on the form to me and back.

"I'm not marrying Mark David Gerson," she announced with grim finality. "I'm marrying Akhneton Yoseyva."

I swallowed hard and turned to the clerk. I had never planned to go through a legal name change. Calen hadn't. But now... "If I were to legally change my name," I asked haltingly, "what would I have to do?"

The clerk explained the procedure, which in pre-9/11 Arizona was liberal enough that even a nonresident Canadian could do it. She handed me the necessary forms. I could do it, but would I?

"I need to think about this," I pleaded.

"Here's what I can do," the clerk offered. "I'll make the license out in your birth name. If you decide to change it, come back with your papers and I'll issue you a new one at no charge."

Two days later, I was back at the same counter, this time with completed, notarized name-change forms. Two weeks later, Mark David Gerson legally ceased to exist. I was Akhneton Yoseyva, in law. A few years afterward, in Hawaii, another legal procedure would turn Akhneton into Aq'naton (and Kentia into Q'nta).

I remained Aq'naton until January 2005, two months after our marriage ended. Having sold our household goods and split the proceeds with my ex, I was back on the road. On this day, I was driving along California's Pacific Coast Highway near Refugio State Beach when, suddenly, it felt was as though there was no longer an Aq'naton. As I had experienced with "Mark" seven-and-a-half years earlier, the name no longer fit. Only this time, I had no handy replacement. I swerved into the next pullout and, shaken, stared at the ocean, steel-gray on this overcast day. If I wasn't Aq'naton, who was I? Was I David again? Mark? Neither felt right.

"Maybe I should just call myself 'The Nameless One,'" I joked to a friend over the phone a little while later. I laughed, hollowly.

Over the next days, I called myself, variously, Mark, David and Aq'naton. None seemed to express who I was. Perhaps, I thought sinkingly, nothing can. When I drove into Sedona a week later, it was once again as David. This time, I knew it was the wrong name, but there was no KA'Ryna to guide me through another name-replacement experience.

"What about 'Mark David,'" Martha Martyn asked. Martha, my ex-dentist's ex-wife, had introduced me to both Diana and Kentia in my early weeks in Sedona, when Steve Baer was still my dentist and she was still his wife and office manager. We were having lunch at Wildflower Bakery in Sedona and I was explaining my name predicament.

"Mark David?" I repeated it a few times. It felt odd, an unusual compound name that seemed to stumble out of my mouth rather than flow easily. I forgot that I had considered it as an option back in Toronto, when Mark became David. Martha's rapid calculation of its numerological significance did not immediately sway me. Even so, "Mark David" felt better than any other known option, so I adopted it...and once again reintroduced myself, once again somewhat anxiously, to the world.

A few days later, I drove back to the Camp Verde courthouse, to the scene of that first legal name change. In Arizona at the time, name-changes did not require legal notices in a newspaper. They involved a summary hearing before a judge. The first time, my court appearance took place a few weeks after I handed in the paperwork in a session filled with uncontested divorces and other quick-gavel decisions. This time, I was only passing through Sedona with no plans to stay beyond the next few days.

"I'll be traveling," I told the clerk when she offered possible court dates weeks out. "Are there no other options?"

"Hang on a sec," she said and disappeared into a back room. Five minutes later she reemerged. "Can you be back here in two hours?"

I nodded.

She grinned. "I found a judge who will give you a private hearing."

Three hours later I was in Division Six of the Superior Court of Arizona.

"Why are you changing your name?" the judge asked.

I told him Aq'naton had been a pen name and that I now wanted all my affairs back in my birth name. It was the simplest piece of a larger truth.

He scribbled something on his pad.

"Are you changing your name to avoid debts or to hide from creditors?"

"No, sir."

He scribbled something else on his pad, signed the name-change order and passed it to the clerk. She stamped it.

It was 11:11 on January 27, 2005. Six years and eight months to the day after Akhneton Yoseyva had been legally created in this same building, he ceased to exist. Mark David Gerson had been reborn.

How I Met My Wife

I WAS SINGLE, I was still officially a Canadian resident and I was an accidental celibate with an indeterminate sexual orientation when I drove into Sedona that September morning in 1997. By the time I left for the Big Island in February 1999, I was a married, soon-to-be-father, rabidly sexual for the first time in my life and with a US green-card application pending. In between... Well, here is some of what happened in between...

If Francene Shoop took on the role of my adoptive Earth Mother in Sedona, Martha Martyn's role was more prophetic, as both the agent and harbinger of change. Slim with gray-streaked reddish-brown hair and an unmistakable New York accent, Martha had been Martha Baer when whichever gods rule Sedona threw us together for the first time. I had only been in Sedona a few weeks when I saw Steve Baer's ad for his holistic dentistry practice and realized I was overdue for a check-up.

When I called for an appointment, two things happened that shouldn't have. First, Martha picked up the phone. Martha never picked up the phone. As Steve's office manager, she kept out of view in her back office, doing whatever it is that dental office managers do. Second, she gave me an appointment. The Sedona of 1997 was a haven for transients. Spiritual seekers of all types made their pilgrimage to the red-rock vortexes. Many stayed for several months or a year; only a minority settled in for the long-term. The legend was that if Sedona wanted you to stay, she would make sure you couldn't leave. Something like that had happened to me, of course, but I heard even more radical stories: of relationship breakups, cars breakdowns, medical issues and flight cancellations. Then, the story went, when Sedona was through with you, she would spit you out, sometimes with head-spinning rapidity. For that reason, the Baers had a strict policy: no transients as patients.

When I arrived for my appointment, Martha, again uncharacteristically, was behind the reception desk. She was intrigued by the story of how I got to Sedona, and we immediately hit it off. The following Saturday, we met for brunch then crossed West Highway 89a to the Hampton Inn for a craft fair-cum-metaphysical show that would be a pivotal Sedona event for me.

Martha's reason for taking me to the Hampton Inn was so that I could meet Diana, the sound-healer who would soon become Irlianna and help trigger both my own work in the sound-energy field and my name change. The event's organizer was Kentia Kazantzis, another friend of Martha's and an artisan who designed elegant hand-painted silk clothing. This was the same Kentia who, seven months later, I would reconnect with at a Beltane bonfire organized by another Hampton Inn booth-holder, Heidi Madsen, who would soon change her name to Dunnea. In fact, between Kentia, Dunnea, Irlianna and Lee Graham, who was also at the event, I connected with the core of my first Sedona life in a single, Hampton Inn afternoon, thanks to Martha.

Although I had arrived in Sedona vague about many things, I had absolute clarity about one: I needed to remain in the US. While I could think of no logical way that could legally occur, I trusted (mostly) that if I continued to surrender, a way would be found. A few mornings before the Hampton Inn event, I was on the patio at Desert Flour when Bruce Sanderson wandered by. I knew Bruce from the local Mailboxes, Etc., my new Sedona mailing address. Tall, lanky and handsome, with longish hair and straggly beard, Bruce joined me at my table and explained that he was on his way to the library to research immigration law. His fiancée was East Asian, and he was determined to find a way for her to stay in the country legally. As soon as Bruce walked off, I had an *aha*: Love and marriage would keep me in the US. I didn't know who she was or how I would meet her, but I knew she was out there.

After that, of course, I couldn't help but wonder about every woman I met. "Is she the one?" I would ask silently. When Martha introduced me to Kentia, something deep inside me shouted *YES*. Then I discovered that Kentia wasn't single, and I questioned the accuracy of my intuitive radar. As it turned out, my radar was flawless; it had just neglected to add a date-stamp to its reading.

Beltane, celebrated May 1, is the Celtic feast of optimism and fertility. Although Dunnea's version had no maypole, her blazing fire would have done the ancients proud. She had been secretly amassing wood for weeks and had been planning the event for even longer. I almost didn't go. I woke up that morning feeling depressed and not at all optimistic. By evening, I had shaken off enough of the pall to drive down to the Cathedral Rock area for the bonfire. When I arrived, the flames were already dancing up into the darkening sky. I saw no one I knew apart from Dunnea, so I sat off to the side. Fifteen minutes later, Kentia, recently split from her partner of six years, arrived with a woman friend. She scanned the crowd, picked me out and strode over. I hadn't seen her since a week after our Hampton Inn meeting but was still surprised when, not seeming to recognize me, she stuck out her hand and announced, "Hi, I'm Kentia."

"I know," I said. "I'm Akhneton." She knew who Akhneton was from Dunnea, who had told her about my local writing workshops. But she didn't recognize me as the David she had met seven months earlier.

We talked solidly for the next three hours — about Sedona (her arrival had preceded mine by a year) and about writing (she was struggling with a novel). During that time no one else existed, and when it was time to go, we agreed to meet again on Sunday for a typical Sedona date: a hike.

Perhaps I shouldn't have been surprised when Kentia didn't recognize the David I had been. A few weeks after I adopted the name, I was sitting meditatively on a large rock at Sedona's Soldiers Pass hiking trail when Arctur, my old friend from the Boise steam room popped into my consciousness and offered a prediction that was the most accurate I had ever intuited. "You will marry, soon," I heard, "by June...an American woman you will meet in Sedona. You will know her when you meet her, and she will know you as Akhneton.

You will be a father before the final bell tolls this year away." Kentia could not recognize me because it was Akhneton not David she had been fated to meet. As it turned out, I was a father by year's end, although neither of us would know until a week into 1999, when we discovered that Kentia was pregnant.

Arctur also had other information for me. By late January 1998, I was weeks away from the expiration of my legal stay in the US and I was considering driving thirteen hundred miles to the nearest border crossing, near Glacier National Park. My plan would be to stay on the Canadian side for a day then return to Sedona, thereby resetting my six-month clock as a visitor. "Don't," I heard Arctur say, as clearly as if he were physically next to me. "Stay in Sedona. Spirit knows immigration law." Spirit did, in fact, know immigration law. When it came time to apply for my green card, the penalty for overstaying my legal welcome was minimal.

Not only did I not leave Sedona for Canada that month, I had trouble leaving Sedona at all. Every time I tried to travel any farther afield than a day trip to Phoenix, something intervened. My first overnight trip out of town wouldn't occur until my honeymoon.

A final Arctur story...

When less than a week after the bonfire, Kentia and I — to our mutual surprise — were discussing marriage, I kept insisting on a June wedding.

"That's next month," she exclaimed incredulously.

"I know. But June feels right."

Kentia argued, insisting that it would be impossible to plan any sort of wedding in that time, and I argued back, with intuition as my sole ammunition. Then I mentioned my January "conversation" with Arctur.

"What did you say his name was?" she asked, her eyes wide.

"Arctur. It's an odd name, isn't it."

"I thought so too," she said, "when an Arctur came to me a few years ago, when I was channeling. I said to him, 'What kind of name is that?' He didn't explain." She paused. "What are the odds of an Arctur coming to both of us, before we'd even met?"

Not only was our connection now even more firmly cemented, but Kentia's respect for my intuitive abilities deepened appreciably.

"Okay," she said. "Let's say we were to get married in June, what date would it be?"

Without thinking, I picked June 21, the summer solstice. Kentia ran to the other room to find a calendar, convinced that my choice would fall midweek and thus be disqualified. It fell on a Sunday and that was the day we married, in a deeply moving if unconventional outdoor ceremony just across Oak Creek from the Beltane bonfire site and within view of Cathedral Rock.

Martha Martyn would show up in Sedona for me at three more pivotal moments. Just as she had been there when I first arrived in town and met Kentia, she would also be present at the end of both my marriage and my time in Sedona.

It was August 2004 and Kentia (by then Aalia) and I needed to move. Although our financial situation had improved steadily since our return from Hawaii in June 2002, we had been consistently late on our Zane Grey Lane rental. The owners warned us that unless we left voluntarily we would likely be evicted. The new house we found was on a different Zane Grey: Zane Grey Circle, at the other end of town. And in one of those last-minute miracles that always seemed to follow us, the precise sum we needed for the move turned up unexpectedly. We moved Halloween weekend, unaware at the time that the only reason the house had become available was because Martha Martyn, then divorced, had backed out at the last minute.

Just a few days later, not long after the polls closed on America's fifty-fifth election, Aalia sat me down in our new living room, surrounded by stacks of unpacked boxes, to tell me that our marriage was over. She had fallen in love with Marcus Gilhart, she said. While she still loved me, she felt she had no choice but to follow her heart.

In the first of another series of synchronistic ironies, our daughter, Guinevere, then five, played a key role in the breakup. It was through her school friendship with Marcus's daughter, Teshna, that the two families initially met. The second irony was that Marcus shared my birth name, my initials and my citizenship. He was born Mark and he, too, was Canadian. The third and most prescient irony also came from Guinevere.

When I returned home that election-night evening from Lemuria Calling, the failing metaphysical store we then co-owned with our friends Karen and Larry Weaver, I found Doreen Virtue's *Magical Mermaids and Dolphin Oracle* deck on my desk, where Guinevere had been using it to practice her writing. In clear view on a yellow notepad, scratched out in her preschool scrawl, were the words "Time to Move On," as copied directly from the mermaid card of the same name. A few hours later, it would be.

Six weeks after that, I was gone from Sedona, having launched what I expected to be a replay of the 1997 road odyssey that had brought me to Sedona. I anticipated a few months on the road. Instead, I spent thirty-three months of cross-country traveling before landing in New Mexico.

Martha and I would run into each one more time in Sedona, five years later, at another key moment in my life.

Married...with Kids?

GROWING UP, I GAVE little thought to marriage and kids, although at some unconscious level, I must have assumed that that's how my life would play out. It was, after all, a reasonable expectation for a boy growing up in the fifties and sixties, and I had no role models for any other outcome. Even my bachelor uncle, as we called my still-single Uncle Danny when I was little, eventually married and started a family.

Once I came out as a gay man in 1975, children were not an option. In those days gay activists lobbied for basic nondiscrimination rights; same-sex marriage and adoption were nowhere on any agenda. And when four Naches friends, a lesbian couple and gay male couple, announced that they were going to form a single household and have kids together, it was considered startlingly revolutionary.

It wasn't until Penetanguishene, with my sexual orientation already in question, that the first hint of something as radical as fatherhood showed up. I had barely moved into Jim and Angela Emery's flat when my first stream of *Dialogues with the Divine* writings produced this interchange.

"I'm afraid," I wrote. "Afraid of what I don't know, of what I can't see, of what I can't imagine...of what I *can* imagine."

"What do you imagine?"

"Married," I replied, "with kids."

"That may or may not happen. If it did, would it be so bad?"

"No. Yes and no. All at the same time."

After a ten-month house-share with Fred Henderson, I thought I had come to Penetanguishene for solitude. What found me instead was Jeremy, young enough to be my son and a constant presence. A few months into my stay, on one of my regular visits to Penetang's tiny New Age store, I bought a black-and-white photo-poster of a young father cradling an infant to his chest. I saw myself as the baby and the poster as a way to heal unresolved feelings toward my father. While that perspective may have been accurate, what I couldn't yet acknowledge was that I could also be the father in the poster. Twenty-two months later, I would be.

By the time Kentia and I reconnected at the Beltane bonfire, I had been sexually inactive for five years. I hadn't been homosexual or heterosexual. I had been asexual. Now, to my amazement, I felt a whole-mind, whole-body attraction toward this woman that I had never experienced with anyone else. At the same time, I had never had sex with a woman. How would I handle it?

On the Monday evening after our Sunday hike-date, not ready to take the sexual plunge that I was certain was coming, I left Roxy at home when I went to Kentia's for dinner, in order to give me a credible excuse to leave by eleven. Before I left, though, I nervously told Kentia that I was — or had been — gay. She took it well, and we agreed to meet two days later to make love. Given my history, we both needed to know whether the "sex thing" was going to work between us.

To my surprised relief, it did. Magnificently. Through those early months of our relationship, the lovemaking was the most profound I had ever experienced. Not because I had been unconsciously straight and was finally expressing my natural sexual self. Rather, our connection felt so cellular, soulful and unbreakable that it dissolved all conventional norms of attraction. I wasn't having sex with a female body. I was making love with someone I felt I had known intimately through lifetimes. Physiology was irrelevant.

After that first afternoon of lovemaking, Kentia turned to me. "I've just had an intuitive hit that we're going to have a son and his name will be Ben."

I jerked up. "Say that again."

She did.

Without explaining, I leapt out of bed and raced across the

house for my *StarQuest* manuscript. I had begun my sequel to *The MoonQuest* eight days earlier. The day before the bonfire, I had written a scene involving the story's main character, Q'nta, and a young man named Ben. As words flew onto the page and the story revealed itself to me, I knew what Q'nta and Ben did not themselves yet know: that they were mother and son.

Dumbfounded, I read the scene to Kentia. She was astounded too — as much for the similarity between Kentia and Q'nta as about the son named Ben. It wouldn't be long before Kentia would take on the name Q'nta, first as a spiritual name then as a legal name. Strangely, it wasn't until Q'nta became Aalia after we split up and in a sense gave the character's name back to me, that I was finally able to finish *The StarQuest*, the fictional Q'nta's story.

Even with Kentia's intuitive sensing and my *StarQuest* story about Ben, neither of us was enthusiastic about parenthood. Kentia stayed on the pill, and over the next months we would alternatively surrender to the notion of having a child and, generally after witnessing a parent-toddler interaction, rebel. Ben-Guinevere had other ideas. One day the cook at the restaurant where Q'nta worked as a server looked at her strangely and asked, "Are you pregnant?" She wasn't, and he wasn't the only one asking her the question. Then, a few weeks later while we were attending a workshop together, one of the exercises involved blindly drawing a card from *The Mayan Oracle* deck. I drew the card titled "Ben."

Our unconditional surrender occurred soon after, over lunch at Sedona's India Palace Restaurant. We had just returned from a trip to Los Angeles, where we visited two old friends of Q'nta's, both parents. One confessed that his marriage was a wreck, but that he and his wife were staying together for the sake of their daughter. The other barely noticed us during our afternoon visit, so focused was she on her infant and toddler.

"No kids," we swore on the drive back. "Never."

The occasion for our India Palace lunch was an opportunity to meet Francene Shoop's cousin, Courtney Eves. Courtney, a metaphysical powerhouse who was visiting from Connecticut, had once worked at Simon & Schuster. Perhaps she could help get *The*

MoonQuest and *Dialogues with the Divine* published? In the middle of telling me that there was likely little she could do, she turned to Q'nta, sitting across from her. Her fork dropped from her hand, clattering onto the table. Her eyes widened, watered.

"There's this being," she began, her voice cracking. "This amazing being. It's sitting just above your right shoulder." She stared at Q'nta. "It's waiting to come through you. It's waiting for you to let it come through you."

That was it. All our resistance dissolved in that powerful moment of revelation and surrender.

"I'll stay on the pill until the moment I feel guided to stop," Q'nta said when we got home from the restaurant. The moment came soon.

When Q'nta stopped taking the pill, we didn't know that for someone who had been on it as long as she had been, it was wise to wait ninety days before conceiving. We learned this only after we found out that she was pregnant. For fun, we counted back from the date of conception, amazed to discover that it had been *exactly* ninety days. Spirit Ben-Guinevere, crossing off the days on a celestial calendar, had waited for the first safe moment to drop into Q'nta's womb.

By then, we had already been discussing a possible move to Hawaii and were planning an exploratory visit for the spring. Q'nta's pregnancy limited our options: We could either move right away or wait until after the baby was born. With little debate, we chose to go immediately. In less than two months, having sold everything, we were living on the rainforest slopes of the Mauna Loa volcano in rural Captain Cook, a thousand feet up from the dolphins of the Big Island's legendary Kealakekua Bay.

Roxy

BEFORE Q'NTA AND I could move to Hawaii, we had to decide what to do about Roxy. Through the two years since she and I had left Fred, Roxy was my constant companion, sometimes my only companion. She had traveled with me to Penetanguishene and back to Toronto, and then on the ninety-day road odyssey that had carried me along many thousands of miles of meanderings to Sedona. Getting her to Hawaii would not be as simple.

Although Hawaii had moderated its once-onerous mandatory quarantine for pets by early 1999, it would still have been punishing for a dog as social as Roxy: thirty days in a state facility on Oahu. There was a quarantine kennel on the Big Island, but it was run privately and was beyond our means. As Q'nta and I continued to plan our move, I sought out local pets owners who had lived in Hawaii. Most confessed that their dogs were never the same after having been sequestered for a month in quarantine. I was torn. Intuitively, I knew that Roxy would not do well in that situation and that it wasn't right to subject her to it. That same intuition, however, insisted that Hawaii was the right next move for us and that, with Q'nta's pregnancy, we could not delay our departure. My journal of the time is filled with tearful pleas for a third option. The guidance that showed up day after day in my *Dialogues with the Divine* format generally went like this: "Roxy has her destiny. You have yours. That they have come together for a time — a blessed time — does not mean they are stuck together for all time. Free her to live her destiny. Just as she frees you to live yours."

I didn't want to hear it and initially threatened to cancel the move. In the end, I surrendered, sobbingly.

If Roxy wasn't to come with us, what were we to do with her?

Perhaps Betty Tentschert would take her? Betty lived in a small apartment underneath our Zane Grey Lane flat with her husband, Fritz, and was the property manager for the two-unit building. She had been a surrogate mother since we moved in and loved Roxy. However, Betty's Lucy-red hair and youthful spirit belied her age, which was some indeterminate number in the eighties — too old, she said with regret, to deal full-time with our rambunctious and not-always-obedient cocker spaniel. We asked a few other friends if they would take her. None could.

In the end, Roxy would find her own home. It was during the final Saturday of our three total-selloff garage sales, with only a few weeks left before we would take off on our one-way transpacific flight. Roxy was tied up on the driveway as Q'nta and I haggled with the bargain-hunters who had responded to our "Moving to Hawaii. Everything must go" ad in the *Sedona Red Rock News*. From the corner of my eye, I noticed a young blonde girl on her knees, playing with the dog. The two were totally involved with each other. When the girl's mother, Leah, shared that she and her husband had been thinking about getting their daughter a dog, I mentioned our Roxy predicament. Leah was intrigued. We talked some more, then I offered to send Roxy over to their house for the day the following weekend to see how everyone got along.

The drive to the Weatherbys' in Cottonwood, twenty minutes from Sedona, was emotional, but not nearly as emotional as our arrival. When we pulled up to the house and opened the car door, Roxy shot out. She raced across the lawn and up to the front door as though it had always been her home. This was not normal Roxy behavior. I was startled, relieved and heartbroken. Q'nta went up ahead. I sat in the car and wept.

The visit was a success, and a few days and many more tears later, I wrote this farewell to Roxy in my journal: "Goodbye, Roxy. Thank you for all you have given me and done for me. Thank you for all you have shared with me and taught me. Thank you for all the times you have comforted me and made me laugh, all the times you have reminded me of the joy of simplicity and the simplicity of joy. You have taught me well, and I honor and love you for that. With both joy and sadness in my heart, I release you. I release you from my future that we may both continue to live in the present. I release you to Savannah and Leah and Don. I release you fully to them, knowing that they will love you as I have, but in their own way, and that you will love them with the fullness you have loved me. I honor you for your journey. I honor you for your love. I honor you for your heart, for your truth and for all that you are. I honor you, love you and release you. Goodbye, little one. Goodbye and thank you."

Our next visit to the Weatherbys' was more difficult still. It was a few days before our flight and we were delivering Roxy and her gear to Savannah and her parents. As hard as I cried on the drive over, I was inconsolable on the way back. Little did I know that this emotional departure from Roxy and Sedona would mirror an even more emotional leave-taking five years later — again from Sedona, but this time from my not-yet born daughter.

Act 11.
Hawaii

Only he who has lived in darkness truly knows and values the light.
Stephen Lawhead

Faith is the strength by which a shattered world shall emerge into the light.
Helen Keller

The Land of Aloha and Uē (Crying)

FOR ALL ITS PICTURE-postcard beauty, Hawaii was a difficult place to be...and not only because of a cost of living that made Sedona's inflated food and land prices seem reasonable. Some metaphysical writers link each of the Hawaiian islands to one of the chakras — from the first or root chakra for the Big Island, through the second or sacral for Maui, all the way up the chain to the seventh, the crown chakra, for Niihau. The root chakra, as I mentioned earlier, governs identity, security and survival; sexuality, fertility and creativity are the domain of the sacral chakra. We lived on both the Big Island and Maui during our three and a half years in Hawaii, and on each island I experienced chakra-linked upheavals that felt as explosive as the volcanic eruptions that originally created the islands.

They began almost as soon we got off the plane. In the middle of one of our first nights, I was stung in bed not once but twice by a poisonous centipede. I should have known then that this was not going to be the paradise we had anticipated. In fact, so challenging were those early months that I joked that it had been tears that turned Hawaii's once-solid land mass into islands. My tears alone might have been enough.

Within days of the centipede incident, the independent, MLM-type income that we had expected would support us in pricey Hawaii collapsed. Soon after, and for the first time since surrendering to my Muse in Carole Leckner's workshop, it felt as though my identity as a writer was also disintegrating. Not for the last time during those years, my faith in my spiritual path crashed.

"I don't know what to call God anymore," I wrote in my journal. "I don't know what to trust anymore. I don't know what to believe in anymore. I'm angry and I'm scared."

Our first priority once we found a place to live — a rustic cabin on an organic coffee and avocado form — was to find jobs. We would both work until Q'nta was too far along in her pregnancy. From our first job, doing food demonstrations at the Kailua-Kona Costco, we went on to become OPCs. If you have ever visited a community where timeshare is big, you will have encountered an OPC: an aggressive, sometimes obnoxious street-hawker who tries to bribe you into attending a timeshare sales presentation. Our jobs, for the Mauna Loa Villages resort in Keauhou, were commission-only. We started in booths on the street, where neither of us performed with great success. After a few months, I was transferred to the resort itself, where my lobby role as quasi-concierge better suited my personality.

By early 2000, I had not looked at my aborted *StarQuest* manuscript in over a year, and despite the early assault on my writerly sense of self, I attempted to move forward with it. We had moved by then, from the mosquito- and mold-spawning Mauna Loa slopes to the town of Waimea. Tucked in a high valley between the Big Island's Mauna Kea and Kohala mountains, Waimea straddles two opposing climate zones. To the east is the wet side, where a clear day means mist instead of rain. To the west is the dry side, where nonstop gales gust violently through the Kohala/Mauna Kea wind tunnel. We lived in Kamuela View Estates, on the dry side.

On days off, I would often drive ten minutes up Kohala Mountain Road, park at an ocean-vista lookout and try to work on *The StarQuest*. Few words came. On work days, I would leave early, park for a different postcard view by the gates of the Pu'u Wa'awa'a cattle ranch, and when no *StarQuest* scenes emerged, seek guidance in that same dialogues format that had served me since Penetanguishene. I didn't get much further on *The StarQuest*, but the reams of inspirational writings that resulted would later form the foundation of *The Voice of the Muse: Answering the Call to Write*.

I hated my job — and I hated myself for being good at it. Fortunately, it paid the bills, if barely. Meantime, I was making no progress on *The StarQuest*. In Sedona, with its abundance of public land and hiking trails, I could always walk off my frustration. Here, although we could easily sneak into open Parker Ranch land, the Waimea winds turned even a simple stroll into an unpleasant slog. We didn't have much of a social life, and with a three-month-old, there was rarely any money for diversions. I may not have had island fever, but Hawaii was as challenging as ever. I was miserable and depressed.

"If you could do anything else right now, something that would bring you joy, what would it be?" Q'nta asked me one day.

Without thinking, I replied, "Teaching."

I had taught a handful of writing workshops in my early days in Sedona, but none since. Excited, I scheduled a free class at a local community center. It was so successful that I began to offer longer series from home — now, to paying students. The students loved my classes, many returning for session after session, I felt the reemergence of a passion I had barely experienced since leaving the mainland, and more material for a *Voice of the Muse* book I didn't know I was writing began germinating within me.

Sweet Surrender

IF THE BIG ISLAND challenged my sense of self, at least it provided us with a bare level of financial support. Maui never bothered with that. After our brief visit to the island for the Maui Writers Conference, during which all signs seemed to point to abundance and opportunity, we packed our things and crossed the Alenuihaha Channel to our new home. Perhaps had we remembered all the ways in which the Big Island had mercilessly shattered our expectations, we would have been less sanguine. As it was, we settled into our Kihei Villages condo convinced that Maui would be our ticket to success and that Kihei would be but a stepping-stone to the more scenic and much more expensive Kula highlands.

It wasn't. Despite two concurrent jobs — as an OPC, where I was never able to recreate my Big Island sales moxie, and as a taxi driver at the helm of an aging mud-brown Ford Aerostar held together with prayers and duct tape — our monthly income rarely met our monthly expenses. The noncredit writing classes I taught at Maui Community College, our weekly crystal-selling stall at the Maui Swap Meet and my occasional sound-healing client sessions all helped. Yet nothing, it seemed, could halt a downward financial spiral that only worsened when 9/11 stripped the island of its tourists. It would take more than two years and a return to the mainland for our finances, shaky at the best of times, to recover from the shipwreck that was Maui. To make matters worse, a Clinton-era law had stripped immigrants of the right to most federally funded social assistance. I was ineligible for unemployment insurance, and although my wife and daughter were American citizens, they could not receive food stamps or welfare as long as we were all part of the same household.

The first to be sacrificed to our financial implosion were my

Canadian credit cards. I simply stopped paying, in the hopes that my American cards could be salvaged. We soon defaulted on those too. Food and rent had to come first. If I had arrived on Maui with exemplary credit in two countries, my credit by the time we left was so bad that First Hawaiian Bank, which held the lien on our car, refused to sign the papers required by the shipper. We would not be allowed to take our car back to the mainland with us.

I had experienced many "voluntary surrenders" over the years; this was my first involving a vehicle. Our plan was to arrive at the airport ultra-early, check in and get our luggage handled. We would then drop our Subaru Forester at First Hawaiian's Kahului branch and have our friend Anita return us to the airport in time for our flight. We never got out of the terminal. Still in the grip of heightened 9/11 security, the airport was a congested mass of molasses-like lines. Ours took two hours, slowed even more by the added risk suggested by my unusual name, which sounded vaguely Arabic, and by our one-way tickets, which suggested martyrdom-focused terrorists. By the time we were cleared, all we had time to do was board. Once on the plane, we convinced the purser to drop our car keys at the ATA counter while, long after cellphones were to have been switched off, I made frantic calls to Anita and First Hawaiian.

By then I had grown largely immune to the humiliation of this, my first financial collapse. Until Sedona, when the Canadian savings I was living on lost thirty percent of their value against the US dollar but had to support me and a pregnant wife, my fiscal life had been controllingly ultraconservative. I had lived not within my means but beneath them. Keeping my expenses well below my income had seemed a sensible strategy. In truth, it was a fear-based one: I was terrified of lack. Although the savings generated by that fear had helped fund my spiritual journey, they were depleted by the time we reached Maui.

As our credit card bills went past due then long past due, the collection calls began, first sporadically then multiple times a day. I answered each and tried to explain our situation. Yet nearly every call seemed designed to make me feel irresponsible, unworthy and a failure. It worked. I felt irresponsible, unworthy and a failure.

Somehow, through a succession of miracles, we managed to meet our most basic needs. One day on a taxi run, a customer topped up a sixty-dollar fare with a forty-dollar tip. On another, a check for eighty dollars arrived in the mail. Although it was made out to me, we never found out what it was for. The owner of our condo was a monthly miracle. A pilot-cum-realtor, Lane never pressured or penalized us, even though we generally paid our rent in bits and pieces and rarely on time. Our biggest Maui angel, though, was a client. A powerful Defense Department administrator with an insatiable appetite for the metaphysical, he became a regular consumer of my sound-healing work, always booking sessions precisely when our cash flow was at its most meager. And when it came time for us to leave the island, he fronted us the cash to get us back to Arizona.

Through all the disintegration, hopelessness and helplessness I experienced on Maui, a constant bulwark to my wavering faith was the island's Unity Church and its then-minister, Mary Omwake. Unity had been a solid anchor for me when I first arrived in Sedona. But Kentia wasn't much of a churchgoer and I rarely returned once we were married. Unity of Maui changed that. More to the point, Mary did. A blonde powerhouse of passion, vision and charisma, she had already overseen a dramatic expansion of her previous congregation and was in the midst of doing the same on Maui. Mary infused her services with the same vibrancy that her friend Michael Beckwith was already bringing to the Agape International Spiritual Center in Los Angeles, and her Sunday talks, never scripted, were rousing calls to the empowered action that only derives from profound inner work. She wasn't perfect, but she was perfect for that time in my life, creating a sanctuary where I could recharge a spirit that seemed nearly always under assault.

It was at Unity that Q'nta and I first learned of Kukuipuka, an ancient Hawaiian temple, or heiau, hidden high up in the East Maui Mountains. What distinguished Kukuipuka from other of the islands' surviving heiaus was that it sat on private land, had been privately restored and received few visitors. We immediately felt called to go. But when we asked how to get there, we were given vague, typically Hawaiian directions that ended with, "If you're meant to find it, you will."

We were meant to find it.

It was late on a March afternoon when we stumbled onto the crude parking lot and made our way up a short path to the heiau, a large, grassy enclosure surrounded by a low rock wall, barely knee-high. Directly across from the opening, at the far end of the heiau, was an altar, also of rough stone. The views were open to the ocean and to the lights just starting to blink on down in Kahului harbor. No one else was there, and the stillness was complete.

We left Guinevere, then two and a half, to play outside the wall. I don't know what Q'nta did. All I remember was being so transfixed that the only thing I could do was slowly circle the heiau's inner perimeter, chanting whatever vocal sounds I felt called to make.

This spontaneous blend of toning, chanting and wordless singing had formed the basis of my sound-healing work since Sedona and would further evolve when we returned to Arizona. If by Maui it came easily and spontaneously, its origins five years earlier had not been so effortless. When I left Diana's Sedona home from the powerful sound session sparked by our meeting at Kentia's Hampton Inn event, I remember a feeling of unhappy foreboding as I sensed that this was work I, too, would be called to do. The sounds Diana made during our session — she hadn't yet changed her name to Irlianna — were peculiar enough that others might think she was a bit crazy and, like my mother before me, I did not want to be judged. Better not to be a sound healer.

My resistance was short-lived.

Soon after, vocal sound work distinct from Diana's became part of the Reiki-initiated attunements I was already offering. Not long after that, sound became their focus. Always unusual and sometimes off-key, my sounds ranged from grating to melodic, often carrying elements of Middle Eastern, Hawaiian and Native American tones and rhythms. I never knew what would come out of my mouth and over time learned to trust that whatever I sang was perfect in the moment. As with writing *The MoonQuest*, it was a training in judgment-free surrender. And as with *The MoonQuest*, it was not always easy to still my doubting, critical monkey mind, even as clients reported powerful physical and emotional results.

My monkey mind was not present at Kukuipuka that March evening, and the sounds I sang as I continued around the inside of Kukuipuka's rock wall were only for me and for whatever ancient spirits still dwelt in that sacred place. I don't know how long I continued or when my singing turned into a five-word mantra. "I surrender to the land," I repeated, over and over. "I surrender to the land."

My relationship with Hawaii had been troubled and ambivalent, almost from the moment in February 1999 when our plane touched down at the Kona airport, amid a stark desert of black lava rock. Yes, the beauty and spirit of both Maui and the Big Island were incomparable. Through our three and half years, we explored constantly and were never less than awed by the islands' physical diversity and splendor. The land, too, breathed a numinous quality that was electric...and addictive. Yet the pollution — natural on the Big Island from the active Kilauea volcano and manmade on Maui from the ash-producing sugar-cane harvest — was hard to live with. The volcanic smog, or "vog," could be so thick some Big Island days that it obscured nearly everything. On Maui, we would often wake to find our white car black with fallout from that morning's cane-burning. If I experienced island fever, it was not from living on a hunk of rock in the middle of the Pacific. It was from unrelenting emotional assaults that ensured that one eye was always cast back to the potential of an easier life on the mainland. I had never surrendered to being in Hawaii.

"I surrender to the land," I chanted softly, moving away from the wall and spiraling toward the center of the enclosure. Suddenly, I collapsed to the ground, sobbing. "I surrender to the land," I continued, my face pressed into the moist Maui earth. After three years of struggle, I had finally given myself over to this land of paradox. Unconditionally. In return, the land let me go. Three months later, having once again stripped our possessions down to an affordable-to-be-shipped minimum, we were on an ATA flight to Phoenix.

As the plane took off and I watched Maui disappear into the

turquoise waters of the Pacific, I sobbed again, harder if possible than I had done at Kukuipuka. Two years would pass before I could remove the word "aloha" from my voice-mail greeting or could listen to Lei'ohu Ryder sing "Maui Loa" without feeling a tug back toward the land whose tough love had bruised, battered and ultimately strengthened me.

Act 12.
Return to Sedona

*There is no creativity, no originality, no success,
no progress without risk.*
Judith Weston

*Only when he no longer knows what he is doing
does the painter do good things.*
Edgar Degas

The Right Place

WE HAD EXPECTED to trade Maui for Tucson. We loved the Arizona desert but weren't keen on Phoenix, and after our financial meltdown, we couldn't see the sense in returning to Sedona. Instead, we would move somewhere with a more diverse economy, one that was independent of tourism. Regardless, Phoenix, with its larger airport hub, would be our port of entry.

Our Tucson plan began to unravel three weeks before our departure date. It started with a phone call from Betty Tentschert, our former neighbor on Zane Grey Lane. While not extraordinary in itself — Betty did contact us occasionally — her call kicked off a rapid-fire succession of unexpected calls in the next days, all from or about Sedona. Many relayed news of former Sedona friends who had left town around the time of our exodus. Several of those, we learned, had already moved back; others were plotting their return.

The final call in the sequence was from Linda Shay. A spritely master of dolphin-energy healings, Linda had been one of my first Sedona friends and had officiated at our wedding. Her husband, David Rosenthal, had bailed me out when the Immigration Service threatened to reject my green-card application because my primary sponsor, my wife, lacked the income to support me — not surprising, given that I was the one supporting her. As the only person in our circle of metaphysical misfits with a real job and declarable income, David had agreed to act as my financial sponsor, and the green card was issued. Unlike Betty, Linda hardly ever called. On this Maui afternoon, she telephoned to let us know that she and David had recently returned to Sedona after several years in Southern California. The moment we hung up, Q'nta and

I looked at each other. There was nothing to say. We both knew that Sedona was calling us back and that we had no choice but to obey.

When Q'nta, Guinevere and I landed in Phoenix on the evening of June 24, we had two hundred dollars spending money, enough extra for a few weeks' car rental, a free temporary billet with Linda and David and lots of doubt. Sedona hadn't supported us particularly abundantly the first time around. Would this be any different?

Q'nta had a strong entrepreneurial streak and throughout our marriage she never lacked ideas for new businesses that might keep us afloat. During our first stint in Sedona, she encouraged me to create watercolor art around inspirational sayings from my *Dialogues with the Divine* manuscript. Although she had abandoned her line of silk clothing, she continued to produce hand-dyed scarves, and soon after we married she launched a line of hand-painted wood furniture and accessories. We took our artsy inventory and joined the Arizona craft-fair circuit, not entirely successfully.

One of those unsuccessful days took place in a dusty vacant lot on the Saturday of my forty-forth birthday. Sales were sparse through the morning and when close to noon a powerful gust scooped up our E-Z Up canopy and slammed it into a fortunately empty part of the fairground, we considered packing up and leaving. Before making a final decision, we each tuned in meditatively for the highest course of action. As was often the case through our time together, we received identical guidance: Stay. Things had improved only slightly by mid-afternoon, when an auburn-haired young woman with a Québecois accent showed up. She loved my inspirational art and promised to see about getting it into the California metaphysical store where she worked. Perhaps the day might turn around after all. As Chantal was saying goodbye, a tall bearded man with graying hair stopped to browse.

"Is this your writing?" he asked, picking up one of the magnets.

I nodded.

"I like it." He selected a few different pieces and as he was paying asked, "Do you have a book with these in it?"

Of course, I did. I had two: *Dialogues* and *The MoonQuest*, both ready for the world, or so I thought. Who was this man?

"I'm sorry," he said, holding out his hand. "I'm Neale Donald Walsch. I've just started a publishing company and I'm looking for manuscripts."

Neale Donald Walsch? The Conversations with God *Neale Donald Walsch? Thank God we stayed!*

I stole a glance at Q'nta. She looked back with that gaze of love and support that always sustained me. I squeezed her hand under the table.

I knew enough about the publishing industry to know that Walsch probably wasn't talking about a company of his own. Likely, he had been given a Neale Donald Walsch Books imprint by Hampton Roads, his publisher. It didn't matter. Either way, this was the break I had been waiting for. And on my forty-fourth birthday! Walsch gave me his local address — a few boxes away from mine at Mailboxes, Etc. — and promised to be in touch once he had looked over the manuscripts.

First thing Monday morning, I dropped them off and began the wait. Weeks went by. Nothing. I checked with Mailboxes, Etc. My package had been picked up. More weeks passed. Still nothing. By the time we reached Hawaii four months later, I began to worry. After many calls, emails and months, the word from Walsch's office was that there was no sign or record of my manuscripts. The only explanation offered was that they might have been destroyed in a flood months earlier. None of that mattered. Books for the imprint had been selected long ago. The project was over. Walsch's assistant apologetically offered to forward the two manuscripts to Hampton Roads. Both were rejected.

Already feeling betrayed by Hawaii, this seemingly pointless series of events pushed me over the edge. Not for the first time on the Big Island, my faith evaporated. For days, I stomped around the house in a rage, refusing to believe anything that I couldn't see or touch. Then, also not for the first time, I reluctantly surrendered to a higher purpose than I was able to understand, and my faith limpingly returned.

Now that we were back in Sedona, Q'nta and I weren't sure how we would manage. We were still living rent-free with Linda and David, but our car-rental money was running out, and although I had applied for several jobs, we had no prospects. Our only certainty was that we were finished with craft fairs. Had we made the right decision in choosing Sedona? Should we have gone to Tucson after all? It was hard not to second-guess ourselves.

"You'll never guess where the Chamber of Commerce is holding a mixer," Q'nta said to me one morning. She was browsing through the *Sedona Red Rock News*.

"Where?"

"The Earth Mother Father Foundation. Can you believe it?"

The Sedona we had abandoned in 1999 had been a segregated town where mainstream and metaphysical businesses rarely mixed. The Earth Mother Father Foundation was a sprawling metaphysical center in the heart of West Sedona. I had offered writing workshops and *Dialogues with the Divine* readings there in my early days in town and had occasionally attended its Sunday morning services. It seemed inconceivable that the Chamber of Commerce could be meeting there.

"Let's go!" she said.

I was skeptical. There was an admission charge, and cash was tight.

"Maybe we'll get some ideas or make some contacts."

Reluctantly, I agreed.

When we arrived, we were surprised to discover that our tickets entitled us each to a free psychic reading from one of Earth Mother Father's intuitives. We wandered around for a while, then chose our first reader, someone whose name I recognized but who I didn't know personally. It was clear that she didn't recognize us either as she shuffled her tarot deck. She turned over a series of cards, studied them for a few moments, then looked up at us.

"You're wondering if you're in the right place." She paused and glanced back down at the cards, as if to confirm what she was about to say. When she looked up again, she stared at each of us in turn and nodded. "You are."

We were. Despite a shaky start, we found jobs, a place to live and a beater of a Ford to get us around town. The car was so old that it lacked power windows, an FM radio and, more important in a Sedona summer where temperatures can exceed one hundred degrees, air conditioning. It lasted five months, only to die the following winter on the steep grade leading up into Sedona from Cottonwood. Its successor, a newer-but-still-old Taurus wagon, met an even more inconvenient end six months later, stranding us on a deserted stretch of Navajo highway on Father's Day. Beyond cell range, we left the car at the side of the road and hitchhiked into Flagstaff.

From Linda and David's, a serendipitous encounter with the Hunter family moved us into the ground-floor studio of the house they rented, known locally as the Russian Teahouse for its Kremlinesque cupola; it was Calen Hunter who four years earlier had helped precipitate my name change to Akhneton. After six months with the Hunters, we moved again, this time to a small cottage around the corner from Betty Tentschert and Zane Grey Lane. A few months after that, we found our way back to our former Zane Grey Lane home. That house, our second together as a couple, would also become our second-to-last together. Two and a half years after Sedona brought us back, it would be time to leave again, this time on my own.

Changing Channels

SOME MIGHT DESCRIBE the *Dialogues with the Divine*-style writing that entered my life in Penetanguishene as "channeled." I did too, initially. But as I grew to see writing as a co-creative act not as something separate from the writer, I dropped the term. Here's how I would later put it in *The Voice of the Muse*: "Even the most conscious act of creation is not yours alone. Nor is the most unconscious act totally separate from you. There is a quantum oneness that's always at work."

During my first Sedona sojourn, however, I continued to explore the traditional channeling I had experienced in Boise. Early in 1998, I took a channeling class and discovered that I had a gift for it. More accurately, perhaps, I was deepening my gift of surrender and learning to own my voice and trust it. I had always been too frightened of other people's judgments to risk speaking up or speaking out. Even in school, I was not a hand-raiser and rarely participated willingly in open discussions. That was why I had always preferred math with its single right answer to English class. I had moved past much of that fear by the time I participated in Helene Rothschild's Sedona channeling class. Still, it felt presumptuous to announce to the group that I had just received a message from Jesus. Earlier, Helene had guided us into a meditation to help us connect with whatever entity or energy was ready to speak through us. Afterward, we would be free to share any message we received.

Timidly, I raised my hand.

"Akhneton?" Helene nodded at me.

My knees shaking but my voice strong, I shared both what I had heard and its source. A few moments' silence followed. Did no one believe me? Finally, a fellow student spoke up.

"Oh, my God," she exclaimed. "I saw Jesus too. He walked in this direction and I thought he was coming to me." She looked at me. "Then he walked right by me and went to you."

However exciting and validating it felt to be channeling celebrity entities, it rarely worked that way for me. Even in those early *Dialogues*, the Divine never identified itself. When I asked for a name, the response inevitably would go something like this: "I am part of you. Yet I am apart. I am love. I am truth. As are you. We are one." For someone as insecure as I was, such answers were not helpful. For someone learning deeper levels of trust and deeper levels of truth, they were perfect.

Our one-room flat at the Hunters' was cramped for two adults and a toddler, but its location at the edge of the National Forest land that surrounds Sedona more than compensated, at least for me. Most mornings, often before Q'nta and Guinevere woke up, I would slip out for a hike. Sometimes, I would carry a pen and pad, park myself on a rock and dialogue. More often, I would take our portable cassette recorder and channel as I walked. It was on one of the latter days that I found myself speaking a message so unlike any I had ever received, in both tone and content, that I insisted on a source. The name that I sensed was Melchizedek.

The Biblical Melchizedek is a king and priest who first appears to Abraham in Genesis. In metaphysical circles, he symbolizes a powerful source of ancient wisdom. Hearing the name Melchizedek that November morning was nearly as startling to me as channeling Jesus had been four years earlier. When I felt pushed by that same energy to make this and future Melchizedek messages public, I was just as reluctant.

After a few weeks' resistance, I surrendered. I emailed that initial message to a small selection of friends, clients and students, encouraging them to pass it on. Within two days, I had received more than forty requests to be added to a Melchizedek mailing list — all from strangers. Within a few months, the email list had mushroomed to more than six hundred people in twenty-five countries, and the messages were being reprinted on metaphysical websites around the world. Some months after that, I collected the first thirteen into a self-published volume titled *The Book of Messages*.

If the early messages were popular, the thirteenth, titled "Choose Empowerment" and distributed four months later, was less so. In it I was urged to drop Melchizedek from the "Messages from Melchizedek" subject line and claim ownership of and responsibility for all the words that flowed through me. It didn't matter how those words showed up; they were all part of me now. In the email accompanying number thirteen, I explained that future messages would carry my name, not Melchizedek's. Not all subscribers were pleased. Some, missing the self-empowering, integrative point of all the messages, viewed Melchizedek as a more trustworthy source. Others took issue with two of the message's urgings: that readers stop going into trance when channeling ("there is no time or space or place for unawareness") and that they stop separating meditation from the rest of their life ("your call now is to be conscious at all times"). Little did I know that before long, two other of number thirteen's declarations would propel me into the next phase of my spiritual journey: "It is now time to embrace *your* voice and power, publicly…out into the world" and "You are God and God is you."

Yes...Minister?

Q'NTA AND I FIRST met Isa de Quesada after a Sunday service at the Agape International Spiritual Center in Los Angeles. Guinevere and Isa's twins had met in the Sunday School, bonded instantly and introduced us all when we came to pick them up. Just back to Sedona from Maui, Q'nta and I were in LA to collect our few pallets of household goods. We had wanted to experience Agape ever since Mary Omwake convinced its minister, Michael Beckwith, who was on Maui for his honeymoon, to deliver an impromptu sermon at Unity of Maui. This was our first opportunity.

Isa's family and ours grew closer when Isa moved to the Sedona area, a friendship that in late 2003 would see the three of us launch a nondenominational metaphysical Sunday service. We called it The Oneness Center and held it at the Rainbow Ray Focus religious center on Airport Road. Our initial plan was for Isa to deliver the minister-like message, for Q'nta to lead the music and for me to guide congregants in a meditation. When Isa later offered to step aside so I could give the Sunday talk, I readily accepted. Not only was inspirational speaking a direction I wanted to pursue, but the opportunity also reminded me of a peculiar portent I had experienced in the Agape parking lot a few years earlier, before we moved to Hawaii.

It was a Wednesday morning and the parking lot was largely empty as Q'nta and I returned to our car from an appointment at the Agape bookstore. Out of nowhere, a harried woman rushed up to us.

"Are you the minister?" she asked me, breathlessly.

Now I would be.

Much as I had tried to do with my first writing class at the

University of Toronto, I scripted out my initial talk. This time, mercifully, my hand didn't cramp up. For my second and third sermons, I spoke from detailed notes. When it came time for my fourth talk, on Thanksgiving Sunday, the inner guidance was unequivocal: no script, no speech, no notes.

Not even notes?

Not even notes. Nor was I to let myself give any thought to the talk during the week leading up to it. I was to stand at the lectern, open my mouth and speak — ironically, on "surrender." A few years later, giving a presentation with neither text nor notes would be my standard practice. It wasn't yet, and I was terrified.

Q'nta and I had arranged to have preservice brunch with Linda Shay and David Rosenthal up the road at the Sedona Airport Restaurant. I ordered but couldn't eat. All I could do, as my stomach turned double somersaults, was worry about how humiliated I would be when I stood before the congregation, opened my mouth and no words came out.

My legs were nearly as wobbly as they had been for my bar mitzvah as I made my way to the lectern. I remember little about the next twenty minutes, other than that one part of me spoke while another part criticized the first part for being unstructured, unfocused and uninspiring. When I was finished, I sat down next to Q'nta, waiting for her to murmur a few words of congratulations. She said nothing. She didn't even look at me.

Oh, my God. It was worse than I thought.

An hour later over lunch at Mago Cafe, as the conversation swirled around me, I still felt lilliputian, certain that I had made a fool of myself.

Then, between bites, Q'nta turned to me. "That was the absolute best I've ever heard you speak. You were awesome!"

I was? Maybe there really is something to this surrender thing...

Apparently, there was. I had achieved what I needed to achieve and there was no need to repeat it. A few days later, Isa, Q'nta and I closed our Oneness Center.

The God That You Are

In March 2004 we returned to Zane Grey Lane. It was both odd and comforting to be back in the old place. Betty still lived downstairs, as lively and feisty as ever, but alone. Sadly, Fritz had died the previous year. There was no Roxy this time but we had two kittens, although we lost one to a coyote early in our stay. And we had a daughter. Guinevere was four and a half, and the house was now noisier and more filled with life than it had ever been.

One thing had not changed: the picture-postcard view of Cathedral Rock, the quintessential Sedona tourist site, from our back deck. If Cathedral Rock was a favorite with hikers and spiritual seekers, Schuerman Mountain, around the corner from our house, was so anonymous that it was only known by name to a handful of locals. Yet it had always intrigued me. How could it not, when I bore the name of an ancient pharaoh and Schuerman resembled a giant red-rock pyramid?

One Sunday, with Q'nta and Guinevere away for the afternoon, I felt the call of Pyramid Mountain, as I liked to call Schuerman, and knew it was time to explore. As I began to clamber up, a notepad in my backpack and my cassette recorder in hand, I could see no sign of a trail through the low scrub and loose rock. It didn't matter. I was certain that I would reach the summit, four hundred feet above Chavez Ranch Road. Why the tape recorder? Although I had not recorded any new messages recently, I woke up that morning panicked by our financial situation, deteriorating yet again, and I was desperate for guidance of any sort. Perhaps I would find some on my climb.

About a third of the way up, I sensed something starting to come through and switched on the recorder. The message was low-key at first. Within a few yards, though, it was exploding out of me with an evangelical fervency that stunned me, as much for its fiery passion as for its preacher-like exhortation, one that echoed the final message in my *Book of Messages*: "Be the God that you are."

When I got home, I immediately transcribed the recording and sent it out to my email list with "The God That You Are" as the subject line. The response was electric and immediate. Even more stunning was the response to my follow-up a few days later.

It was another difficult morning, for the same reason: money or, rather, the lack of it. The previous afternoon I had been out on a sales call. I was repping a merchant-services provider at the time, not with great success. All the way to my appointment, I repeated, "I am the God that I am." I was certain I would make the sale.

I didn't.

"What am I supposed to do?" I cried into the shower stall.

"God Activations," I heard back. "All about 'the God that you are.' Teleconferences. Paid teleconferences."

I didn't know which to doubt first. I had tried my hand at teleconferences in the past, with even less success than I was experiencing selling credit-card systems. As for activations, I was open to that. I had been offering various sorts, mostly to individual clients, since my Reiki attunement days, under varying metaphysical monikers. But God Activations? *God* Activations? If I had felt presumptuous channeling Jesus and Melchizedek, I felt beyond arrogant to be offering any kind of event that invoked the name God. Who did I think I was?

The God that you are.

Oh, yeah. Right.

Feeling more pompous than empowered, I emailed invitations for a God Activation event to take place five days later. The response was again immediate. More than a dozen people paid to attend. Most registered, as well, for the follow-up, even better-attended, and for the next one and the one after that. A handful of the original dozen participated in every teleconference I offered until I phased out the twice-monthly blends of sound-healing, meditation and inspirational talk nearly three years later.

As with other aspects of my metaphysical and creative work, these teleconferences were pure acts of surrender. All I knew in advance were the dates and topics, both intuitively chosen. When I began a God Activation, I never knew what words I would speak or what sounds I would sing. Nor could I know how my odd sounds and spontaneous talks and meditations were being received. All I could do was trust that whatever I was being called to do was precisely what those on the phone line needed in that moment.

Did I never judge what I was speaking or chanting? Did I never cringe when I sang off-key? Hardly. Instead, I learned to notice the judgment and allow it its voice, without letting it get in my way or in the way of the work. As I had learned from Carole Leckner in that first writing workshop, my critical, left-brain mind could not be in charge. Only my analogical, right-brain mind was wise enough to see beyond the logical. Only my intuitive mind was visionary enough to see the possible in the conventionally impossible.

My faith wasn't totally blind. I received many email testimonials and sold event recordings to at least half the participants on any given teleconference. Still, each God Activation was a deeper training in the same intuitive skills I had learned while writing *The MoonQuest*: breath-by-breath surrender to the imperative of the moment. As with my novel, this story, too, was smarter than I was.

The Art of Surrender

Although I had created watercolor backdrops for the inspirational sayings that Q'nta and I marketed at craft fairs and to metaphysical bookstores, I did not consider myself an artist. Rather, I was a writer who splashed swishes and swirls of color onto paper to pretty up his writing. That changed in January 2004, when Courtney Eves, on another of her regular pilgrimages to Sedona, caught sight of one of my doodles. At least to me they were doodles: complex, rune-like squiggles, scratched without thought onto any piece of paper with any pen.

"That's-that's language of light," Courtney sputtered. "That's incredible. It gives me goosebumps. Do you have any others?"

Language of light, a metaphysical term, can take many visual forms: calligraphic, runic, geometric, hieroglyphic or a blend of any of those. Like my sound-healing, itself a vocal form of light language, it touches places in our psyche far beneath the conscious mind, and any interpretations come from that same place. In an energetic-vibrational sense, it carries the same transformational potential as crystals, working subtly — sometimes not so subtly — at physical, emotional, spiritual and mental levels.

Did I have other drawings? Of course not. These were mindless squiggles. Why would I keep them?

"Is there an art store in town?" she asked before I could respond.

"Uh, yes. Why?"

"Are you doing anything right now?"

"I—"

"Let's go."

The moment we stepped into Sedona Art Supplies, Courtney hustled me to the colored pencils and had me choose a dozen. She then asked the sales clerk to pick out a suitable sketch pad and paid for the lot.

"Start drawing," she commanded.

I did, that afternoon. Once I started, I couldn't stop. I drew two, three, four, five drawings a day, from the simple to the complex, all from that non-thinking place that had produced my doodles. The more I drew, the more I trusted what was emerging and the less, for the most part, I judged my output. Courtney loved them all.

Once I began offering themed God Activation teleconferences a few months later, the ever-entrepreneurial Q'nta wondered whether I could create a drawing for each event, one that would amplify the energy of its topic. I could and did: With the week's theme in mind, I drew as intuitively as I sang and wrote. Before long, I was selling nearly as many energy drawings, as I dubbed them, as I was teleconference recordings. Soon after, from that same place of surrender, I began offering custom energy portraits, again created intuitively. These were not physical likenesses. I lacked the technical skill for that. Rather, they were symbolic representations of the next level of an individual's potential that she or he was ready to access and activate. Often, I would record a short sound healing to accompany them.

Most fun of all, when it came to my art, were my interpretations — some vaguely realistic-looking, others more abstract — of the places I encountered on my travels. I was attracted mostly to mountains, rock formations and other natural features — from Virginia's Shenandoah Mountain to the Joshua trees of the Southern California desert. Now and again, something manmade would also catch my eye or touch me deeply: Monticello did that, as did Santa Fe's Saint Francis Cathedral and the medicine wheel in Wyoming's Bighorn Mountains. One of my favorites was Oceanside Pier north of San Diego. I titled its drawing "Walking on Water" because every time I would step onto the pier and walk over and past the beach, past the waves, past the surfers and out over open sea, I always felt as though the pier wasn't really there, as though nothing stood between me and the water. If I could walk on water, anything was possible!

Almost anything. I still couldn't call myself an artist. I created energy-enhancing tools and just happened to employ the same instruments used by "real" artists. One day, though, I dropped into the Red Door Bookstore in Corrales, just outside Albuquerque. Local artist Barbara Besser was installed there that day, exhibiting her paintings. We struck up a conversation and I showed her some of my drawings. A few nights later, I met her and a few of her friends for a jazz night at an Albuquerque cafe.

"I'd like you to meet Mark David Gerson," she said to the rest of the table when I arrived. "He's also an artist."

I am? Really? An artist? Oh, I guess I am.

It reminded me of the afternoon in Grand Rapids, Michigan, when a woman approached me after a God Activation event.

"That was incredible," she said, of my singing. "Where were you trained?"

Trained? Me?

For someone who had grown up painfully insecure about his voice, this was the ultimate validation.

Whether it was sound-healing, inspirational speaking, writing, teaching or art, every element of this journey was conspiring to deepen my faith in myself and in the invisible, and was helping me to surrender unconditionally to that inner wisdom that knows more than my physical self could ever touch on its own.

I would need all the wisdom, faith and surrender I could muster by the end of the year, when without warning my marriage imploded.

Act 13.
Scenes from the End of a Marriage

There's one thing worse than change and that's the status quo.
JOHN LE CARRÉ

*A genuine odyssey is not about piling up experiences.
It is a deeply felt, risky, unpredictable tour of the soul.*
THOMAS MOORE

Ringing Out the Old

My marriage didn't quite implode without warning. In retrospect, disturbing portents were present as early as a week before the wedding. They weren't indications that our marriage was a mistake. They did, however, belie our shared fantasy that this union had been divinely ordained and would last forever.

Rachel's Knoll is now part of the gated Seven Canyons golf community at the end of Long Canyon Road, about fifteen minutes north of Sedona. In 1997, even though privately owned, the knoll was open to the community, a peaceful hilltop oasis for meditation and other spiritual pursuits. My first day in town, when Alison guided me through Sedona, Rachel's Knoll was our first stop. That night, Long Canyon Road leading toward the knoll was where I chose to sleep. It didn't take long for Rachel's Knoll to become a favorite spot, and I visited often. So when in May 1998 Kentia and I were discussing marriage, that's where I proposed to hold our outdoor wedding ceremony. Kentia was skeptical. Parking was limited and climbing the uphill path might prove daunting for some guests. But bowing to my passion, she relented.

In the meantime, the Rachel of Rachel's Knoll died. Her family did not share her vision for the property and sold it to a company proposing to redevelop the surrounding land. For the time being, though, access remained unrestricted. On the Thursday before our Sunday wedding, we drove out to the knoll to finalize some last-minute plans for the ceremony. But when we reached the end of Long Canyon Road, a locked swing gate bearing a "Private Property" sign blocked public access. Ours was to be an open ceremony, and we had passed out cards all over town inviting anyone to attend. Now what would we do? In the end, we moved the wedding to the place that had been Kentia's first choice — by Oak Creek at Red Rock Crossing — and we hastily posted signs and flyers throughout Sedona to redirect our guests.

If seeing our planned wedding site disappear three days before the event wasn't omen enough, the ceremony itself disappeared into an unrecorded void when our videographer, an accomplished and experienced filmmaker, produced a work of uninterrupted snow and static. Still, although there is no official visual record of the event, the afternoon continues to stand out for me as one of the most moving of my life, and I remember being close to tears many times as Linda Shay officiated over the ritual Kentia and I had created to cement our relationship.

There was little about our marriage that at the time I wouldn't have characterized as ideal. We shared a spiritual outlook, rarely disagreed on anything significant, had many similar tastes and, at least in the early months, enjoyed a passionate sex life. Yet the cement must not have been as strong as it seemed, for disturbing signs continued to show up.

We had been married only three months when the first of three peculiar wedding-band incidents occurred. Q'nta and I had just returned from Roxy's evening walk. As we took off our coats, I noticed that my wedding ring was missing. My logical thought was that the cold of an autumn night had contracted my fingers and that the ring had slipped off while we were walking the dog. I remained calm on the outside, but on the inside I couldn't help but worry that this might be a sign, and not a good one, about our marriage. We grabbed flashlights, ran outside and retraced our steps. No ring. On hands and knees back in the house, we sifted meticulously through the carpet. No ring.

The following morning, as I walked across the living room, something glinted up at me from the rug. My wedding band. Relief washed over me. Confusion too: We had searched this spot multiple times the night before. If the ring had been there, it would have been impossible to miss. If it hadn't, where had it been? What could the disappearance mean?

It would be another six years before my wedding band would

again symbolically suggest a problem with our marriage: In the spring of 2004, the ring developed a visible crack. If in 1998 it had been off my finger for only twelve hours, this time it was off for a few weeks, an absence that was both uncomfortable and prescient.

The final ring incident — a sign of a different sort, for the marriage had ended the previous evening — came during one of the closing exercises in a class at Sedona's Dahn Yoga Center. As I lay on my back, shaking out hands, wrists, ankles and feet to release tension, my wedding ring flew off my finger, sailed across the room and bounced off the far wall, miraculously hitting no one. This was a regular Dahn exercise, one I had practiced two or three times a week for more than a year. Never before had my ring flown off. This *was* a sign. I slipped the ring into my pocket and never put it back on.

Never Forever

Before I met Kentia, I had not led a particularly sexual life. Despite having come out as a gay man in the pre-AIDS era of unfettered promiscuity, fear of intimacy had limited my sexual escapades and, until Kentia, denied me a live-in relationship. It wasn't that I didn't want a romantic partner. It was that I had never been willing to surrender into a life with someone else deeply enough to make such a partnership possible.

Life with Q'nta changed that, perhaps to a codependent extreme. We were inseparable, so much so that it sometimes seemed that we were a single person. Constant financial struggle contributed to that. Or perhaps overdependence helped create our persistent money problems. Regardless, we were like two playing cards leaning together to form a tent: If one fell, the other would have been challenged to stand on its own.

A few months after we separated, Aalia began to hint at the possibility of a reconciliation. Her relationship with Marcus was volatile, and I couldn't blame her for seeking an exit. Yet I wasn't sure that I was ready to serve as her way out. Possibly not ever, certainly not yet. I ignored her hints until one day she asked directly.

"I would never say 'never,'" I began slowly, unsure how to respond. I took a deep breath. "But until we can come together as two independent, empowered individuals, it's premature to even consider it." Without realizing it, I was characterizing our marriage as having been codependent.

I didn't see that while we were married. While we were together, it felt as though I dwelt in a safe, comfortable, if financially precarious cocoon. But caterpillars can't live in their cocoons forever, and if the butterfly-in-becoming won't push its way out, some force of nature will step in to do the job. Some force of nature did. His name was Marcus Gilhart. I don't blame myself for not having seen it coming. I have wondered in the years since, though, how I missed signs even more direct than wedding weirdness and missing rings.

As I experienced while creating *The MoonQuest*, I knew little about *The StarQuest* and *SunQuest* stories, except as I wrote them. And as I was writing all three, I often failed to recognize what the stories might be revealing about me and my life. One revelation suggested by *The SunQuest* grew out of the moment in the narrative when Ben reveals that his beloved wife, Y'glana, died in childbirth, a surprise to me as I wrote it. Even more surprising was when, in rereading that scene a few months later, I recognized a connection between the end of Ben's relationship with Y'glana and the end of Aq'naton's with Q'nta. Q'nta, of course, did not die when Guinevere was born. In some ways, though, our marriage did.

If our lovemaking was extraordinary at the beginning — so much so that it often moved us to tears — both its passion and frequency fell away once Q'nta was pregnant. It never returned. It wasn't just that we opted to have Guinevere sleep in our bed with us, a not unexpected damper to an active sex life. Rather, co-sleeping gave us each permission to be less interested in making love. Q'nta's focus, naturally, was on Guinevere. For me, the unprecedented and explosive sexual desire I had experienced when we first met, continued to dissipate through the months until it extinguished altogether.

We still loved each other deeply, but it almost seemed as though our marriage had been orchestrated from above by a powerfully assertive spirit-entity not yet named Guinevere. Had she thumbed through a celestial catalog of potential parents, picking Kentia from Column A and Akhneton from Column B? Had she first conspired to move me six thousand circuitous miles from Toronto to Sedona, then arranged for Kentia and me to meet, fall in love and get married, then relocated us to Hawaii for her birth and, finally, washed her hands of the whole, now-unnecessary arrangement? Regardless, the "arrangement" continued to unravel, first invisibly and then more visibly than I was prepared to acknowledge.

Throughout our marriage, we had always insisted to each other that Aq'naton and Q'nta were forever, that we were perfectly matched and that nothing could ever separate us. But names are more than letters on a page. It had taken my name change to Akhneton, for example, for Kentia to be drawn to me and for the two of us to come together. Perhaps it took the name Aalia for us to come apart. As soon as she adopted it, a few months before our breakup, there was no longer an "Aq'naton and Q'nta," and not only in name. Some tectonic plate in our relationship had shifted. That something brought her to Marcus, first for work, then for more.

Ironically, soon after Q'nta ceased to exist, so would Aq'naton.

Signs of Dissolution

AALIA WAS ALREADY spending time with Marcus in the months leading up to our breakup. Marcus had been trying to finance several movie projects and Aalia, who now felt a call to work in a film industry that she had rejected while growing up in Hollywood, was helping him. In exchange he was teaching her how to be a film producer. This seemed to be more than a passing enthusiasm, and I was excited for her.

That spring we had opened Lemuria Calling in a funky West Sedona building around the corner from the Gilhart home. If our early months in the metaphysical store were wildly successful, Sedona's always-quiet summer season proved deathly. By fall, business had picked up, but not enough to resuscitate the store and not enough for Aalia's increased absence to be a problem. Most of the time, co-owner Karen Weaver and I could easily manage sales and intuitive readings on our own.

One September afternoon, Aalia picked me up at the store after her day with Marcus and excitedly related how she had given him an energy-healing treatment to help him clear issues that they had determined had been holding back his success. "I took him to the Nefertiti trail," she gushed. "We did the energy work there."

Q'nta and I had first explored Sedona's Jim Thompson hiking trail early in our relationship and had dubbed it the Nefertiti trail because of a cliff formation that resembled a bust of the ancient Egyptian queen. Nefertiti being the wife of my namesake, Akhenaten, we both felt a powerful connection to that area. For Q'nta, now Aalia, to have taken Marcus to what I viewed as a special place for us as a couple felt like a betrayal. I said nothing, but my stomach churned. That was the first of three signs that autumn that should have indicated to me that something was amiss.

The next occurred a short while later when Marcus repeated an oft-made, oft-declined invitation to me to write screenplays for him. I had never considered writing for the screen, which was one of the reasons I always said no. My other reason had nothing to do with his partnership with Aalia. Rather, there was something about the idea of working with him that always left me indefinably uncomfortable. Marcus was a natural salesman, and in his presence I was always tempted to say yes. Once removed from his aura of charm, I always wondered why I would have considered it.

This time, I did something different. I didn't say yes or no. Instead, I closed my eyes and, in a meditative way, tried to visualize what life might be like if I were a screenwriter. Not necessarily one working with Marcus. Just a screenwriter. The first image to emerge was of a stunning, modernist house perched at the edge of a low cliff overlooking the Pacific. *Not bad. Maybe there's more to this screenwriting thing than I thought.* The next view was inside the ocean-view room that was my writing studio. I was liking this. A lot. Then I stopped liking it. A lot. Because my next sensing was that I lived in this architectural gem alone. No Aalia. No Guinevere. My eyes shot open and I shook my head to clear the nightmare. I told no one what I had seen.

The final sign came in a dream, a dream I also dared not share. In it, Aalia was leaving me for another man. Through my years of dreamwork, I have experienced few predictive dreams. The most dramatic was in the mid-nineties when I dreamt that a friend's husband had died. Within days of my dream he had, unexpectedly. That was the exception. While my dreams are rich with metaphor and symbolism, rarely can they be taken literally and make any sense. Perhaps had the man in my dream been Marcus, I might have viewed it as a warning. Likely not. I still couldn't imagine anything that might tear my marriage apart. A few weeks later something did.

As I sleepwalked through the days following Aalia's announcement in a haze of shock and depression, part of me knew with absolute certainty that the end of our marriage was the best outcome for all of us, including for Guinevere. My mind couldn't grasp how this was possible, yet I knew it to be true. Even if from some aerie of advanced consciousness I could acknowledge the higher good and, from the same place, honor Aalia for following her heart, Aq'naton the man felt betrayed. It wasn't until five years later in Albuquerque that I could see that the betrayal I had assigned to her was really mine, to myself.

It was a Sunday in January 2009 and I had woken knowing that I needed to attend the morning service at the Albuquerque Center for Spiritual Living. I hadn't been a regular churchgoer since Maui, but I followed the imperative to the Louisiana Boulevard sanctuary. As soon as I heard Rev. Julie Interrante's talk, I knew why I had come.

"No one can betray you if you haven't first betrayed yourself," Julie said in the only eleven words of her sermon that I retained.

In that moment, I realized that my marriage was already over before Aalia left. I realized, too, that I had spent much if not all our relationship weighted down by self-destructive, guilt-ridden hyper-responsibility, a situation eerily similar to that of my mother, also the sole breadwinner for her family. In my blindness, I could never have allowed myself to even admit that I had unfulfilled needs, let alone consider ending the marriage to realize them. When had I sacrificed my soul to the relationship? I didn't know. Perhaps as far back as its inception. Regardless, the instant I did was the instant I betrayed myself, the same instant the clock began ticking toward the moment when Aalia would have no choice but to betray me by leaving.

In those early days after the breakup, Marcus and Aalia spoke often about relocating to Virginia, where they hoped to convert a century-old abandoned prison into a film studio. Initially, I assumed that I would follow them so that I could remain close to Guinevere. Then one day, in a replay of my thoughts around leaving Toronto for Nova Scotia, I realized that I couldn't plan my life around the externals of other people's plans, especially plans as erratic as theirs. What to do?

"Hit the road," I heard.

Too numb to question or analyze the intuitive feeling, I made plans for another car journey, naively assuming that I would find my new home within three months, just as I had done when I left Toronto in 1997. Six weeks after election night, having once more sold everything, I was back on the road, knowing little other than that once again I would begin by heading west, this time to Southern California. Had I realized then that three months would balloon into thirty-three, it might have been harder to leave.

Act 14.
On the Road...Again

Not all those who wander are lost.
J.R.R. Tolkien

*I was a child of these roads
A child of these roads
A black wide river shinin'
I rode her everywhere she wanted to go
Just a child of these roads...*
Joshua Kadison

Guinevere

I'M NOT GOING to see Guinevere grow up. We were living in Hawaii when that intuitive impression struck me. I don't remember where I was or what I was doing, only that I had heard few phrases in my life as heart-stoppingly painful as that one. What could it mean? Was something going to happen to Guinevere? To me? Even divorce, then an unimaginable option, could never separate us that radically. Could it? As much as I tried to analyze and rationalize what I had sensed, I could come up with no explanation that wasn't deeply disturbing. This premonition, too, I shared with no one. It was a premonition that in its own way would come true.

It was just past eleven o'clock on September 10, 1999. Q'nta and I were asleep. The night outside our rainforest home in Captain Cook was still. Inside too. Even the giant flying cockroaches, ubiquitous on the Big Island and seemingly unextinguishable, were, unusually, not rattling around our front room, itself now dominated by a large, circular birthing tank. In our bedroom, jammed between our bed and the window was a crib outfitted with baby-boy blue fittings, stuffed animals and a Noah's ark mobile — blue because with no evidence to the contrary, we were convinced that were having a boy: the Ben of Q'nta's intuition and of my *StarQuest*.

Suddenly, Q'nta jostled me awake. "I think my water just broke."

I leapt out of bed, called our midwife, Roxanne, began to fill the birthing tank and banged on our neighbor Kathy Sue's door. Q'nta went into labor while Kathy Sue fussed and attended to both of us. She mopped the sweat from Q'nta's forehead and poured over-sweetened black coffee into me. Initially out of reach on another birth, Roxanne and her assistant showed up near dawn and, soon after, directed us both into the birthing tank. Q'nta leaned back against me, breathing and pushing according to Roxanne's direction, and I held her, too high on caffeine, sugar, adrenalin and wonder to do anything else. Fortunately, there was nothing else for me to do. As much as we always did most things together, only Q'nta could do this one.

When the final push came and Roxanne held up the new baby for us to see, I was astounded, and not only by the miracle of birth. "Oh, my God!" I exclaimed. "It's a girl!"

The baby boy of all our intuitive sensings was not a boy after all.

I quickly glanced up at the clock. It was 9:11 on September 11. Guinevere had arrived with Virgo-like punctuality, right on her due date — a date that two birthdays later would take on global significance. A tsunami of emotion washed through me, a supercharged blend of awe, humility and love. I had never expected to be a father, never thought I wanted to be a father. And now... Now this tiny creature was my child. Forever.

"Forever" did not play out as expected, especially on Friday, December 10, 2004, when I headed out of Sedona one last time as a resident. I was on my way to Tucson, where a teleconference regular had offered to host me for a week of God Activations, writing workshops and private sessions. From there, I would continue to Southern California and beyond that to wherever the road would take me.

The car packed yet again with all my belongings, I drove west out of town, feeling nothing as I left Sedona and its red-rock formations behind. As Hawaii had done, Sedona had birthed some of my greatest joys and sorrows. My heart was too muddled to make sense of it all in that moment. Besides, I was focused on Murphy's Restaurant in Cottonwood. There, Marcus, Aalia and Guinevere were breakfasting with friends. There, I would make my farewell to Guinevere.

It's hard to know what five-year-old Guinevere felt or understood during the weeks leading up to that day. The night after Aalia broke the news to me about our marriage, we sat her down and tried to explain that the love Mommies and Daddies feel for each other is sometimes different than the forever-love they feel for their children. I added that even though we would no longer all be living together — I didn't yet know that I would be leaving town — I still loved her as much as I always had, and that that would never change. In a private conversation with Guinevere a few days later, Aalia took full responsibility for the upheaval.

The next ten days were awkward and strained, as the three of us remained in the Zane Grey Circle house, still surrounded by unpacked moving boxes. Aalia had expected to move in with Marcus immediately, but Marcus's ex-wife, Denise, had returned from Hawaii and was staying with him in their old house. Separated but not, Aalia and I slept at opposite ends of our king-size bed those first few nights. Then, uncomfortable with the arrangement, I moved into the guest room. A few nights later, wondering why I should be displaced, I insisted that Aalia and I switch places. Sleeping arrangements remained unchanged until Denise returned to the Big Island and Aalia moved with Guinevere to Marcus's. We did our best to reassure Guinevere through it all. Still, it must have been confusing.

I parked in front of Murphy's but couldn't bring myself to go inside. Instead, I sat in the car for a few shaky minutes, unsure what to do, then called Aalia on my cell. She brought Guinevere out to the car and left us alone. I must have told my daughter that I loved her, that I would love her always and forever, wherever I was, and that I would see her soon. I must have reminded her that she could hear me on the CD I had recorded for her of all the bedtime songs I had sung to her nightly since she was born: "Puff, the Magic Dragon" and "Maui Loa"; "Bushel and a Peck" and "You Are My Sunshine" from my own childhood; and one I had written myself when she was only weeks old: "Sleep, Little Guinevere." I must have said all that but I remember nothing. All I remember is watching my daughter walk back into the restaurant with her mother, then driving away, sobbing.

My second Sedona leave-taking was equally painful. I had returned to town from California in late January and was spending a week with friends before continuing on to New Mexico. I didn't understand why I was feeling called to Albuquerque, a city I didn't know in a state I had never visited, any more than I knew why it had been important to launch my journey in California. But if that's where my heart was pulling me, that's where I would go. Meantime, my heart had pulled me to Sedona and Guinevere, and I had to force back the tears when I saw her for the first time in five weeks — the longest yet we had been apart. I didn't bother holding back the tears a few days later as I drove past her school on my way out of town, The Rankin Family's "Rise Again" blasting out of the CD player: "We rise again, in the faces of our children." For years, that song would always carry me back to that emotional morning and to a photograph of a dejected-looking Guinevere curled up on my lap. That the photo wasn't taken until the following Christmas doesn't alter my memory.

However Guinevere felt during that first visit back, her despair was clear a few weeks earlier, during our first Christmas apart. I was spending mine on California's Central Coast, with Geri and Art O'Hare, elderly friends who had insisted that I not be alone through my first post-family holiday season. A few days after Christmas, I was sitting in an easy chair in the O'Hare living room when my cellphone rang. I picked it up to the sound of sobs.

"I want you here," Guinevere wailed. *"Now!"*

My heart broke. It would take many more calls like that one before I discovered that nearly all were sparked by one of Marcus and Aalia's rows. On one hand the knowledge helped me see that as much as she missed me, the trigger for Guinevere's outbursts had nothing to do with me. On the other, I felt helpless. Like most parents, I wanted to fix what was broken for my child. I couldn't fix this one, even if I were in Sedona. It took time, but I began to understand that my job as a parent was not to fix anything. Rather, it was to be emotionally available — in all the ways that my two absent fathers had never been.

I hadn't yet reached that place of surrender and deeper understanding a few weeks later when, lying in the bathtub of an Albuquerque hotel, I was immersed not only in steamy water but in self-reproach. The lights out, my mood was as dark as the bathroom.

What kind of father am I? Other fathers don't leave town when their marriage ends. Other fathers put their children first. Other fathers are physically present for their kids. Other fathers act like real fathers. I'm as bad as my own father!

I didn't see a physical representation of Guinevere flutter into view in front of me, just as I had not seen a physical Arctur in the steam room in Boise's Shilo Inn. Nor did I hear a physical voice. What I sensed that February evening was an expression of what I would call Guinevere's higher self, that infinite-mind presence that I knew to be wiser than my five-year-old child, by then asleep in her Sedona bed.

"Don't worry about me," she said. "I'm fine."

I started to cry.

"Do what you have to do," she continued. "Whatever it is will be the best thing for me too."

I didn't stop worrying. Does any parent ever stop worrying? I did begin to trust more fully in the path I felt called to follow, the path I knew to have chosen me as much as I had chosen it.

Pennies from Heaven

My mystical bathtub experience with Guinevere's higher self took place at the Howard Johnson Express on I-25, the closest thing I would experience to an Albuquerque home during my time on the road. I stayed there often when I was in town, and I was in town often. Mostly, I asked for Room 133 because it had the fridge and microwave I always insisted on in my hotel and motel surrogate homes and because it was located as far as possible from the noisy rumble of the freeway.

On this particular stay, it was the Saturday night of a holiday weekend and I had been in Room 133 for more than a week. I had already spent my share of the proceeds of our Sedona contents sale, and my only income now came from my teleconferences, private God Activations and related sales. Nervous about my accumulating hotel bill, I asked the front-desk clerk to charge through what I owed to date. My credit had not yet recovered from its Maui malaise and I was operating, somewhat stressfully, on a cash-only basis. The clerk did as I requested but neglected to first cancel the authorization that had been placed on my debit card when I checked in. The result? Not only was my checking account technically overdrawn, but because of the holiday Monday I would have no access to cash until Wednesday morning, when the authorization would lift and pending credit card payments from clients would show up in my account. Even as part of me flew into fear, I knew that my empty bank account was an illusion, the creation of a banking system that shut down on weekends. More important, I saw in the incident an eloquent reminder that my anxieties around money were all equally illusory. As if to cap the experience, the hotel's owner fronted me fifty dollars to get me through the weekend.

Still, in those early days of my journeying, I was so emotionally and financially on edge that it took little to push me into panic. On one of those days, somewhere on some anonymous highway, I began to fret. Perhaps fewer people than expected had paid for an upcoming teleconference. Perhaps a hoped-for client session had failed to materialize. Regardless, my heart began to race as I ran the figures through my similarly throbbing head. An inner voice interrupted my fretful calculations.

Is there gas in the tank?
Yes... What was this about?
Do you have money for food for today?
Uh-huh.
Do you have a place to stay tonight or money for a hotel room?
Ye-e-s.
Is there anything that's in immediate danger of being taken away from you because you haven't paid a bill?
I shook my head. Nothing was imminently problematic.
Then focus on today, and let tomorrow take care of itself.
Of course.

I would recall this experience frequently in the months and years ahead. Through 2005, I would always call it up around the due date of my car payment, then my single largest monthly expense. Somehow, I managed never to be more than a few days' late on either this car payment or on the higher one I took on a year later when a miracle made it possible for me to trade in my used Pontiac Aztek for a new Mercury Monterey.

I experienced many money miracles while I was on the road. The first occurred just after I left Sedona, when I needed a new computer. My iMac, while still functional, was not portable enough to carry in and out of hotel rooms. Enter a loyal teleconference participant who had read about my Sedona exodus in one of my newsletters; her cash gift went toward a new laptop.

An even more dramatic miracle involved the Mercury Monterey. I was in remote Nevada in 2006 when the Aztek began to exhibit peculiar symptoms. Its temperature gauge would show that the car was overheating, even when the vehicle was comfortably cool.

Because both our Ford wagons had died from overheating, I was particularly sensitive to the issue. A string of mechanics, however, could find no problem with the gauge, the engine or anything else.

"What do I do?" I asked silently as I drove into Utah on my way back to Sedona.

It's time for a new car.

A new car? How? It's not possible.

Has any car you have ever bought in this country been conventionally possible?

Some quirky miracle surrounded every vehicle I had purchased, all the way back to the first: a Nissan Quest that replaced the Dodge Caravan that had brought me into the US. The fortunately empty Dodge had been rear-ended and totaled while parked in Phoenix. I didn't discover the Nissan dealer's questionable dealings until I was buying the Quest's Hawaii replacement, itself a far from ordinary transaction.

From the road, I called the Cottonwood salesman who had sold us the Aztek.

"Would you be interested in getting your Aztek back in a trade?"

"Sure."

"Then do me a favor. Look up its value, then check my credit to see if it's even worth your time and mine for me to come in."

Could my credit really have repaired itself enough to get me a new car loan? Apparently, so. Or at least that's what Joe intimated when he called me back. But where would I find a down payment?

I was still having my mail sent to a Sedona UPS Store at that time. My friend and former Lemuria Calling business partner Karen Weaver would pick it up for me and let me know if she spotted anything important. Nothing in the batch waiting for me at her house had prompted a call. As I sifted through the envelopes when I got there, I noticed one from Diana, a Midwest client. She had called a few weeks earlier for my mailing address: "Bob and I want to send you a tithe."

I had expected a few hundred dollars. When I ripped open the envelope, a check for four thousand dollars fluttered out, the precise down payment needed for the Monterey deal to close.

* * * * *

Lemuria Calling offered its own spark of a financial miracle, long before I knew that my marriage would end and that I would leave Sedona. I had never been enthusiastic about becoming one of the store's intuitive readers. Not only did I not trust my ability to make the kind of predictively specific statements that Sedona's New Age tourists expected, I had already dropped the word "channeling" from my metaphysical vocabulary and was increasingly uncomfortable with the whole "psychic" approach. Too much was changing too quickly, I believed, for any prediction to have much value beyond the moment in which it was made. At the same time, our struggling store needed help. My in-store sound healings, God Activations and energy portraits — edgy, even in metaphysical circles — were attracting few customers. Intuitive readings were more popular. I became a reader.

One afternoon, three women from Michigan wandered into the store. Patti and Christine wanted readings. Joan was dubious but agreed to join them. I shuffled my preferred deck and began. Joan's questions were probing and skeptical, so I was surprised when they extended their reading for a second twenty minutes. When our time was up, all three not only signed on for my next God Activation teleconference, they became regulars.

A few months later, Joan urged me to come out to Michigan to facilitate live group events. "You can stay with us," she offered, "and I know I can get you at least one more event, in Lansing."

Soon, I was facilitating events throughout the Midwest on a twice-yearly pilgrimage that boosted my income and provided a skeletal focus to my travels.

I still taught the occasional writing workshop, but I wasn't writing. I hadn't looked at my *StarQuest* manuscript since Maui, nor was I journaling. It wouldn't be long before my Muse would feel the need to take corrective action.

America the Beautiful

I NOW HAD something of an annual itinerary: I would spend Guinevere's birthday in Sedona, then begin the eastward trek for my Midwest events. Sometimes, I facilitated activations at a client's home in South Dakota along the way. Sometimes, I continued past Michigan, Wisconsin and Ohio to offer more events on the East Coast. By early December, I would be on my way back south and west to avoid the harshest winter weather zones. I would then repeat the sequence between March and May. As for the routes I traveled and where I roamed in the in-between times, I relied on my inner, intuitive GPS. That "God Positioning System," as I called it, carried me through more than forty states and two Canadian provinces during those thirty-three months on the road. As I had done nearly a decade earlier when I left Toronto, I rarely knew from one day to the next where I would go, what I would see or where I would sleep. I simply trusted that my car would take me to the appropriate place and find me an appropriate billet. Even when I thought I was lost or missed a planned freeway exit, or when it took longer than was comfortable to find a hotel room, I knew that I was always where I needed to be, and I trusted that I was always being taken care of.

What I saw and experienced through that extended time was a daily reminder of the magnificence not only of this land but of the earth itself. Hardly a day passed that failed to present me with another marvel. Some, like Yellowstone and Grand Teton National Parks, Washington's volcanoes, California's redwoods and much of Utah, were almost clichéd in their splendor. Many others were surprising treasures, at least to me: the deep, numinous blue of Oregon's Crater Lake, the alien rock formations at Wyoming's Vedauwoo, California's

Avalon-like Mono Lake, the granite bulwark of New Mexico's Sandia Mountains, the stately majesty of the Columbia River, the natural amphitheater of Colorado's Red Rocks, and the craggy outcroppings of Nebraska's Legend Butte. A handful of others were welcome replays of my earlier road journey, among them Nevada's Pyramid Lake, South Dakota's Badlands and Black Hills, and the medicine wheel and Powder River Pass of Wyoming's Bighorn Mountains.

Those were just the natural wonders. Despite not being American, I found myself profoundly moved at the Statue of Liberty, Gettysburg and the Liberty Bell. Monticello was so magical that I returned to the famed Thomas Jefferson house two years in a row. I felt similarly and mysteriously drawn to the McDonald Observatory in the remote Davis Mountains of West Texas, so much so that on a third, much shorter road odyssey in the fall of 2008, I would choose to spend my fifty-fourth birthday there.

Arizona's Painted Desert fell into its own category. Kentia and I had visited the national park as part of a 1998 honeymoon trip through eastern Arizona that carried us up into Hopi lands and down to the lake country near Pinetop. Once I was on my own and on the road, I would pass Painted Desert frequently. Just off I-40 some forty miles west of the New Mexico state line, it was impossible to miss for someone who spent as much time as I did traveling the Albuquerque-Flagstaff-Southern California corridor. It's a stunning spot, its rocks and dunes layered in various hues of red, pink, brown, blue, gray and white. But even though I always carried a national parks pass, I could never bring myself to use it there. Painted Desert remained too tied up with my marriage for me to be comfortable stopping there.

During those years, Guinevere would sometimes stay with me in an Albuquerque hotel while she was on holiday breaks from school. It was a way for me to have her to myself and to not have to spend time in Sedona to see her. On those visits, Aalia and I would meet in Gallup, New Mexico for lunch to do the daughter-exchange. Heading back to Albuquerque on one such drive, having left Guinevere with her mother, my car pulled me off I-40 at exit 311, the turnoff for Painted Desert.

"It's time," I heard, "time to reclaim this spot for *you*."

It should have been easy to drive up to the gate, flash my pass and enter into the technicolor-desert realm. After all, I had revisited many other sites linked to my marriage in the months and years since its end. Most had been in and around the Sedona of our daily life together, which to my mind should have been more difficult to experience. This was harder, perhaps because it represented the earliest, most hopeful stages of the relationship, when our love for each other seemed eternal and when the horizon of our time together seemed endless. I drove to a scenic pullout and gazed out over a different kind of endlessness, the endlessness of the desert — as much an illusion as the eternal nature of marriage.

I was certain that Q'nta and Aq'naton would go on forever. We both were. We kept telling each other that this would be the lifetime when we wouldn't be separated, when love would triumph. What happened?

A rare Arizona cloud blocked the sun, pasting a shadow on the desert floor below.

Maybe Q'nta and Aq'naton are still together, in some other realm. Maybe the energy that is Q'nta still lives, separate from Aalia. Maybe the energy of Aq'naton lives on too, separate from the Mark David I have become. Maybe those energies are still together. Maybe we were right...

Could this be true? Or was it a creation of my metaphysical imagination? It didn't matter. Now Painted Desert could still belong to Aq'naton and Q'nta, and to Mark David as well. I smiled and returned to the car. I started to follow the loop road that would have taken me through the entire park, then turned around and instead headed back to I-40. I had done what I came to do. I could visit another time, any time.

That wasn't the only time a deeper purpose would reveal itself to me through my travels. On my first visit to Madison, Wisconsin, for example, I drove from hotel to hotel through the traffic morass of rush hour, searching in mounting frustration for a place to spend a night or two. I had grown increasingly fussy about my accommodations as my weeks and months on the road lengthened into years. Why not? I had no home to return to. Every night's lodging was my home. This wasn't a vacation. This was my life, and I was working along the way. As with Albuquerque's Howard Johnson Express, a fridge and microwave were mandatory. Reliable wifi was also a must. When, tired and frustrated, I finally checked into a Microtel off I-90 and studied the city map to get my bearings, I realized that I had just driven three concentric circles around Madison and its State Capitol.

One of the things Laurie Ward, my first Reiki master, stressed during our classes was that, like crystals, we are all energy transmitters. Whatever we say, whatever we do, however we simply *are*, we are always having an impact on everything around us. If, then, we are all energetically connected, if we are all truly one, that impact, like the hundredth monkey effect, ultimately affects everyone everywhere. As I crisscrossed the country, I knew that I was not only doing energy-healing work on those who attended my events or booked private sessions. I was also performing some form of energy work, however unwittingly, on myself and on everyone I encountered, as well as on the land itself. When the Madison map showed me the geometry of my route, I realized that in the midst of my frustration, I had been doing something energetically significant with those three concentric circles, whether or not I ever came to know what it was.

I would have a similarly geometric experience a few years later, during a shorter road journey. After living in Albuquerque for thirteen months, I put my things into storage and took off for parts unknown, uncertain whether I would ever return. Once again, I freed my God Positioning System to take charge. From Albuquerque, my GPS sent me south into West Texas. From there, I looped up to the Mississippi side of the Mississippi River and continued north and west into Arkansas and Oklahoma before dipping down to Albuquerque. Then, after continuing south toward San Diego, I shot straight up to Sacramento and completed a second loop, back down through Nevada and Arizona and into Albuquerque. When I later retraced my unconscious itinerary on a map, I realized that I had driven an infinity symbol, with Albuquerque as its pivot point. Did it mean something? I was certain of it — both for me and the land route I had driven. Did I know what it meant? No. Yet if I had learned anything on my spiritual journeying, it was that my "want to know" was not the same as my "need to know." I still hungered for answers, but I could live with the mystery.

I trusted the mystery too as my full-time travels continued beyond Painted Desert. I trusted it but didn't always welcome it. Despite the magnificence of the land and my deepening sense of purpose, I couldn't help but wonder as first months then years flew by, how long this itinerant life could last. When I asked, the reply was always the same: "When it's time to stop, you'll know."

When the time came, I did know…in a characteristically uncomfortable way.

The End of the Road

THAT INNER GPS of mine could be persistent, especially when I tried to ignore it. By mid-2006, attendance for my teleconferences and live events had begun to slip. By fall, what would turn out to be my final Midwest tour brought in only a sprinkling of people. And by the end of the year, even teleconferences I offered for free attracted minimal participation. Clearly, this brand of metaphysical work had run its course. What would replace it...and my income?

An answer would soon make itself known. Now, though, it was late February 2007 and all month I had been trying to avoid the vague pull I was feeling toward Texas. I had crossed the state multiple times in what was by then my two years of full-time travel. In all those times, I had never felt a call to stop, never felt an urge to explore. It couldn't be about God Activations. I had no active clients in Texas.

Yet that GPS kept on beeping.

"Why would I want to go to Texas?" I asked the Divine Void one day on the drive between Santa Fe and Albuquerque.

No answer.

"Okay," I said. "If Texas is to be my next stop, I want a sign. Make the next license plate I see be from Texas."

It wasn't.

Ha!

A few minutes later, I passed a truck. Replacing it in front of me on the freeway was a burgundy sedan from...Texas.

Oh.

In case I missed it, the next vehicle also carried Texas plates, as did a half dozen others after that.

"You know," I remarked acidly, "Texas *is* right next door to New Mexico..."

I was even more skeptical the following day after I polled the handful of Texans on my email list to gauge their interest in private sessions or a group event. There was none. I knew that there could be myriad other reasons for a trip to Texas but still I resisted.

Two mornings later, I walked out to the hotel parking lot. The car next to mine was from Texas.

Hmm...

Soon after, I maneuvered into the tight parking lot at the Montgomery Avenue Satellite Coffee to meet a friend. As I passed the car that was squeezed in next to mine, I glanced down at its license plate. Texas.

Nothing miraculous happened on my trip to the Lone Star State. I had no instant revelations, nor did the experience resuscitate my moribund metaphysical practice. Yet I had barely crossed back into New Mexico when I knew what my next steps needed to be: It was time to bring back my Muse, refocus on my writing and push *The MoonQuest* out into the world.

When four months later I felt a call to return to Texas, I was just as resistant as I had been in February. By then, *The MoonQuest* was published and I was immersed in a hectic round of book-signings and other promotional activities. I still had no serious contacts in Texas and there would be no time to set up any book-related events. So why go? This time, I was on I-40, returning to Albuquerque from Sedona and the road was littered with Texas plates.

"If you want me back in Texas," I muttered, "you'll to have to do better than license plates."

Two nights later, I was back at the Howard Johnson Express, chatting with the owner about *The MoonQuest*, which she had just begun reading. I never mentioned Texas. She did. Her husband, she noted in passing, had family there. An hour passed and I returned to the front desk. Kay had been replaced by Josh, her new front-desk clerk.

"Are you a native New Mexican?" I asked him.

"No," he said. "I'm from Dallas."

Texas.

I was close to surrender...but not quite. Capitulation would arrive twenty-four hours later in an OfficeMax parking lot. Once again, the car next to mine, a black Toyota, had Texas plates.

That's not going to work this time. Show me people, not plates.

When I left the store, I was a few paces behind the man who had been ahead of me in the checkout line. He headed straight for the Toyota, got in and drove off. To Texas, no doubt.

Was I convinced? Almost. Then, as I crossed the Texan's now-vacant parking spot, something flashed up at me from the pavement. A penny. The instant I picked it up, I surrendered. I knew I would be going to Texas.

"But why?" I asked. I couldn't help myself.

In answer, the title of a talk I had given the previous Sunday in Santa Fe flashed through my mind — "Too Much Knowledge Is a Dangerous Thing: Giving Up the Need to Know." On that day, at least, I gave it up. A few days later I left for Texas.

Once again Texas offered me no immediate guidance or inspiration, even as I soaked in its unexpected natural beauty. My earlier trip had introduced me to the grandeur of the Guadalupe Mountains and the low-key ruggedness of the Davis Mountains, as well as to a pair of manmade marvels: the surprisingly urbane and culturally rich town of Marfa and the McDonald Observatory. On my second trip, I focused on the south. I started out in the remote ruggedness of Big Bend National Park, then moved to the endless stretches of ocean and beach of Padre Island National Seashore before driving a circuit around Austin that took me to the Monastery of the Poor Clares in Brenham and past the surprising protuberance of Enchanted Rock.

If my first Texas trip had activated the return of my Muse, this second one was about to activate the end my life on the road. I had just returned to Albuquerque and was asleep in Room 133 of the Howard Johnson Express when my room phone rang. It was a few minutes past seven.

"Mr. Gerson?"

"Yes?" I croaked through my morning fog. I have never woken up easily or quickly.

"You'd better come to the front desk."

"What?"

"Someone broke into your car. The police are here."

Some things easily focus the mind. This was one of them. Moments later I was dressed and in the lobby.

Through thirty-three months of travel, I had never worried about the safety of my car or its contents. And if I had ever parked in the one spot in a hotel parking lot out of range of security cameras, as I had apparently done the previous night, I had no awareness of it.

A guest at the next-door Clarion Hotel had called 911 when she had seen two young men smash my driver's side front window. By the time the police arrived, the malefactors had vanished — fortunately, with nothing of real value: personal documents, my inexpensive point-and-shoot camera and, significantly, the now-dusty digital audio recorder I had used to record my God Activation events. Not sophisticated enough to recognize the marketability of my Canadian passport, they had left it on the front passenger seat before fleeing.

As I filled out police reports and called banks, credit card issuers, insurance companies and auto-glass outlets, I wondered what it meant. By the end of the day I knew: If I had lost my itinerant identity in the break-in, it must be time for a new identity, a more established identity. I realized in that moment that my full-time traveling days had come to an end. My new ID, then, would need to reflect my newly settled state...as soon as I could figure out which state to settle in.

Act 15.
Canada

*All journeys have secret destinations
of which the traveler is unaware.*
MARTIN BUBER

*There is no passion to be found playing small, in settling for a life
that is less than the one you are capable of living.*
NELSON MANDELA

Stranger in a Familiar Land

BY THE TIME I arrived in Michigan for my first round of God Activation events, it was April 2005, nearly eight years since I had "accidentally" crossed into the US. I had not been back to Canada since. When I was married, the cost was too great, especially when there were three of us and we lived in Hawaii. Now that I was in Detroit, I was looking forward to seeing friends in Toronto and family in Montreal.

Detroit is so close to Canada you can almost touch it. You can certainly hear it. The CBC radio signal is as clear on the Michigan side of the Detroit River as it is on the Ontario side. All it takes to get from one country to the other is a drive through the Detroit-Windsor Tunnel or across the Ambassador Bridge. A passport is also necessary, as is a valid green card, if you happen to be a non-citizen resident of the United States. I was ready: I had a brand-new passport inscribed with my restored birth name and I had a green card. There was only one problem: The name on my green card was Aq'naton Yoseyva, but all my other papers identified me as Mark David Gerson. Would court documents proving Aq'naton and Mark David to be the same person be enough to overcome the inconsistency? Would I be permitted to reenter the US after my Canadian visit? Logic suggested yes. Logic wasn't necessarily relevant. This was the Immigration Service. I decided to call to make sure.

I would spend most of my free time in Detroit on the phone, much of it on hold, trying to get a straight answer to that simple question. Many phone conversations later, each offering conflicting information and each preceded by a recorded message warning me that any advice I might receive was not guaranteed to be legally accurate, I chose to postpone my cross-border visit.

My weeks within sight and sound of Canada carried an eerie Cold War feel about them. Like in Berlin before the Wall came down, I could see over the border and hear radio broadcasts from the other side. But I couldn't cross. In the end, Canada would come to me: my friends Fred and Dov met me for an afternoon in Niagara Falls — on the American side.

By the following fall, I had updated my green card and was back in Michigan for another round of events. When they were finished, I drove up I-94 to Port Huron and over the Blue Water Bridge into Canada. A few official questions, a glance at my passport, green card and license plate and I was waved through. Suddenly, I was crying. Was it a rush of affection for my long, lost homeland? Or was it a realization that my homeland was no longer home?

In a paradoxical way, it was both. Thirteen years earlier, when I moved to Toronto, Montreal quickly stopped feeling like home, even though I had grown up and spent twenty-nine years there. My first impressions of Canada when I returned in 2006 were similar. I had lived nearly forty-three years in Canada and only nine in the US. But although everything I saw was familiar, everything also felt foreign.

When I drove into Baudette in 1997, one of the first things I noticed were the speed limit signs. The numbers back then looked freakishly huge, thick and bold to me. Nine years later, when Michigan's I-94 morphed into Ontario's 402, the first speed-limit sign I passed seemed quaintly delicate. Then there was the metric system. Although I had been measuring my world in liters, kilograms, kilometers and degrees Celsius since the 1970s, when Canada went metric, I discovered that I forgotten most of it. The money was alien too. All the banknotes had been redesigned in my absence. My new country also conspired to make me feel like a foreigner in my old one: My cell provider had me on a foreign calling plan, my bank was adding a three percent foreign-exchange charge to each debit-card transaction, and my auto insurer insisted I carry a foreign-travel insurance card. If I would always be something of an outsider in my adopted land, I was now also destined to be an outsider in my native country.

Larger Than Life

My first stop in Canada was the Arabesque restaurant, an hour north of Toronto in downtown Barrie — a visit that offered not only a ghostly reminder of my past but a spectral presentiment of an event yet to come. Dov and I had planned to meet at Arabesque before continuing on to a friend's summer cottage for a few days. This would be our second time together at the Middle Eastern restaurant; the first had occurred while I still lived in Penetanguishene. During that earlier visit, the music accompanying our dinner was from Cirque du Soleil's *Alegría*. *Alegría* wasn't playing when we returned to Arabesque in 2006 but it had remained a favorite, and the recording was one of the few CDs I still owned from that era. Four years later in 2010, off the road in Albuquerque and preparing to move to LA, I saw that *Alegría* was coming to town. Unable to resist the synchronicity, I went to the show, my first-ever Cirque experience. As the trapeze artists flew through the cavernous Santa Ana Center seemingly unassisted, I began to weep. With my upcoming move, I felt that I too was poised to take off in flight. A week later I did...during my first-ever flying lesson.

Dov (now going by Sander, his middle name) had two homecoming treats for me in 2006: tickets to see, first, Cyndi Lauper in a casino near Barrie and a few nights later Barbra Streisand in Toronto. Cyndi Lauper put on an energetic, musically exciting show, and I couldn't help but cry all the way through her signature song, "True Colors." It felt as though she knew everything about my journey and was singing the words directly to me.

I see your true colors
Shining through
I see your true colors

And that's why I love you
So don't be afraid to let them show
Your true colors are beautiful...

If Cyndi Lauper's show touched the places in me that could easily get disheartened, Barbra Streisand's breathtaking performance reminded me to reach for the stars...and then soar beyond them. "She's larger than life," I gushed at intermission. She was. Despite our seats in the highest reaches of the Air Canada Centre, I was startled by how fully and personally her energy filled every corner of the vast hockey arena.

I recalled the experience a few months later while listening to a CD recording of the concert. "That's what *I* want," I heard myself blurt out loud and was so startled by what seemed such an unspiritual, ego-driven thought that I was embarrassed. It would be a few months more before I was able to recognize the deeper meaning of both the Streisand experience and my response to it. "Larger than life," I realized, was not about having Barbra Streisand's fame. It was about continuing to shed whatever self-imposed limitations I still carried within me in the mistaken belief that they could protect me from some undefined evil. Even if I couldn't detail all the ways I was holding myself back, I knew that I was. I knew too that I would have to continue stripping away those constricting comfort zones if I was to live out the limitlessness that my soul yearned for. I would have to speak my truth, regardless of consequences. I would have to fling open the shutters to my heart wherever they had slammed shut. I would have to face down my ghosts.

I had already made a start on those ghosts during my Toronto visit. One evening, over dinner at a restaurant around the corner from my old Gloucester Street apartment, I stared, Ebenezer Scrooge-like, at the different versions of myself who wandered past the window in this, my lifetimes-ago neighborhood. There were still more ghosts to come — three hundred and fifty miles away on the streets of my hometown.

Hometown Ghosts

IT IS SAID THAT ghosts are spirits who are stuck between planes, not free to move to the next world because they have yet to complete something in this one.

Is that what this time-travel trip back to Montreal is for me? Am I here not to exorcise my ghosts but to bring them to the kind of completion that will release them, and me, to move forward?

I asked myself those questions on my first night in the city as I strolled the streets of the McGill Ghetto — the same streets I had walked as I struggled to come out, the same streets that, soon after, were part of my daily life in Montreal.

At first my mood was detached, almost tourist-like.

Oh, yeah, here's La Patisserie Belge. And The Word. It's still here and it looks just the same...

Then out of nowhere, a panic gripped me in a vise so tight I could barely breathe. In that moment, all I wanted to do was flee Montreal as quickly as possible. I had tripped over a ghost, one I had never known was there. I steadied my breathing and continued walking. Block after block after block. In the dark. In the rain. But my ghost wouldn't fall back. Even as I tried to avoid it, it walked beside me, insisting I acknowledge its presence. Finally, I did.

You! You pushed me out of Montreal and always made me not want to come back, including this time.

I walked faster, but it kept pace, refusing to let me escape.

Suddenly, I knew its name: "Not Enough." We had been born together, this ghost and I, and it had haunted me in various guises ever since. When I least expected it, it would trigger the feeling that whatever I was doing could never measure up, that whoever I was could never be enough.

If you're not Canadian, you may not realize that French is the dominant language in Montreal and all of Quebec. My ghost showed up to remind me that whenever I would speak French in this city, I would always feel inadequate. Not good enough. Not perfect enough. It also showed up to point out that my second-language skills were not the root of my feelings. Rather, they were a constant and painful reminder of their presence.

I see now another reason why I had to move away. I see now one of the reasons I had to come back. This ghost is ready to complete its transition. We're both ready to move on. Only I can free it. Only by freeing it can I free myself.

As I left the Ghetto and continued toward my hotel, I knew that it was time to make peace with this piece of my past, still so uncomfortably a part of my present. I knew too that more pieces, and ghosts, would be waiting for me the next day when I met my sister and when, together for the first time since our mother died, we would visit the house in which we had been raised.

Growing up, my relationship with Susan was volatile, occasionally violent and often ugly. From my child perspective, she was a demon, responsible for many of my fears, scars and traumas. From her point of view, I was probably the kid brother from hell. None of this was subtle, and Edith always swore that one of us would end up in jail for the murder of the other. Those childhood terrors remained with me into adulthood and, not surprisingly, colored my ties with my sister, from whom I always maintained what I considered to be a safe distance. We spoke rarely, except during our mother's declining health and subsequent death. My physical departure, first from Montreal and later from Canada, did nothing to increase the frequency of our contact.

By the time I crossed into Canada in October 2006, getting the house on Atherton ready for sale had produced more communication but no more closeness, at least not for me. In fact, the thought of seeing Susan for the first time in nearly a decade contributed to some of my resistance to the visit.

Then two things happened to shatter my decades-old patterns. The first was when Susan told me that in order to spend more time with me, she had not only freed up her entire weekend but would be taking a day off from work. I was stunned. This was the sister I had avoided all these years? The second occurred as I drove into Montreal and, visualizing the next day's planned reunion, saw myself crying. I did cry when I saw her. To my surprise, and perhaps for the first time in my life, I was happy to be with my sister and felt safe and comfortable in her presence.

What had shifted? Me. In an instant.

Of course, Susan had grown and matured since our childhood battles. Yet as we hugged for the first time in nearly a decade, I realized that I hadn't — not in relation to her. Whether twenty-five, forty-five or fifty, I was still always five or eight or twelve whenever I thought about her, talked to her or spent time with her. I was still the put-upon little brother. It was sobering to realize that, just as with the ghost named Not Enough, I had spent much of my life living a lie. In that moment of revelation and acknowledgment in our childhood home, another ghost was gone.

We were meeting at the Atherton house to see if any additional work needed to be done to hasten its sale. When Edith died in 1984, she left the house to me and Susan but gave my stepfather the right to live in it as long as he wanted. By spring 2006, Jack was ready to leave. The house had now been on the market for six months, empty for about half that time. A conventional walk-through was the surface reason for my visit. The deeper reason had to do with energy — mine and the house's. The longer it sat unsold, the more I grew to believe that something in me was holding on to it. I needed to say goodbye. More than that, I needed to set it free.

Ours was the only family this house had ever known. It was also the only family home I had ever known. When we moved into it in January 1955, the streets of this new subdivision were still mud, and I was only three months old. Photos of that long-ago Atherton suggest the promise of young families and new life. Fifty years later, new families had replaced the old ones, and Susan and I were the sole links to that prehistoric time.

It's clichéd to say that the house seemed smaller than I remembered, but it did. Sadder too. Empty houses always seem sad and lifeless. Even the mature maple in our front yard didn't give our house the authority of age so much as shroud it in gloom. A few years ago, one of my students shared a brilliant piece of prose from a book she was writing. It described an empty house waiting to be sold, but from the point of view of the house. Listening to our empty house that October morning, I heard a plea to be freed so that it could move on to embrace life again.

As I wandered slowly from room to room and then into the back and side yards, many lives flashed before my eyes, all enclosed in the frame of this modest bungalow, all viewed through the lens of every age I had ever been. My childhood memories may be sparse, but what wasn't embedded in those walls and floors was lurking among the dying grasses of autumn, including all that had I long ago forgotten.

"Thank you," I repeated just under my breath as I moved through and around the house. "I'm grateful for all you were and still are. I'm grateful for all the ways you sheltered me when I lived here and for the memories you have held for me, even in my absence. Now it's time to relieve you of those memories, to free you to scrub them away. It's time to move on. For both of us." Soon after, Susan and I left to have lunch. A few weeks later, the house sold.

A few days after that, I crossed back into the US at a spot where another of my ghosts resided: the border crossing at Champlain, New York. We still had a car, a white Vauxhall, and Sydney had not yet been hospitalized, when in the early 1960s we made regular family pilgrimages to the Montrealers' shopping mecca of Plattsburgh, twenty miles south of the Champlain crossing.

The Champlain ghost was a friendly one that day. Casper-like, it waved at me as US Customs gestured me through...and home.

Act 16.
The Writer I Am

It's the story that has the power. I'm what follows it.
Ursula K. Le Guin

*I have only one story to tell, and that's my story.
But mine is large and encompasses much,
and it can be sliced into myriad tales of truth and fantasy.*
Elizabeth Engstrom

The Story Knows Best

A YEAR AFTER WE returned to Sedona from Hawaii, and with Neil Donald Walsch and Hampton Roads long out of the picture, I began approaching literary agents to see if I could find representation for *The MoonQuest*. Although most agents today insist on email queries, few would accept them in 2003. The Nancy Ellis Agency was an exception. Within twenty-four hours of my email, Nancy had requested the complete manuscript. That, too, was exceptional. When an author query piques their interest, agents generally ask for only the first twenty or thirty pages. I was ecstatic. I was even more ecstatic a few months later when Nancy and I signed a contract. I now had an agent, *The MoonQuest* was being pitched to all the major fantasy houses and I would soon be a published author…or so I thought.

Meantime, I recalled all the writings on writing I had penned back on the Big Island. Could they be a book too? I called Nancy. Would she be interested in a book on writing and creativity?

She would. The problem was, I had no book on writing. All I had were reams of random inspirational vignettes and a vague sense that a book might be buried somewhere within them. The next morning, I took my laptop, a mountain of printouts, a pair of scissors and a roll of Scotch tape to Sedona's Ravenheart Coffee.

"If you're a book," I declared to the papers spread out over my table, "it's up to you to show me what you're about."

It did.

I have often claimed that my books are smarter than I am. That afternoon, for the first time, I consciously experienced that concept. Doing my best to keep my mind disengaged from the process, I read through each piece, intuitively stacking them by theme. I then read through each individual pile, looking for redundancy and more commonality, merging some pieces and discarding others. Slowly and to my surprise, the skeleton of a book began to emerge. I continued sifting and organizing over the next week, creating sections, adding exercises and filling in obvious gaps. I nearly had a book.

"Meditations," Q'nta said a few days later.

"What?"

"You always use guided meditations when you teach. Why not include some in the book?"

She was right. I created a half-dozen to add to the manuscript. Q'nta also suggested a title when one continued to elude me. The book would be called *The Voice of the Muse: Answering the Call to Write*.

When, a few months afterward, Nancy opted to focus only on *The MoonQuest*, Q'nta and I designed a PDF version of *The Voice of the Muse*, I recorded the meditations in a friend's garage studio, and we packaged the result on two CDs: a music disc for the meditations and a data disc for the book. Now I had two books; one was out, sort of, and the other was represented by an agent. What more could a writer ask for?

He could ask for a sale. After more than two years of searching for a home for *The MoonQuest*, Nancy conceded defeat. She had made all the approaches she knew to make and reluctantly resigned as my agent. Now I had two books and no agent. I was on the road by then, focused more on my God Activations than on my Muse. Another round of queries seemed impractical. *The MoonQuest* would have to wait.

"What's happening with *The MoonQuest*?" Aalia asked me one afternoon in 2006 as I was driving back to New Mexico from Wisconsin.

"Nothing." I told her that Nancy and I had parted ways.

"You should adapt it as a screenplay."

Although I had always seen *The MoonQuest* as a movie, secretly fantasizing about Steven Spielberg as director, I couldn't see writing the screenplay myself. I had never accepted Marcus's screenwriting invitations, knew nothing about the medium and assumed that getting produced would be even tougher than getting published. Aalia had made the suggestion before and I had always ignored it. This time, the idea stuck. My writerly self had returned.

One of my first stops when I reached Santa Fe was Borders. I knew that traditional screenwriting methods were highly structured and unlikely to work for me. Could I find a handbook that was more intuitive? As I scanned the shelves, Viki King's *How to Write a Movie in 21 Days: The Inner Movie Method* caught my eye, and not only because I found the idea of finishing in three weeks difficult to resist. Rather, an "inner movie method" suggested something more organic than the other screenwriting books, all of which felt suffocatingly rule-bound. King's book was a good start. It presented me with the basics and inspired me to continue…even if, when I finished reading it, twenty-one days seemed unrealistically optimistic and even though a key component was missing: King had said nothing about how to adapt an existing work for the screen. How was I supposed to do that? Days of online research delivered no answers.

"You know everything you need to know," an inner voice insisted. I was doubtful. Screenplays were technical, demanding creatures. Where would I begin? How would I begin? Then I laughed. That had been Toshar's dilemma in *The MoonQuest* book. Both Na'an and M'nor had helped him, and me, a decade earlier on the first draft of the novel. I would have to trust that they were also ready to help me on this film version of the story.

They were. Once again, I got out of my own way and listened. I tried not to worry about three-act structure, beats or plot points and did my best to let the story tell me how to make it work for the screen. As with all my writing, it was an intuitive process. And as with all my writing, it came with many moments of doubt, distrust and self-judgment.

A few halting weeks later, I was in Albuquerque flipping through the city's alternative weekly when an ad leapt out at me — for a screenwriting conference. This wasn't just any screenwriting conference. It was a major conference happening up the road in Santa Fe, and it opened in a week's time. Although nervous about the cost, I couldn't ignore the synchronicity. I registered on the spot.

I left the conference exhilarated and ready to commit to this *MoonQuest* screenplay, even if I still couldn't see how it would ever get produced. My single pitch session at the conference didn't help: "I love the story...but get the book out first," a young Hollywood producer advised me.

"I will," I retorted silently, "as soon as you find me a publisher."

Regardless, I was determined to finish the screenplay. The spirit of the story would have to take care of the rest. What I needed most, in the meantime, was uninterrupted writing time, not easy for a full-time traveler to find. Then I remembered Sunrise Ranch, an intentional community just outside Loveland, Colorado. I had attended a metaphysical retreat on the property the year before, and its setting in the rural Rocky Mountain foothills was magnificent: open fields bordered by craggy hills and a broad, blue reservoir. As well, the energy had been open, peaceful and uplifting. I booked in for a week's writing retreat.

It took me more than a week. But I continued working on it after leaving Sunrise and by summer's end I had completed two drafts of a *MoonQuest* screenplay. I didn't know whether it was any good. I did know that writing it had already improved the novel. Viewing *The MoonQuest* from a film perspective had sparked a handful of shifts to the story and its characters, which I knew I would have to incorporate into a new draft of the book.

The MoonQuest would soon be readier for publication than ever. Where was the publisher? The answer would have to wait until one more eastward journey, for a final round of God Activation events.

Cover Story

By early 2007, with my God Activations at an end, I sent out another round of agent queries for *The MoonQuest*. This time, no one asked to see the manuscript, and when I left for Texas, I wasn't sure what to do about the book. Soon after I returned, I was: If no agent or publisher would take it on, I would publish it myself. It was time, and I now had the money to do it. The sale of the Atherton house had closed a few months earlier, rescuing me at the last minute from pennilessness. With little income, I had been living on the credit cards that began trickling in a year earlier. I was days away from running out of both cash and credit when Susan called to let me know that my share of the proceeds was on its way into my bank account.

Now, I was a publisher. The process was more mundane than magical, except when it came to the book cover. My relationship with Angela Farley, the gifted graphic artist I contracted with to produce *The MoonQuest*'s cover art was testy, almost from the outset, as my perfectionism clashed with her prickly temperament. But when she sent me an early idea that featured two colored horses on either side of a chalice I knew that despite our increasingly strained relationship, she was the right artist for the job. The horses were *The MoonQuest*'s Rykka and Ta'ar and were, as best as I could then recall, an exact match for their original models: the horses on the Chariot tarot card that had inspired the story thirteen years earlier. Somehow, Angela had magically tapped into the same creative essence I had when I conceived the book.

A month later, I emailed the tarot deck's artist, Courtney Davis in the UK, to let him know that I would be mentioning him in *The MoonQuest*'s acknowledgments. When he heard how his card had inspired my book, he asked if I would write the story as a caption for a planned retrospective of his work.

"Of course," I replied, "but you'll need to send me a copy of the Chariot card." I no longer had a copy of the deck. I had gifted it to a tarot reader friend when I left Toronto in 1997.

What Courtney sent was even more like Angela's cover than I remembered. Not only were the horses identically colored, they were identically placed. There was even a tiny chalice just above the wording on the card. Angela was as startled as I was. She had never seen the deck, nor had she heard of it.

Two months and many details later, an advance copy of the printed book arrived in my UPS Store mailbox in Santa Fe. Of course, I had seen proofs of the cover and all the pages. But a printed book was different. *The MoonQuest* had been part of my life for more than a decade and now, finally, it was in form. I carried the FedEx envelope to the car and tremblingly ripped it open. The moment I saw the book, I burst into tears. Holding this copy of *The MoonQuest* was in its own way like the moment I first held Guinevere in my arms. Both were sentient, fully independent entities that had emerged from some mysterious place within me. And although both would live their own imperative, in that first moment of miraculous revelation, both were physical expressions of my deepest self. I was awed...and just a little bit scared.

The MoonQuest book was now out, and though I was still on the road, I was doing whatever I could to promote it. My screenplay adaptation, largely forgotten, wouldn't remain in the shadows for long. For now, though, my Muse had other plans.

The Voice of My Muse

MY BOXES OF *MoonQuest* books had barely settled into their new Albuquerque storage-unit home when I was back on the road and in Sedona. Once again, I sat in Ravenheart Coffee with *The Voice of the Muse*. Now, I was rereading the ebook that I had birthed there with a view to updating and expanding it. With my sound-healing days over, it felt time to reinvent myself as a published author and refocus my energy on writing classes. *The Voice of the Muse* would be part of that.

I was astounded. I had not looked at *The Voice of the Muse* in years and not only was it better than I remembered, it was a perfect companion to *The MoonQuest*. If among its other themes, *The MoonQuest* was a call to live a more authentic life by telling our stories, *The Voice of the Muse* demonstrated how to do it. Perfect!

A few days later, driving north on US-93 toward Las Vegas and still thinking about ways I could improve *The Voice of the Muse*, I heard the voice of *my* Muse.

Forget the ebook.

What? Why?

Publish The Voice of the Muse *as a physical book. Not in a year. Not in six months. Now. Start the process now.*

But-but—

A few days earlier, I had taken Guinevere to see the movie *Evan Almighty*, the story of an ambitious newscaster-turned-Congressman whose life is turned upside-down when God tells him to prepare for an impending flood by building an ark. I had laughed, of course, at Steve Carell's comedic brilliance. I had cried, too, when I saw myself in Evan. Like Evan, I had been guided along roads that appeared bizarre — to myself and to others. Like Evan, I had initially cursed and resisted, only to ultimately surrender. And like

Evan's, my higher guidance had always proven itself wiser and more knowing than my limited, control-crazy mind could ever be.

"But *The MoonQuest*," I shouted into the windshield. "It's just barely out. This is insane!"

No more insane than building an ark.

I cursed and resisted, but not for long. A month later, even as I continued to schedule book-signings and media appearances for *The MoonQuest*, I began to revise *The Voice of the Muse* and plan its publication. Once again, I asked its essence to guide me and, when I was done, the new *Voice of the Muse* was fifty percent longer, with many new chapters, meditations and exercises.

I knew I couldn't use Angela Farley again for the cover. By the end of *The MoonQuest* experience, we had barely been on speaking terms. At the same time, I was having difficulty finding someone whose work seemed as though it could connect to the spirit of the book. Then I stumbled onto Richard Crookes. A mutual Facebook friend had been soliciting opinions on her proposed book cover; Richard's comments were posted above mine. When I went to Richard's website, I knew that I had found my designer. Everything about his work suggested just the grounded spirituality that was at the core of *The Voice of the Muse*.

One obstacle remained: What to do about the meditations? Assuming that a professional studio would be beyond my means, I bought some basic equipment and used Garage Band on my Mac to record them myself. The result was not even good enough for a digital mastering facility to fix. I was faced with a tough choice: Trust that a solution would present itself or immediately scrap the CD aspect of the project. Immediately, because the book, now twenty-four hours away from being sent to the printer, would have to be stripped of all references to the recording.

I opted for trust. Within days, I was in a sound booth at Albuquerque's Shepherd Studios, being expertly coached in the best use of my voice by owner Michael McDade. A while later as we listened to one of the tracks I had recorded, Michael slid over to the electronic keyboard.

"I think it would sound even better with something like this," he said and began to improvise a track of contemplative music.

He was right. It sounded incredible. But...

"What would something like that add to the cost?" I asked hesitantly, my fearful mind insisting that my resources were limited.

Michael looked directly at me. "Does it matter?" he asked back, clearly channeling the spirit of the project.

It did matter...but it couldn't. In the end, my final Shepherd bill, including original music, barely exceeded what I had planned to spend on mastering my computer recording. The result was more professional and inspirational than anything I could have imagined, the perfect companion for a book whose primary message called for unconditional surrender to the greater wisdom of the Muse.

I had not been surprised to burst into tears when I first held a printed copy of *The MoonQuest*. I didn't expect a repeat performance when, eight months later, I opened another FedEx delivery from my Michigan book printer. But cry I did. If *The Voice of the Muse* wasn't my firstborn, it was still my child, and I was overcome.

Act 17.
Albuquerque

As to me I know of nothing else but miracles.
Walt Whitman

What is essential is invisible to the eye.
Antoine de Saint-Exupéry

Hello, Albuquerque

If I realized after my car was broken into that my full-time traveling days were over, what I didn't know was where I would live. Nearly three years of journeying had carried me through some forty states, yet only two places in the country had ever felt like home: New Mexico and Southern California. New Mexico and California were the first two states I visited after leaving Sedona, and both had competed for my heart and mind ever since. Would I move to LA or San Diego? Or would I stay in New Mexico and choose between Albuquerque and Santa Fe?

I struggled with the decision for days as I replaced compromised bank accounts and bank cards. In the end, Albuquerque's call was strongest. It made no sense. Santa Fe was not only New Mexico's state capital but its cultural capital. And Los Angeles was more dynamic than both. But when had I lived according to conventional sense?

Once I decided to stay in Albuquerque, choosing a part of town was easy.

The Sandia Mountains form the city's eastern boundary, rising through park and National Forest land to a craggily sky-scraping 10,678 feet. I can't say for certain that it was the Sandias that drew me to Albuquerque that first time. Regardless, they definitely kept me coming back. Something about the mountain spoke to me and all I wanted to do, whenever I was in town, was spend time walking its city-side trails, driving its streets or, if the weather wouldn't cooperate, sitting in my car in its trailhead parking lots. I knew that I couldn't live anywhere but in its foothills. But where, specifically? The foothills include a large swathe of territory and many types of housing.

What made most sense would have been a house small enough for one but big enough for Guinevere to have her own room, and reasonably close to a hiking trail. What I ended up with, of course, made no sense: a spacious, four-bedroom, Santa Fe-style home with a three-car garage. Even before I saw the house, I felt that it was mine. After all, it was on Moondance Place. Then I drove by. It was bigger than I needed, more than I wanted to furnish, and its rent lay well outside my comfort zone. But *Moon*dance? I closed my storage unit and my cartons of *MoonQuest* books and I moved in.

Two weeks later, with a few of those cartons in the back of my Monterey, I pulled into the parking lot of Albuquerque's westside Borders for my first big-box bookstore book-signing. It was September 16, the ten-year anniversary of my arrival in Sedona and a date that would continue to show up for me in significant ways in the years ahead.

When you're not a well-known author, no lengthy queues of readers eager to meet you snake through a bookstore during a signing. Rather, the reverse is true. Customers make a point of detouring to the next aisle to avoid having to face an unidentifiable writer peddling an anonymous book. At the regional Hastings chain, customers couldn't avoid me. The book department managers always placed me near the front door. Eventually, I learned to call up my OPC experience from Hawaii, engaging most customers as they entered the store and forcing myself to be charmingly aggressive. Because few Hastings customers were readers — most came in to rent or buy DVDs — I often needed a harder sell. On the other hand, if they hadn't come in looking for books, I didn't have to compete with other authors when I made my front-door pitch. Borders was more urbane, its customers mostly readers, and its book-signing tables more discreetly placed...and easier to dodge.

It had been a quiet Sunday afternoon at Borders, with few conversations and fewer sales. After an hour, a red-haired woman walked up to my table, intrigued, she said, by the colored horses on the giant *MoonQuest*-cover poster on an easel next to me. She picked up a copy of the book, glanced at the cover to make sure it matched the poster, flipped it over and began to read.

"Oh," she exclaimed suddenly, glancing from the author's photo to me and back again. "You're the author!"

I nodded, masking both my hopefulness at the prospect of a sale and my irritation at her surprise. Why else would I be there?

I held my breath. Would she buy?

She looked up. "Would you sign it for me?"

I breathed again. "Of course. What's your name?"

"You know," she said as she passed me her business card, "this might make a really good movie."

Her card read: "Kathleen Messmer, Script Supervisor." I didn't know what a script supervisor was. I knew only that it had something to do with filmmaking. I perked up.

"Funny you should say that," I said, handing her back the book but keeping her card. "I've written a screenplay adaption."

She glanced back at the cover, then at me. "Funny you should say *that*. I've just launched an independent film production company, and I'm looking for projects."

My eyebrows shot up, if cautiously. I remembered Neale Donald Walsch.

"If I like the book," she added. "I'll want to see your screenplay."

She loved the book and, to my amazement, the script.

Not much happened in the next while, other than occasional coffee meet-ups with progress reports on Anvil Springs Entertainment's sluggish journey to launch. Little did I know that four years later I would be living in her Albuquerque home, an associate producer as well as the screenwriter of not one film but three in a newly dubbed *Q'ntana Trilogy* of fantasy features: *The MoonQuest*, *The StarQuest* and *The SunQuest*.

Goodbye, Albuquerque

By spring 2008, as I intensified my promotional efforts with now two books and a CD, the owners of my Moondance house decided to sell. They offered me the option of staying on month-to-month, which I did. Then, in a gentler echo of my experience on Toronto's Gloucester Street fourteen years earlier, where balcony-rebuilding ultimately pushed me out, life at home grew increasingly less home-like. I had never felt the need to fully furnish the house. One of the bedrooms was empty, for example, as was the dining room. The house was also mostly devoid of wall hangings and knickknacks, except in Guinevere's room. The look was spare, too spare for the realtor, who kept bringing in new pieces and accessories, none to my taste, to fill out the house for showing. When, unlike on Gloucester, I didn't take the hint and leave, a higher power stepped in: The realtor convinced the owners that the house would sell more quickly without a tenant. I was given my notice. Thirteen months after moving in, I would have to move out.

Now what? In another echo of yet another Toronto experience — this time when I left Pauline Avenue — I explored other rentals, but without enthusiasm. The only option that felt right was to hit the road again. Now, however, it would be pointless to sell off my household goods before leaving. If my cartons of *MoonQuest* and *Voice of the Muse* books and CDs would have to go into storage, my furniture could join them.

Like the Aztek before it, my Monterey was beginning to show signs of wear, not surprising given the tens of thousands of miles I had put on it through each year of my travels. I was reluctant to subject it to the rigors of another full-time open-ended journey, but it was starting to look as though I would have no choice. Although my credit had recovered since Maui, several frustrating all-day outings to car dealerships proved that it had not recovered enough for me to get a car loan. I abandoned my new-car quest. I would have to take my chances with the Mercury.

Then, the car angel that had been looking after my automotive needs since I arrived in the US stepped in with another miracle: I received an invitation to a local Chevrolet dealer's employee-pricing event. I was being invited, the email said, because of my previous inquiry. I had made no previous inquiry, to Galles or to any GM dealership. Six hours after I arrived at the Lomas Boulevard showroom, I left — behind the wheel of a new 2008 Chevy Trailblazer.

The miracle didn't end there.

Ever since I experienced a bait-and-switch at a Hawaii dealership — our low interest rate was increased two days after we drove our Subaru Forester off the lot — I had been wary of car dealers and their finance managers. I warned my Albuquerque salesman that I would return the Trailblazer immediately if Galles Chevrolet tried something similar. So, when the morning after the sale I got a call from Galles, I was primed for a fight.

"This is the finance manager at Galles Chevrolet."

"Yes?" I asked warily.

"Can you come down to the dealership today?"

"Why?" Now I was certain that I had been scammed.

"We'd like to lower your interest rate."

Lower my interest rate? Who lowered interest rates? I was back at Galles within the hour, signing the revised paperwork.

In a final echo of journeys past, I left Albuquerque a few days before my birthday, now my fifty-fourth...once again, driving a new vehicle.

Coming Out (Again) for Christmas

ALONG WITH MY "Who is Aq'naton?" question after my marriage ended, I also asked about my sexual orientation. Was I gay again? Was I straight? Was I bisexual? Had I ever been straight? Had I ever really been gay? Who was I? What was I?

It seemed disingenuous to call myself straight. With few exceptions, my wife was the only woman I had ever been physically attracted to. After she and I separated, my eyes tended to again linger on the men around me, never pausing to take sexual note of the women. That likely eliminated bisexuality too. Yes, I was functionally bisexual, as are most people, even if that innate potential is hardly ever expressed. At the same time, it didn't feel right to call myself gay. So what was I? Unlike my Aq'naton question, which resolved itself within weeks with Martha Martyn's help, my sexuality remained uncomfortably open. Meantime, I reverted to my pre-Sedona definition: primarily attracted to men, open to all possibilities, reluctant to label myself. In one sense it was irrelevant. As in the years leading up to my marriage, I was sexually inactive. Nearly four years passed like that, with little change.

Then, everything changed. It was December 14, 2008. I had recently resettled in Albuquerque after my six-week road trip, and I was sitting in Starbucks with Kathleen Messmer. We had just come from the New Mexico Gay Men's Chorus "Come Out for Christmas" concert, our second year attending the holiday show together. The first year, I had attended more because I like choral and seasonal music than because it was a gay event. This second year felt different, almost as though I was twenty again attending my first gay-community event in Montreal.

"Have I ever told you my 'gay story?'" I asked Kathleen over coffee.

She looked at me quizzically. "No..."

I took a deep breath and told her about coming out at twenty, about the spiritual journey that had led me to Aalia, about the end of my marriage and about my still-undefined orientation. When I drove off an hour later, I felt the same rush I had experienced thirty-four years earlier when I came out as a gay man to straight friends. I also felt lighter, as though a weighty burden had dissolved from my shoulders.

It felt, too, as I so often would in the months that followed, as though I was reconnecting with the thirty-two-year-old I had been before my spiritual awakening. Somehow, I was taking all that Mark, David and Aq'naton had encountered through more than a decade of spiritual growth and bringing it back to earth as Mark David — into the practical, into the physical. "Perhaps," as I wrote so presciently of Toshar in *The MoonQuest*, "it is time...to allow the boy I was to touch the man I have become..."

Four days after the concert, I was at the High Ridge Cinemas to see *Milk*, the story of Harvey Milk, the first openly gay elected official in the US, who was assassinated in 1978 by a fellow San Francisco city supervisor. I cried during the film, and not only because of Sean Penn's compelling portrayal. I cried for a more personal reason: The film's time frame covered the period of my coming out, and the gay activism it portrayed was a bolder version of my activism in the Montreal of the mid- to late seventies. When I got into the car, I began to sob uncontrollably. I sat there — crying, heaving, releasing — until long after the parking lot had emptied. When the tears finally stopped, I realized that I had come full circle, that like Toshar, I had allowed the Mark I had been to touch the Mark David I had become. And I recognized that as open as I still was to the infinite realm of possibilities in life, I was a gay man. Again.

All That Matters Is That I'm Writing

WHEN I RETURNED to New Mexico from my six weeks on the road and realized that Albuquerque had formed the pivot point of the infinity symbol I had unconsciously driven, I knew I would stay. Still addicted to the Sandias, I found a two-story condo nestled in the foothills and located on the last street before open space swept up toward the summit. My new home not only offered kingly views of both city and mountain but was across from the Piedra Lisa hiking trail.

That was the good news. The other piece of good news was that I had just won a New Mexico Book Award, *The MoonQuest*'s fifth literary honor. The bad news was that days after I moved into the condo, I realized that my savings were spent, my credit was exhausted and I had no income prospects other than paltry amounts from book sales. It was the week before Thanksgiving. I was broke.

Finding a job in your mid-fifties is not easy when the economy is crashing, when you're a writer and spiritual wanderer with no recent stable employment history, and when you're either unqualified or overqualified for everything advertised. Despite a handful of interviews, I received no callbacks. Finally, my friend Marisha Diaz sent me to Hobby Lobby, a regional craft mart with three local stores. An artist and intuitive reader, Marisha had signed up for my mailing list shortly before I left Sedona. She lived in Denver at the time, and when she heard about my open-ended road trip, offered to put me up if I ever found myself in her area. When we finally met, the connection was instant. She felt like family and would be an anchor in my life for the next several years. By November 2008 Marisha was an Albuquerque neighbor and had herself returned to the Hobby Lobby sales floor that had sustained her off and on over the years.

Bob, her store manager, was at least fifteen years my junior and only agreed to meet me on Marisha's recommendation. The afternoon of our interview, we stood at the front of the store as he glanced between my application and me, silently sizing up my physical strength for the only opening he had: in the store's stockroom. A week later, following Guinevere's Thanksgiving visit to Albuquerque, I began my new working life as a fifty-four-year-old stock boy. The pay was poor, the hours were long and I hated it. Some days I was grateful, some days I was angry. Most days, all my muscles ached as I crawled into bed soon after dinner.

By the week before Christmas, I felt desperate and hopeless. My paycheck didn't begin to cover my expenses, and I couldn't see how I would be able to keep up with my car payments. Not sure what else to do, I scouted the neighborhood for bus stops, in case I had to give up my car, and I scoured the listings for better jobs, but found nothing. My friends were all sympathetic, but only one had a suggestion. It arrived via email on the evening of the winter solstice. "Write, write, write," Sander Freedman urged from Toronto. "It is your soul work. It is your gift." Sobbing, I read his words over and over. Then I remembered a commitment I had made to myself on the drive back into Albuquerque from my road trip, that after a decade of fits and starts, it was time to complete *The StarQuest*. "Regardless of what it takes and what is required of me," I had declared, "I commit to getting it done. It's time, and I'm ready."

Now, I resolved, I had no choice but to transcend all disruption and distraction and act on that commitment. Now, at a time when I had no time, I had to make time. That meant writing every day, something I had not done since early drafts of *The MoonQuest*, when all I had was time. Now, writing was the only thing that could matter — more important than job, more important than car, more important than condo. In *The Voice of the Muse*, I had quoted Abraham Lincoln as saying, "Determine that the thing can and shall be done, and then we shall find the way." I made the determination. Now I had to find the way.

My first question was, *When?* Morning or evening? I have always been slow to get going first thing in the day, and mornings have never been my best time. Still, I had made it through the first draft of *The MoonQuest* by working on it as soon as I woke up, before any opportunity to procrastinate could arise. Mornings would be tough, but evenings, when I was physically exhausted from my day at Hobby Lobby, would be tougher.

My next question was, *How long?* Many job-bound writers wake up at four or five in the morning. Could I do that? I had to be realistic, and honest. I was trying to create a schedule I would stick to, not one that would melt away after a week…or a day. I knew myself. A four-in-the-morning routine would never last. What would, then? After many internal negotiations, I chose to set my alarm fifteen minutes earlier than I needed to. I would stay in bed and write during that time. Fifteen minutes wasn't much, but I had to follow the same advice I gave workshop participants: I had to set myself up for success. That meant establishing goals that I could meet easily and, perhaps, exceed. Setting the bar too high was a recipe for disappointment, failure and giving up. As well, I would take the manuscript to work and try to squeeze in a few minutes more during my breaks. And I would write for longer periods on my days off.

It worked. Progress was slow at first. But by July I was finished. After two false starts, the first dating back ten years, I had finally completed a first draft of *The StarQuest*. I had left Hobby Lobby by then. Rather, Hobby Lobby had left me.

Although my recommitment to writing had brought with it my first coaching client in years, I was still financially challenged. I didn't want to break my lease, but I seemed to be running out of options. One Friday in late January, stressed by my bank balance and gearing up to break the news to my property manager that I would have to move out, I decided that I would spend the day in Santa Fe. Perhaps a change of scenery would offer some perspective. As I left the house, I noticed that the mail truck had just pulled up. I walked over to the group mailbox and chatted with the letter carrier as he filled the boxes. This wasn't our usual mailman. I had never seen this one here before. "Nothing for you," he said, when he got to my box, "but there's always a chance for good news tomorrow."

There's always a chance for good news tomorrow. His words replayed in my head as I drove out of the complex and along Tramway toward the freeway. *There's always a chance for good news tomorrow.* Within moments, I knew: I would not call the property manager and I would not leave. Somehow, things would turn around.

They did. Suddenly, I was signing up more coaching clients. Not enough to fully support me but enough to satisfy the bill collectors. By mid-February, after I had asked Hobby Lobby for a week's unpaid leave to visit Guinevere in Sedona, I felt a leap of faith coming on. I lacked the courage to quit my job outright, although with holiday and inventory rushes over, everyone's hours were being cut. Instead, I dropped a note in Bob's mailbox telling him that I needed an additional four weeks off. I doubted that he would care; most days, he sent me home early. This would be my attempt to wean myself off Hobby Lobby. If other money came in, I would quit; if not, I would stay. Ten days later, when my usually direct-deposited pay didn't show in my bank account, I called the store.

"Your check's here," the office manager told me. She offered no explanation.

As I headed out of the store check in hand, I stopped to chat with one of my coworkers.

"Bob told me he had to let you go," Carla said.

"What? What do you mean?" I looked at her blankly. Bob had said nothing to me and there was no pink slip in my pay envelope.

"Bob told me he had to let you go," she repeated.

I had been fired and no one had told me. Clearly, it was time to move on.

It was certainly not time to look back. A few Sundays later, I came out of the Albuquerque Church of Religious Science to find that the driver's-side rearview-mirror housing was gone from my car.

Not again!

This may have been a first for my Trailblazer, but it was hardly a first for one of my rearview mirrors. I had been at fault when the passenger-side mirror was stripped from my Quest days before the Beltane bonfire that launched my relationship with Kentia. I had driven too close to a construction sign and the mirror was the only major casualty. Seven years later, my marriage recently over, I was driving my Aztek across rural Nebraska on my first trip to the Midwest when a slab of ice whipped off the roof of a Swift semi and popped the mirror glass out of its housing, also on the passenger side. Both incidents occurred at times of endings and new beginnings, and both seemed to be warning me to avoid the rearview mirror of my past so that I could move forward into the next phase of my life — as a husband and father when I was driving the Quest and as an itinerant sound healer with the Aztek.

Losing the Trailblazer's mirror marked another new beginning as I renewed my focus on coaching, teaching and public speaking and launched a different kind of travel. For the next year, as I completed that first draft of *The StarQuest* and launched an initial draft of this memoir, my coaching practice boomed and my newly developed roster of writing workshops thrived. I was in demand, thanks to my Muse and *The Voice of the Muse*. This new persona carried me to Las Vegas in November 2009, Denver two months later and Los Angeles a month after that for a series of successful events and appearances. If I had no rearview-mirror experience in LA, where I was presenting at the Conscious Life Expo, the trip would still mark the beginning of an end I could not yet see.

Act 18.
LA Story

I have learned to use the word "impossible" with the greatest caution.
WERNHER VON BRAUN

All my life, when things have happened that have worked out successfully, it has been because of what has come to me, not from what I have willed.
ANG LEE

Trading Open Spaces

SEDONA IS ALWAYS rich with color. Jagged cliffs shaded from pale pink to vermilion dominate the landscape, and stands of full-size conifers keep it vibrant-looking year-round. New Mexico offers a sharp contrast. The first time I drove in from Sedona and saw nothing but dun-colored earth pocked with scrubby stands of black-green juniper, I wondered why I felt drawn to this drab terrain. Surface appearances, however, can be meaningless, and I would soon fall victim to the unique spell that had given New Mexico its motto: the land of enchantment...or as residents jokingly put it, the "land of entrapment." To make certain that I got the message that I needed to *stop* in New Mexico, I got a ticket that first day, for running a stop sign. Yet even after I chose to make New Mexico my home, Southern California never stopped calling to me. Throughout that time, every intuitive sensing repeated that I would live there one day.

By February 2010, when I drove to Los Angeles to speak at the Conscious Life Expo, California's pull felt stronger than ever. I still loved Albuquerque's lack of density and the open space of the Sandias, but once immersed in the urban hustle of LA, I recalled how much I had loved my inner-city apartments in Montreal and Toronto. Was it time to reclaim that part of me? Was it finally time for LA?

Everywhere I looked, the signs screamed *yes*. On my first morning in the city, as I walked the block back to the conference hotel from a Denny's breakfast, pondering what lay ahead for me that day, an inner voice interrupted with a compelling non sequitur: "LA will support you." I was intrigued. Over the next two days, that prediction played out with satisfying accuracy. I was at the conference because Susan Larison Danz, a coaching client who was now practicing her marketing magic on my behalf, had invited me to be part of her Lighted Bridge Communications booth. I was selling books and offering mini-coaching sessions on the exhibition floor and had been granted two speaking slots in the conference schedule. *The Voice of the Muse* flew off the table, my coaching roster was full and the response to my two talks was electric. I was drunk with success, and it was all happening in LA.

The night the conference closed, I called Sander Freedman's cell from my hotel room. I knew it would ring through to his voice mail. But he would be landing in LA long after I had fallen asleep and I wanted my message to be the first thing he heard when he got in. "Welcome to LA," I said then gasped, muttered a few more sentences about our plans for the next day and hung up. I gasped because as I spoke those three words, it felt as though I was speaking them as a resident not as a visitor. I went to bed afterward, but lay awake for hours wondering if, finally, it was time.

The following day I was certain.

Ojai is a magical, Sedona-like town inland and upcountry from Ventura, north of Los Angeles. That's where Sander and I planned to spend our day together in LA. He had arranged a one-day layover on his way back to Toronto from South America and I had extended my California stay by a day to spend it with him. We hadn't seen each other since my Toronto visit four years earlier and I was looking forward to the reunion.

I was also looking forward to seeing Ojai again. I had last been there in early 2007, when I was inspired to take a break from my travels to work on a new draft of *The MoonQuest* screenplay. Then, I had stayed in a magical hilltop house redolent with synchronicity. Johann Wolf, its regular tenant, wanted to spend a few full-time months in LA seeking out music and filmmaking opportunities and was looking for someone to cover his rent for a month or two. I had been spending another holiday season two hours north in Arroyo Grande with the O'Hares when I saw his ad on Craig's List. A few days after Christmas, I drove down to see the house and meet him.

Johann and I hit it off immediately. We talked for hours about our dreams and passions while we drank tea at an outdoor table and gazed north over a mystical valley. Orange trees heavy with fruit scented the air. If the setting wasn't enough to convince me to take the house, two other curious coincidences were.

A month earlier, I had been staying in LA with my friend Kent Spies. "What's your passion?" he asked abruptly one evening.

"Well," I responded with quintessential Libra equivocation, "I love to do sacred sound, to inspire people. I love to draw, to connect with the earth—"

"No," he interjected. "What's your *passion*? What do you claim?"

My answer was unequivocal: getting *The MoonQuest* published, filmed and out in the world and completing the trilogy of which it was the first part. I wasn't altogether surprised, particularly as *The MoonQuest* had placed third in the New Mexico Discovery Competition for unpublished fiction a few days earlier. But I was surprised by how passionately this desire edged out all others.

So when I learned from Johann that *ojai* means moon in the Chumash language and that Johann's cat, who I would be caring for if I stayed, was named Kenta — almost identical to the Q'nta of *The StarQuest* — I was convinced. In fact, I never left. I spent the night in the guest bed and Johann left on his LA adventure the following afternoon.

Kent drove up to Ojai early in my stay and introduced me to Meditation Mount, a thirty-two acre retreat center in the hills above town. I loved the aura of tranquility that enfolded the property and I returned often after Kent's visit. Sitting in the colorful gardens and gazing out over the surrounding mountains was a meditation in itself. If I was bringing Sander to Ojai, I would have to include Meditation Mount in our itinerary.

We drove up late in the afternoon, and as we walked behind the main building toward the gardens and overlook, we spotted a young man sitting on a low wall, strumming a guitar. The sun setting behind him bathed the valley below in a coppery light and threw a radiant aura around his head. He looked up when he heard us approach, and his long, blond hair glinted in the golden glow of approaching dusk.

"Can I play you one of my songs?" he asked.

Startled but intrigued, we sat next to him and he resumed his strumming, crooning softly in a velvet voice.

I said I wanted open spaces now I'm tradin' them in
Some things are better found within
My heart is the only open space I need to live in

As I listened to the lyrics of Erich Lenk's song, I knew that the desire for physical open space that had so defined my life since I left downtown Toronto in 1994 no longer mattered. What mattered was that I expand the open space in my heart to encompass the dense physical spaces I had so long avoided. What mattered was that I surrender to my heart's desire, however foreign it seemed in the moment.

Even as I sensed all that deeper meaning, what I said, silently, was, "Shit. It's time."

A Time of Signs

ON OCTOBER 3, 1995, the evening of my forty-first birthday, I sat in Ron and Carol MacInnis's castoff rocking chair, the fire in my Nova Scotia wood stove blazing, and knew with incontrovertible certainty that it was time to return to Toronto. It wasn't a surprise, and in the centered calm of meditation, I was okay with it. The next morning, I walked the gravelly mile up Hubbard Mountain Road to the Pereau United Baptist Church to tell my minister friend, Mark Parent, of my plans. As I neared the white clapboard building, I knew that if it was time, I must be ready. I was also terrified.

"What are you afraid of?" Mark asked.

Before I realized what I was saying, I blurted out, "Life."

A year in rural Nova Scotia and two drafts of *The MoonQuest* had changed me. Yet they had changed me within the protective embrace of a solitary cocoon. How would this new Mark David Gerson respond to the world when he returned to it? How would the world respond to this new Mark David Gerson? Despite my fears, I went back. And through those ten Toronto months until my next exodus, I felt expanded and expansive in the midst of all that Canada's largest city had to offer the newly minted me.

Now, in February 2010, I was poised to play out another version of that experience. Albuquerque wasn't rural Nova Scotia. But I did live on the last street before urban subdivisions melted into a mountain infinity of open space. Plus, apart from students, clients and book-signings, my life was nearly as cloistered as it had been in Nova Scotia. I drove back from LA, the Conscious Life Expo and Ojai suspended between exhilaration and panic. I both yearned for this move and was terrified by it. Then, there was the money. After two months of Hobby Lobby and three months on the edge,

Albuquerque had finally come to support me. Still, the Albuquerque cost of living lay below the national average. LA? Well, LA was LA. How would I get there? How could I ever get it to work? I knew it wasn't my job to answer those questions. I knew it was my job to surrender to both my desire and the means of achieving it. That didn't eliminate my anxiety...or the rightness of this next step.

Signs of that rightness kept popping up; the first, even before I got home. I had stopped in Sedona to see my daughter in a school play and was in the New Frontiers health food store a few hours before the show when I ran into Sao, a shamanic astrologer friend I hadn't seen since before I left town. After the usual preliminaries, he launched into an impromptu reading. This was Sedona, after all.

"How old are you?" he asked.

"Fifty-five," I replied.

"When's your birthday?"

"October 3."

He paused, and stared piercingly at me.

"You're entering into the most powerful period of your life," he intoned. "Whatever you truly desire will be yours." He paused again. "Start asking yourself this question: By the time you turn 57, who do you want in your life, what do you want to be doing in your life and where do you want to be living?"

To the first two parts of Sao's question, I felt nothing. At "where do you want to be living," I heard, with crystal clarity from somewhere deep inside me, "Beverly Hills."

Beverly Hills? Of all the areas I was considering as a potential LA home, none was Beverly Hills. Not because of the cost. It just wasn't on my radar. "Maybe," my logical mind inserted, "Beverly Hills is just a stand-in for Greater LA."

Another sign followed a few weeks later when back in Albuquerque, I was trudging through a slushy Target parking lot. On my way to my car, I passed a silver Ford Escort bearing a faux California license plate under the front grill. Instead of a number were the words "Beverly Hills." *Maybe it's more than a stand-in...*

In May and again in July, I returned to LA with no agenda other than to explore the city and feel what it felt like to be there. On my first visit, I walked the few blocks from my hotel to Hollywood Boulevard. As I turned onto the legendary avenue, I noticed a massive billboard looming over the Walk of Fame. "This Is My Town," it read in giant letters. Then I looked down at the star-studded sidewalk and overcome with emotion, I began to cry. In July, as I was again walking up La Brea toward Hollywood, my phone rang. It was my friend Joan Cerio, whose writerly and peripatetic journeyings had in many ways mirrored mine.

"How do you feel in LA?" she asked. "Do you feel joyful? Abundant? Do you feel prosperous?"

I didn't feel any one of those things. But a single word kept popping into my head as she asked.

"Alive," I replied. "I feel alive."

Leap of Faith

THERE'S A SCENE IN *The MoonQuest* where a character who has been living for many years in the safe solitude of a desert oasis hears a voice on the wind. The voice urges him to leave, despite the blinding sandstorm that rages beyond the palm trees ringing his insular retreat.

"You must go," the wind insists.

"Go where?" Kyri asks. "There is nowhere to go. I will die out there."

"Stay, and you are already dead," the wind replies.

I thought about that scene often in the days after I returned to Albuquerque from my July visit to Los Angeles. I thought about it because if I had felt vibrantly alive in LA, Albuquerque for the first time felt dead to me. More than dead. A day after my return, my New Mexico life abruptly stopped working. No book sales. No new clients. No money coming in to meet even the most trifling expenses. It was as though the well of miracles that had sustained me in New Mexico since Hobby Lobby suddenly dried up, with no new ones showing up to get me to LA.

I panicked. I groped for solutions. None appeared. I felt paralyzed, impotent, angry and scared. Mostly scared. Like Kyri in his oasis, my desert sanctuary had ceased to function for me. I knew I needed to leave. I couldn't see how.

"Give notice on your condo," Sander insisted in his tough-love way when he called one Friday morning in the midst of my self-pitying despair. "You have to do it."

I knew he was right. Yet it was a leap of faith I couldn't see taking. How could I give up my home when there was no money to move and no money to land? There wasn't even money to pay my current bills. Even as I argued and resisted, I knew that my resistance was futile. I knew in my heart that the only way to live was to leave. I knew too that the only way to leave would be to leap off the highest cliff I had ever encountered and trust that as I always had been, I would be supported.

I wish I could report that I surrendered joyfully and gracefully. I didn't. I was childish, churlish, petulant and argumentative...more paralyzed by fear than I had been in decades. Soon after I hung up from my conversation with Sander, I recognized this paralysis as the return of a pattern that had ruled too much of my early life. In that moment, I knew I had no choice: I would have to give my notice and step trustingly into the void — as I had done so often in the past, as the Fool does in just about every tarot deck.

The first miracle showed up within the hour, even before I wrote and mailed my letter of notice to the property manager. It was a phone call, from Adam Bereki in Orange County, just south of LA. Adam is a former Huntington Beach police officer who was harassed out of the force for being gay. We had met on a social network a few months earlier when I saw that he had written a book about his experiences. We had spoken a few times since.

"I was driving to the gym," Adam said, "and I knew I had to call you. I don't know why."

I didn't either. We chatted amiably for an hour, and toward the end of our conversation I mentioned that I was preparing to move to LA — on faith, with no sense of how I would either get there or live there.

"I've got plenty of space," Adam surprised himself by saying. "Stay with me." His street name? Spirit.

As I had no money for storage or for much of anything else, I decided to sell most of what I owned to finance my relocation. As I had done in Nova Scotia, I would step into my new life open, naked and ready for whatever fresh beginnings awaited me. All I left behind were cartons of *MoonQuest* and *Voice of the Muse* books and CDs and a scattering of other boxes, stored in a former student's Albuquerque garage. With that letting go, the flow of miracles swelled: unexpected gifts of cash, support and love; unexpected contacts and connections; unexpected validations and confirmations; and assorted serendipities, synchronicities and surprises.

I still didn't know why the LA call was so strong, although I had no lack of logic-based theories: LA would better support my writing, coaching and teaching; LA was the center of the film industry; LA represented my return to the world from the solitude of my Sandia Mountain aerie; LA would reconnect me with an ocean I missed; LA was where my daughter and her mother seemed to be headed.

There was truth in all of them.

Yes, I wrote — mostly on this memoir. Yes, I spent time by the sea, and it was healing. Yes, I spent time in urban LA, and it was exhilarating. And yes, Guinevere and her mom moved out, although they were an hour away and our time in the same region would prove to be short-lived. As for the deeper reasons, some would reveal themselves over the next weeks, others would remain a mystery.

I didn't leave Albuquerque on the same kind of road odyssey that had pushed me out of Toronto and Sedona. Nonetheless, it was the start of an odyssey — one that would continue through my ten weeks in Southern California and carry me right back to New Mexico. I couldn't know that when on Thursday, August 12, I drove onto I-40 and pointed the car west toward LA. That I arrived at Adam's in Costa Mesa on Friday the thirteenth should perhaps have given me an indication of the deaths and rebirths ahead. It didn't. I was too busy being nervous and excited about the new life that I was certain was about to start.

The Heart of Desire

"What do you want?" Adam asked me one afternoon as we wandered along Laguna's West Beach. The surf was gentle that afternoon, pushing toward us with no urgency and with just enough roll for the lone surfer to find some easy action.

I didn't answer right away. I had been in Southern California for a month and had made only one outing up into the urban LA that was supposed to have drawn me here. Most days, Adam and I went to Laguna or Newport to write. If Los Angeles had pulled me here, Orange County's beach communities were seducing me.

"I don't know," I replied after a time. "When I'm in LA and feel the buzz of the city, that's where I want to be. When I'm down here in Laguna, I don't want to be anywhere else. It's as though there are two parts of me competing for my future."

We continued in silence. I had removed my shoes, and the sand squished between my toes. At the asphalt path to the street, I brushed off my feet, put my flip-flops back on and started up the hill toward the tiny Camel Point subdivision at the top. I stopped halfway and gazed back. In the silence of that no-man's land between sea and city, I heard my voice echo back at me from a few days' earlier, when I had accompanied Adam and his realtor to an ocean-view house in this same neighborhood.

If I lived here, I would never leave.

"Shit," I said out loud.

"What?" Adam asked.

"It can't be Laguna. It's LA. It has to be LA." I started to cry.

My tears weren't for Laguna Beach. They were for parts of me that I had outgrown, parts of me that wanted to stay in seclusion but couldn't. Laguna represented a continuation of the years of retreat I had in many ways lived since leaving downtown Toronto in 1994. LA represented my return to the world I had sensed in Ojai the previous winter. Through my tears I was saying goodbye to what remained of the me-in-hiding, a me I could never be again. Laguna represented my past; LA, my future.

The next afternoon I drove into the city, just to feel what it would be like to be there. As I sped up the 405, I kept glancing into the rearview mirror, not at traffic but at my new haircut, the most expensive I had ever allowed myself to get. Making and keeping that salon appointment had an been act of defiance — against a fearfulness that in too many ways still constricted me. Now, the new-look me was racing toward my new city, knowing only that I could no longer settle for less than I deserved.

"Act as though and make it so," I had written in *The Wisdom Keepers Training*, a multimedia personal-growth manual I created during my God Activation days. It was time to live that statement more baldly and boldly than I had ever dared.

The following day I returned to Los Angeles. Aalia and Guinevere had moved there from Sedona a few weeks earlier, and I would be joining them for my daughter's eleventh birthday. First, I planned to do some reconnoitering. Over the next few hours, I drove through neighborhood after westside LA neighborhood, scouting for a part of town that could feel like home. Money was not to be a deciding factor. Rather, I was on a quest beyond the sensible and conventional. I was on a quest to discover the heart of my desire.

More often than not in my life, my passions have resided so far beyond the limits of my imagination that they have been hard for me to see and express. Writing, of course, was one. Even after I had been writing for years, even after my dramatic, Hobby Lobby-era commitment to *The StarQuest*, I didn't realize the full extent of that desire until my harrowing conversation with Sander, the one where he urged me to give notice on my Albuquerque condo.

"Take the rest of the day off," he said, toward the end of the call.

"No," I responded, without thinking. "I think I'll go to Starbucks to write."

Sander argued with me, tried to convince me not to work.

"You don't understand," I countered. "Writing is the only thing that makes sense." Then, to my surprise, I burst into tears. That same visceral desire and response was waiting for me in Beverly Hills.

Even though Beverly Hills sent unexpected signs my way back in February, I hadn't planned to include it in that morning's explorations. Then, unexpectedly, I found myself on its eastern fringes with extra time on my hands. Aalia and Guinevere weren't yet ready for me and I was hungry. Where could I find a quick, reasonably priced meal? Then I remembered the Beverly Hills Whole Foods on North Crescent Drive, only a mile from where I was parked. As I walked into the store, a strange feeling washed over me. It felt as though this was *my* Whole Foods, as though I shopped there all the time. I filed it away as curious and sat down in the deli with a bowl of soup. After lunch, I ambled down the block to The Crescent Beverly Hills, a luxury apartment building I had noticed earlier. The doorman smiled and opened the door. No leasing agents were on duty over the weekend, he apologized. Then he scribbled a name and number for me to call on Monday. As I left, that same at-home feeling I had experienced in the market tingled through me.

Back in the car, I took North Crescent to Santa Monica Boulevard, and then North Beverly to westbound Wilshire Boulevard for the twenty-minute drive to my daughter's. Now, *everything* about the area felt normal, natural, home-like. As I passed the Starbucks on North Beverly, I saw myself sitting inside, working on this book. As I passed an outdoor cafe around the corner on Wilshire, I saw myself on the patio, people-watching over lunch. The *Twilight Zone*-quality of the experience left me bewildered.

Moments later, I crossed the city line back into Los Angeles. I gazed up at the Wilshire Boulevard apartment towers and tried to imagine myself living there. I couldn't. In a flash, I was back in New Frontiers in Sedona, hearing "Beverly Hills" in response to Sao's question. Just as quickly, I started to cry. Somehow, Beverly Hills dwelt within the heart of my desire. What did it mean? I couldn't know. Would I be living there? Only time would tell. Meantime, I couldn't ignore an emotional charge that was as powerful as it was mysterious.

Birthday Presence

I SPENT THE weekend of my fifty-six birthday in San Diego, at the Mind Body Spirit Expo. When Susan Larison Danz had invited me to be part of her Lighted Bridge booth there, I accepted easily. I had been certain that I would already be living in Los Angeles by then and that this Expo, along with another two weeks later in LA, would launch my teaching and speaking career in Southern California. I was right about one thing: The San Diego Expo *would* herald a major change in my life. Just not the one I expected. By the time I drove back to Costa Mesa that evening, another transformative birthday had had its way with me: I knew it was time to leave Adam's.

Until then, life with Adam had been a strange blend of my time with Fred Henderson in Toronto and of my marriage. It was as though the remaining dysfunctions for me of both experiences were stirred into a California cauldron and served up in regular, if sometimes barely digestible portions. Once again, my housemate was a gay man on a similar spiritual path. Once again, I assumed that if the universe had thrown us together, there was a romantic subtext pointing to an imminent happily ever after. Once again, I was wrong. This time, there was even more circumstantial evidence to support my misguided assumption: I found Adam physically attractive, he was also writing a book, we spent most of our time together, and we talked for hours at a stretch. And, of course, we lived together. It could almost have been a marriage, but without the sex. It could almost have been *my* marriage. Unlike my time with Aalia, I was now the financially dependent one. But I was still as emotionally needy as ever.

I had arrived in California with the proceeds of my contents sale but with few coaching clients and no income prospects. Adam provided shelter and much of my food; I took care of my other expenses. While grateful for Adam's hospitality and generosity, I couldn't help but worry about what would happen were he to retract them. I would soon find out.

"You need to leave," he announced one morning three weeks into my stay. "In a week. This whole thing — you, here — it's codependent. It's not good."

Adam was not only forcing me to face my unresolved issues, my presence was forcing him to face his. It was his longstanding "caretaker mode," he explained. It had played out in his previous relationships, it had prompted his initial invitation for me to stay, it was playing out now, and it wasn't healthy. For either of us. I couldn't argue with his diagnosis, particularly once I saw some of the parallels with my marriage. Still, his proposed cure threw me into a panic. I had no money, and by September 16, that landmark date that continued to show up in my life, I would need to be gone. I felt powerless to argue. This was his house and I was a guest. Of course, I would leave, although I couldn't imagine where I would go or how. My only recourse, once again, was surrender.

One of Adam's greatest strengths could also be one of his greatest weaknesses: He would leap fearlessly into whatever situation presented itself without worrying about potential fallout. Ironically, it was the mirror image of one of my greatest strengths and weaknesses: my ability to take the time to go within, sometimes with so much deliberation that a decision was painfully slow in coming. A few days later, Adam changed his mind. Having aired the issue, he declared, we would find a way to move through it. We did, but the mutual button-pushing continued.

"If I don't commit to leaving this house, nothing's going to break open for me," I told Adam the morning after my birthday. "I don't know any more than that."

I did know more. I knew that I had not jettisoned my clingy codependence as completely as I had believed and that leaving was now the only way to cut that cord. What I didn't know was where I would go and what I would do. This time, I couldn't launch a new road odyssey. My shaky finances would not support it. Besides, I was behind on my car payments. Who knew how much longer I would have the Trailblazer?

A month earlier in a coaching session with a client, I had likened the stripping-away process she was experiencing to a demolition that removes everything of a building but its skeletal structure. She was finding the process unnerving, and I assured her that new walls, floors, ceilings, fittings and furnishings could only be installed once all the old ones had been shed. I found myself in that same place in the days after my birthday, just as unnerved as Mary Ann had been.

One of my favorite spots in the area is Los Trancos Canyon View Park on Newport Coast Drive. The park sits high on a ridge overlooking both the desert-y San Joaquin Hills and an endless Pacific vista. You rarely see anyone else there, despite the apparent hopefulness of its two dozen parking spaces. It was no different a few days before my birthday when I drove there for some solitude. As I stepped from the asphalt onto the park's walking path, I saw four tomb-like steel slabs set into the ground. I had never noticed them before, especially the one that leapt out at me: It bore the letters RIP etched prominently into the metal. It took me a moment to realize there was also a D there and that the cover for this irrigation control valve actually spelled out DRIP. In that brief instant, it was as though I was seeing my own grave, as though some higher power with a wicked sense of humor was confirming the death that would need to occur before my birthday could trigger a rebirth I could not yet imagine.

I was back at Los Trancos the afternoon after my birthday. As I sat in the car, an autumn storm pounding into my windshield, I considered stripping off all my clothes and running naked into the canyon, never to return. I had left my New Mexico home and shed nearly all my material belongings. Now, I seemed to be shedding more and more of my personal and professional identity. The void felt overwhelming.

It wasn't the first time. Not long after we returned to Sedona from Hawaii, I tiptoed out of the house for an early morning hike.

Guinevere and her mom were still asleep. As I walked deeper into the trail-less desert scrub, I contemplated never returning to the house. I would just keep walking until...until whatever happened happened. Nothing particular triggered my hopelessness that day. All I knew in those moments was that my love for my wife and daughter could not compete with my debilitating despair. Finally, fear or responsibility did. I turned around and went home.

If the word "suicide" never consciously entered my thoughts that morning, it did six years earlier, when I was living in Penetanguishene. "I'm afraid of the emptiness," I wrote in my journal one gloomy January morning. "I'm afraid it will devour me, destroy me, annihilate me. Emptiness is death." What would happen if I took my life? Who would notice, other than the Emerys? What would happen to Roxy? In logical retrospect, nothing. The Emerys would have adopted her. At the time, though, worrying about the fate of my dog snapped me out of it.

I returned to Los Trancos a few days later, still wrapped in an existential confusion that had kept me up most of the night. The weather was as brooding as I felt: a sky textured in shades of gray and, in the near distance, an ocean of steel. The rain, like my tears, had held off thus far. But for how long? As I stared out toward the ocean, my thoughts turned to *The MoonQuest*, to a coronation scene where Crown Prince Kyri is directed to throw all the jeweled accoutrements of the old king's regalia into the fire as he and his subjects-to-be chant, "The past is passed. We let it go." Only when Kyri stands naked before the crowd, with all that could encumber him to his father's reign consumed in the ceremonial flame, can he begin to chart his own course as monarch...can he truly begin his own life.

What was left for me to toss into the fire? The answer would come the following day.

Sacrifice and Surrender

IT HAD BEEN storming all morning, and I had been counting on a misty, moody beach walk to match my gray frame of mind as I contemplated my uncertain future. However, by the time I pulled into the parking lot at Crystal Cove State Park in Newport Beach, all but scudding white powder-puffs had fled a sky now so blue and deep that it seemed more Southwest than West Coast.

In Genesis, ten chapters past the *Lech L'cha* story that launched me at age thirteen, God tells Abraham that he must offer up his only son, Isaac, as a live sacrifice. Abraham unquestioningly travels three days to Moriah, builds an altar there and binds Isaac to it. Only as Abraham holds the knife to his son's throat does God, through an angel, stay the execution, commend Abraham's obedience and promise him abundant blessings. I pondered that story often in the days leading up to my Crystal Cove beach walk. The more I thought about it, the more I came to believe that God was rewarding not obedience, but Abraham's unconditional surrender to his own authenticity. By acting in a way that was true to his deepest heart, regardless of what he thought or of what the repercussions might be, Abraham was expressing God's will, which, ultimately, was his own highest will, the only genuine will there could ever be. As for the "abundant blessings" of God's reward, they would show up as God deemed appropriate, regardless of what Abraham might think of them. For in God's mind, all outcomes are blessed.

I thought, too, about my resistance, about all the "will nots" I had thrown at God's will over the years and about how conditional my surrender had so often been: If I did such-and-such, I would manifest money, love or success. Or I would be safe. Or, like with Abraham and Isaac, the knife would be pulled away at the last minute, sparing me the dreaded sacrifice. "Moving toward surrender while hoping for a reprieve is neither authentic nor unconditional," I wrote in my journal. I added that I was now prepared to give over *everything* to God, unconditionally, including my writerly identity. "Like Abraham in Genesis, I willingly take the knife to what I hold most dear. God will either pull my hand back at the last minute or not." Then I added, "For now I'm more naked than I have ever let myself be...more empty than I could ever have imagined possible."

Who I was and where I was going were mysteries I couldn't begin to fathom. Was my LA story truly over? Would I remain in the area but find a calmer landing strip away from Adam's? Would I leave the crowded madness of Southern California for some version of the wide open spaces I had only recently jettisoned? Or would Los Angeles call me back once I moved through this death? I had no answers to these or any other questions. All I could do was embrace the void and wait for something to light up the darkness.

I didn't have to wait long. When I stepped onto the deserted beach at Crystal Cove, its sands still damp from the morning's downpour, a series of *aha*'s began to fill in some of the emptiness. My first awareness was of a hand pulling away mine — the one that held the knife of sacrifice to my writing. In agreeing, like Abraham, to give up what I held most dear, the need for sacrifice dissolved. Writing would remain a central pillar of my life. Next came the clear certainty that I was not to wait until October 24, a departure date I had chosen in part to honor my commitment to speak at LA's Conscious Life Expo. As with the Toronto writing class that canceled itself to accelerate my exodus to Nova Scotia, the Expo no longer mattered. I would leave Orange County and California in less than a week, on October 10 — 10/10/10, which in numerological terms would signify a trifecta of new beginnings. I would travel through Sedona to Albuquerque and Santa Fe, revisiting the principal stops on the solo portion of my US journey. Beyond that, I didn't know...couldn't know.

In another replay, this time of the relief I had felt thirteen years earlier when I knew to leave Toronto and head vaguely west, I suddenly felt lighter, freer and filled with possibility. It wasn't so much *what* I was to do that lifted the burden. It was that, finally, there was *something* to do.

Even before leaving the beach, I started calling my handful of Sedona contacts for a place to stay. Ironically, success came not with a call to Arizona, but with a call to Isa de Quesada, twenty miles away in Westminster. Isa had moved back to the LA area a few years earlier, but she had retained her Camp Verde home for retreats and vacations. When I shared my plans with her, she was characteristically enthusiastic and supportive.

"Stay as long as you need to," she said a few days later as she handed over her spare key.

What about Albuquerque and Santa Fe? I trusted that they would sort themselves out. First, I had to get to Sedona.

Act 19.
Retracing My Steps

*No man ever steps in the same river twice,
for it's not the same river and he's not the same man.*
HERACLITUS

The journey is the reward.
STEVE JOBS

Back to the Future

IF MY FIRST DAY in Sedona, in September 1997, marked my entry into a life I could not yet begin to imagine, my return thirteen years and three weeks later seemed at first glance to signify a rebirth of equally dramatic proportions. Without my consciously planning it, October 11 turned into a replay of that first day, including a miraculous pilgrimage back to Rachel's Knoll, closed to the public since 1998 when it was incorporated into a luxury golf community. Seven Canyons was still undeveloped back then. Now, a gate and guard at the end of Long Canyon Road signified its exclusive status.

I had no plan to drive to Seven Canyons. My only reason for being on Long Canyon that morning was to see if I could identify the trailhead pullout where I had spent my first Sedona night all those years before. By the time I had picked out a few possible candidates, I found myself at the end of the road. I pulled up next to the gatehouse to ask the guard if I could drive through to make a U-turn.

"Welcome to Seven Canyons," he said, beaming, as I pulled up.

"Thanks," I said, astonished by a warmth I had never experienced other times I had turned around here. "I used to live in Sedona," I added, "before this property was developed."

He nodded. "That would have been at least seven years ago."

"Nineteen ninety-seven."

He nodded again.

"I used to come up here all the time, to go to Rachel's Knoll."

He paused for only an instant.

"It's still there, you know."

"Oh?"

"Would you like to go up?"

My heart raced. *Would I?* The guard gave me instructions and sent me on my way. Five minutes later, I was standing atop the hill whose panoramic views and sweet, powerful energy had so seduced me from my first day in Sedona. Afterward, no one in town could believe that I had not only been allowed in, I had been invited in. I barely believed it. It had to be a sign...of something.

Running into Martha Martyn at Wildflower Bakery a few hours later felt equally portentous. When I looked up from my lunch and noticed a Martha-like woman at a nearby table, I couldn't believe it was her. As far as I knew, Martha had moved to Portland. I hadn't seen her since the day, in this same cafe, when she suggested Mark David as a replacement for the outmoded Aq'naton. I wasn't even certain that it was her.

It was. Reconnecting with this woman who had been present at every important turning of my Sedona life, immediately after my Rachel's Knoll experience, felt powerfully significant, even if I didn't know in what way.

Albuquerque would be my next stop, but I still didn't know where to stay. With limited cash, my old Howard Johnson Express room was out. Who could I ask to put me up? While I had many former students and clients in Albuquerque, I had only one close friend and her living situation made house guests impossible. As for Marisha Diaz, who had billeted me briefly after my six-week road trip in 2008, not only was she gone from Albuquerque, she had somehow vanished from my life. What to do? As I drove up Hwy. 179 toward Oak Creek and the heart of Sedona, an inner voice replied: "Ask Kathleen."

Kathleen? We had been meeting for coffee semi-regularly since she first expressed interest in producing *The MoonQuest* as a feature film. But she was not a close friend and not at all someone I would feel comfortable asking for that kind of hospitality.

"Ask Kathleen," I heard again. "Think *MoonQuest* movie. Think synergy."

Synergy would be good. For all Kathleen's commitment and enthusiasm, visible progress on the film front had been minimal. Yet I was still reluctant as I dialed her number. It seemed a huge favor to ask of someone I barely knew.

"It's so strange that you're calling," she said. "I had a dream last night that I was angry at you because you hadn't turned in the *MoonQuest* trailer script I'd asked you for."

Kathleen had in fact asked me to write a script for a short promotional trailer. Between the drama I was living in California and the momentum I wasn't seeing on the film project, I had felt no urgency.

"Then, in the dream," she added, "you suddenly turned up at my front door. I think you'd better come."

As I jotted down directions to her house, I discovered that I would be staying a quarter of a mile from the corner of Paradise and Universe. Another sign?

My return to Albuquerque a few days later didn't unfold as dramatically as my return to Sedona had. But it did contain an echo of my first drive into the city in 2005. Then, only twenty miles from Albuquerque, I had been so overwhelmed by a powerful wave of exhaustion that I pulled into the parking lot at the Route 66 Casino for a quick nap. I had the identical experience in the same spot in 2010. It was as though I was being energetically prepared for some major life-changing experience. Little did I know, that first time, that Albuquerque would soon become my home. Little did I know this most recent time, what would be waiting for me: an increasingly unassailable clarity about what was now most important in my life.

My first weeks in New Mexico had me leapfrogging from one guest room to another. I had been at Kathleen's for only a few days when a visiting relative bumped me across town to the home of Karen Walker, a fellow author and former coaching client. From there, I spent a few days in Santa Fe with Shoshana Love, another writer and ex-client. For all the nurturing support I received from both Karen and Shoshana, I felt lost. How long could I continue shuffling purposelessly and, increasingly, pennilessly? I had moved past the financial triage of which bills I could pay to a place where food, gas, cellphone and car insurance were my sole considerations. Soon, I feared, there might not even be a car to insure. I had insisted that I would be okay were I to lose the car, but after witnessing what looked like a repossession around the corner from Karen's one morning, I felt a lead ball drop into the pit of my stomach. *How far from that scene am I?*

Not far at all, as it turned out. I had suspended car payments in California, while praying that I would be able to catch up before it was too late. By early December, it was too late. A few days before I called the finance company to arrange for my second voluntary surrender, I researched Albuquerque's public transit system. The last time I had relied on public transit to get around, I had lived in Toronto. I knew that Albuquerque couldn't compare, but surely there had to be a bus stop in Kathleen's neighborhood. There wasn't. The nearest was two and half miles away. The nearest shops were three miles away. How would I manage even the most basic of errands?

That evening at dinner, I told Kathleen that I would have to give up the Trailblazer. If she wasn't comfortable with me being stranded under her roof, I needed to know before I turned it in. Silently, she rose from the table and walked to the other end of the house. When she got back, she dropped the spare key to her car onto the table.

"It's simple," she said. "You'll use my car."

Once more, I had been take care of — not in a way I would have chosen and not in a way I was comfortable with. It didn't matter. It couldn't matter. Other things would soon prove themselves more important.

Passion's Legacy

WHAT I CAME TO know, in those early days back in New Mexico, even before I gave up my car, was that I was no longer prepared to struggle or make compromises to stay afloat or, if it came to that, to stay alive. This time, I wasn't toying with suicide. I was digging deeper and deeper within myself to identify a life that would be worth living, a life that would expresses my soul's deepest yearning. And I was insisting that I could no longer let fear pull me from its pursuit as I had over the years, despite the great strides I knew I had made. Nor was I prepared to let anyone or anything outside of me pull me from that pursuit.

Two years earlier, faced with a similar brink, I had taken the job at Hobby Lobby and avoided stepping into the abyss. This time, my only choice was to step off the cliff, trusting that, as I had done in that long-ago meditation, I wouldn't go *splat*. This time, my surrender would have to be unconditional. It never had been before. I had never said, "I do this because I know in my deepest heart that this is the right choice. The only choice. I do it with no expectation of reward and with no regard for any possible fallout. And I will let no one deter me from that path." I hadn't said it before. I said it now.

My resolve would be quickly put to the test.

When I revealed to Aalia that I would be leaving California, she was upset. My presence in LA had given her the confidence to move back to her hometown without Marcus. I knew she was scared, but I couldn't take responsibility for either her anxiety or her move. I had to do what I had to do, even as I regretted leaving Guinevere again. Two weeks later, Aalia's fear would explode in a rage-filled tirade. But when I met her and Guinevere for a going-away breakfast on my way out of town, she was her usual supportive self.

I was in an Albuquerque Costco when my cellphone rang, on my final shopping expedition to the warehouse store before my membership expired. It was Aalia. After a few cursory preliminaries, she lit into me. "You have to come back to LA. You have to get a job. You have to live with us. You have to support us."

When Aalia and I divorced, she hadn't wanted alimony and we had agreed to keep child support informal and out of the courts. At the time, I had little income and Marcus was supporting them. Now Aalia was in LA on her own and flailing in fear...just as I was declaring my flailing days to be over. I stood in speechless shock in a Costco aisle as she repeated variations on that theme for the next fifteen minutes. For all my emotional progress, I still carried a legacy of guilt around Guinevere — for having left Sedona in 2004, for having left LA and for my spotty contributions to her upkeep over the years. I didn't know what to say. I didn't have to say much. In her mounting panic, Aalia left few openings for me to reply until the call dropped and she was gone.

Shaking with fear, confusion and impotence, I abandoned my purchases and fled to my car. I had planned to spend the next few hours writing, at a Starbucks up the street from the Hotel Albuquerque, where later that afternoon Kathleen and I were to have a meeting with the director of the Albuquerque Film Festival about *The MoonQuest* movie. I made it to Starbucks, but whatever writing I had expected to do was drowned out by the echo of Aalia's voice. Finally, I began a letter to her that I wasn't sure I would have the courage to send.

"I've reached a point," I wrote, "where I'm either powerful enough to magnetize to me a life that's worth living or I'm not. I'm not looking for anyone to rescue me. I'm doing what I now know I must do if I'm to continue living. I'll either make it or I won't. I'll either sink or a tidal wave will carry me to shore. I'll either go splat or I'll survive the fall. But I'm no longer prepared to shrink from the full-body, full-hearted attempt." I acknowledged my responsibility for Guinevere and committed to a modest but regular support. I also insisted that my primary responsibility to my daughter was to model for her the life choices that would enrich her journey in the years ahead. I would not, I said, be returning to LA from guilt or fear, but only when the highest imperative called on me to.

Halfway through the letter, I knew that I would have to send it. I knew too that there could be repercussions. I believed that Aalia was emotionally and spiritually evolved enough to recognize the truth of my words. I also knew how blinding fear could be. Would she turn her back on me? Would she cut off all future contact with Guinevere? I knew it was a possibility, however slight. I knew too that the only way to be true to myself was to take the risk. "I will never stop loving you or Guinevere," I concluded. "But I can only express that love genuinely by loving myself and by honoring what I know in my heart to be true, regardless of fallout or consequences."

Six years almost to the day after Aalia had left me, I finally left her. The moment I hit *send*, I fell into a panic. What had I done? In declaring myself sovereign — not only from Aalia but, it seemed, from all I had ever been — I had stripped myself of a lifetime of structures and foundations and had threatened my relationship with my daughter. I felt grounded but rootless, detached from an old life, yet with no clear sign of the new one. I had passed through a door, and I heard it slam shut behind me. There could be no take-back. I was scared.

As so often in my life, only one thing still made sense: writing.

There's a scene in *The StarQuest* where Q'nta must pass through The Coil, a serpentine tunnel in which she will be forced to face her deepest fears. To her surprise, and to mine the moment I wrote the words, her greatest fear is the loss of her storytelling ability. "How can losing my stories be my nightmare?" she asks. "How can I put my stories before my son? Before *The StarQuest*? What kind of mother am I?"

Like the Q'nta of my story, I found it inconceivable that writing could be the only thing that mattered. Like Q'nta, I felt parental guilt. And like Q'nta, I knew that the most precious gift I could give myself and my child was the legacy of a life passionately lived.

Movie Magic

MY SEDONA INTUITION, that throwing me and Kathleen together in close quarters would create a *MoonQuest* movie synergy, was proving accurate. Within weeks, I had produced not only the promised *MoonQuest* trailer script, but trailer scripts for *The StarQuest* and *The SunQuest* — even though I had no *StarQuest* screenplay to work from and no written *SunQuest* story in any form. I had barely typed "Fade Out" on the final page when I was immersed in a fast-track filmmaking course: My three mini-scripts were to be filmed with a volunteer cast and crew of local professionals. Soon. Suddenly, I was no longer just the screenwriter. I was an associate producer involved in every aspect of production. I participated in all casting calls and choices. I helped interview directors and crew members. I was in on design decisions. And sooner than I thought possible, I was on a film set, awestruck by the process.

I would be lying if I claimed that I always believed in *The MoonQuest* as fully as I know it has always believed in me. Of course, early rejections from publishers and agents eroded my self-esteem. Yet even with excellent reviews, multiple awards and enthusiastic reader response, part of me still doubted not only the book's quality and impact but my gifts as a writer.

Many mocked Sally Field in 1979 when she exclaimed, during her Oscar speech for her *Norma Rae* best-actress win, "You like me. You really like me!" I experienced countless Sally Field moments of my own while the trailers were being shot. It was hard to conceive that everyone present on this film set was there because of me...because of my words and my vision. For large chunks of those four twelve-hour days, my mind struggled to accept that fact. I would hear my dialogue spoken by costumed, in-character actors and not be able to connect the experience with the words I had penned and the scenes I had envisioned. In part, that was a good thing. It afforded me an ego-free objectivity that allowed me to see what worked and what didn't. Often, though, it felt like I was strangely not present, even though my physical body was consuming large quantities of sweetened coffee to keep me functioning after a week's anxious sleeplessness — the same wake-me-up that had kept me going through another birth eleven years earlier: my daughter's.

There were flashes, of course...moments when I did recognize that I had written what I was seeing and hearing. Those moments were indescribable validations of the power of my dreams and imagination, a power that I realized I still didn't fully trust. I had experienced similar moments during our casting calls and rehearsals, when actors proved to my doubting mind that my dialogue worked and my stories were sound. I even cried during particularly powerful readings. Now, with recreations of my characters interacting in recreations of my worlds, the proof was incontrovertible. I was gratified, stunned...and scared. Like a Sally Field surprised by the depth of her gifts, I didn't know what to do with that proof. And like a Sally Field startled by the praise of her peers, I didn't know what to say when, at the end of each shooting day, actors thanked me for my stories and for the privilege of playing my characters. Just as I had wept when I held an advance copy of the published *MoonQuest* book in 2007, so I wept when the second assistant camera operator clicked her slate in front of the camera and called out, "Scene 10, Take 1. Marker." It was Saturday morning, the first take of the first scene to be shot.

The Write Place

During the months and year that followed the trailer shoot, while Kathleen worked her producer magic to bring the *Q'ntana* features to fruition, all I did was write — in an unparalleled frenzy of creativity. I produced a *StarQuest* feature screenplay and, almost immediately, launched into a first draft of a *SunQuest* script, written as I had created the initial drafts of all my books, with no notes, no outline and only a vague sense of the story. Perhaps I should not have been surprised at how easily it flowed, but I was. Over the next one hundred days, in rapid succession, I wrote a new draft of *The StarQuest* novel, a first draft of a *SunQuest* novel and a first draft of this book, churning out the last two in a mind-numbing three weeks each and completing the latter only days before the end of 2011. The first two-thirds of 2012 would bring final drafts of *The StarQuest* and *The SunQuest* books and screenplays, a largely final draft of this book, and ideas for enough writing projects to keep me occupied for several more years.

I still had only a minimal income, provided by a handful of cosmically timed book-editing projects. I was still living under Kathleen's roof and using her car. The *Q'ntana* film project was still unfunded. And I was still in Albuquerque. But I was writing. The passion that had defined so much of my life, a passion that existed within me long before I could acknowledge it, was being realized... and supported.

Through my time in Sedona and Hawaii, through all the turbulence, upheaval and financial insecurity, one mantra continued to repeat itself to me from somewhere deep within: "Your books will support you." Now, in Albuquerque, in the city in which I had finally and unconditionally surrendered to my writerly self, they were.

Coda

*I'm not the one who invents the stories;
I'm like a radio that picks up the waves.*
Isabelle Allende

Where there is no vision, the people perish.
Proverbs 29:18

The Next Surrender...

It's July 9, 2012. I'm driving home from Starbucks after an afternoon's revisions to *Acts of Surrender*. The book is nearly complete, and I'm looking forward to being able to put it aside and move on to other projects. From the moment nearly three years ago when I set down the first words of the first draft, this book has remained one of my most profound and difficult acts of surrender. As Toshar does in *The MoonQuest*, I have had to overcome my reluctance to write my story or risk a form of stasis. As Q'nta does in *The StarQuest*, I have had to accept the predominant role that storytelling plays in every aspect of my life or risk living without passion. And like Ben in *The SunQuest*, I have had to not only recount my past but reexperience its emotions with sometimes disturbing fidelity, or risk betraying my human potential.

More daunting than all those challenges has been my anxiety around releasing this book into the world. In one sense, that's odd. There are few stories shared here that I have not told before — to friends and clients or more publicly in talks and workshops. Some have been disseminated even more widely through my blogs and *The Voice of the Muse*. But my life until now has been compartmentalized. Through the decades of my journey, I have lived very distinct lives as I have traveled from Marky to Mark to David to Akhneton/Aq'naton to Mark David and as I have redefined my sexuality, my spirituality, my sense of self, my work and most things about me — multiple times. Few of you have known me through even half those changes, and the parts of me that still fear judgment wonder how the rest of you will respond to the mosaic that is me.

Fear of judgment is not a new issue in my life, as you will have read in these pages. I picked it up early on from my mother, and as much of it as I have shed through the years, I have retained more than I realized...more than I care to admit. That has been one of my discoveries as *Acts of Surrender* has moved closer to completion. It's a discovery that snuck up on me, masquerading as a weird panoply of physical and emotional symptoms before exploding into full awareness on this twenty-minute drive home.

Until the moment before this one, I have been feeling safe, despite my stress. With no publisher and no resources to produce the book myself, all I can do is finish it, show it to a few friends for feedback and file it away. Its day will come. That day, clearly, is not today.

Then, a voice — once again, the voice of my Muse. Today, it's seductively indirect, recognizing that the blunt tone it has employed in the past would only feed my fear, not usher me past it.

What about all those Acts of Surrender *excerpts you've posted — on your website, on Facebook and elsewhere? Won't all that promotional investment be wasted if you shelve the manuscript?*

I say nothing.

I'm approaching the corner of Paseo del Norte and Unser, four minutes from my front door, and I am not responding as my Muse had hoped I would. A delay is required. When I reach the intersection, a police cruiser blocks the way, forcing a ten-minute, bumper-to-bumper detour. As I crawl through traffic on a street that is never anything but free-flowing, a flash of Muse-inspired insight strikes.

I could produce Acts of Surrender *as an ebook. It wouldn't be as perfect as I might prefer, but—*

In that instant I know that I *must* produce *Acts of Surrender* as an ebook — for reasons that have nothing at all to do with promotional investment. That argument was a devious ruse. If my biggest fear is of exposing myself to the world — of walking the earth naked, clothed only in my truth — then the only way to face that fear is by releasing the book. As speedily as possible. Not for anyone else. For me. That's the only way I will move through and past my terror. And if my only option for getting it out quickly is as an ebook, then that's my best course of action...my only course of action.

✽   ✽   ✽   ✽   ✽

It is now December 2013. In the seventeen months since the ebook release of *Acts of Surrender*, not a single judgmental mob bearing torches and pitchforks has raged to my door. This fear, as so many others in my past, has proven groundless. Yet as I revisit my life and words in preparation for a print edition of this book, a deeper level of those old anxieties surfaces: I'm once again reluctant to walk the earth naked, to expose myself to the world.

No, this is not *Groundhog Day* and I'm not the arrogant weatherman played by Bill Murray. The two sets of experiences appear to be identical, but they're not.

I know I used the expression "coming full circle" elsewhere in these pages, but it's one I prefer to avoid. That's because it suggests a return to a place I have already been, having learned nothing and grown not at all. My preferred image is that of a spiral, where I return instead to a place along the same axis, but at a higher level of consciousness and understanding, and where I am given the opportunity, as I put it in *The Voice of the Muse*, to operate at "a higher level of awareness, mastery, openness and trust."

With the call to get *Acts of Surrender* onto the printed page, I have been given that opportunity once again.

If I were to choose an archetype to describe my life's journey, it would be the Fool, a tarot character often pictured stepping off a cliff into the unknown. His may be a leap of faith, but it's never blind faith. For he knows that even as he trades the certainty of solid ground for the mysteries of the void, the infinite wisdom of his infinite mind will guide him forward. This knowingness frees him to surrender again and again. And again. Not without resistance and not without fear, but in the conviction that resistance is futile, fear cannot stop him and meaning is always present, even when it is invisible.

The tarot Fool may appear to have a choice in his folly: In many decks, one of his feet is still firmly anchored. He could step back. Or could he? In my favorite representation, from *The Osho Zen Tarot*, it's too late: One foot hangs off the edge; the other only barely touches the earth. That's the kind of Fool I am: always in motion, with a momentum that keeps pressing me on to the next act of surrender. Any other choice breaks faith with a choice I made long ago, a choice that banished conventional free will from my life, a choice to live my passion as authentically as humanly possible, whatever the consequences.

As I observe my fears around this new edition, this new coming out, I realize that if Toshar could not move forward until he had set his story onto parchment for all to read, I cannot move forward either, as the Fool that I am, until I take a further step in making mine public. And so I make the commitment — to this next leap of faith, to this next surrender.

There will be more acts of surrender after this one. There always are. Each one will push me harder than the last. Each one will nudge me closer to my essential truth. Each one will require a greater leap of faith. And through each, I will continue to trust in the story. Whether it's the story I'm writing or the story I'm living, it always knows best.

...And the Next

IT IS NOW MARCH 2019 — a few days after the renewal signified by the spring equinox and a few weeks from both the time of death and resurrection represented by Easter and the time of liberation from slavery symbolized by Passover.

It's a powerful moment in which to be reexperiencing the original edition of *Acts of Surrender* — I finished reading it a few hours ago — and an equally powerful one in which to be writing this chapter as I prepare to release a new edition of the book.

In the five years that have passed since I penned the words that close both the previous chapter and that original edition, much about my life has changed. Yet at a fundamental level, everything is exactly as it was, only more so.

Let's start with the changes...

I am no longer in Albuquerque under Kathleen Messmer's roof and I am no longer driving her car. Today, I live in Portland, Oregon, I drive my own car, and my housemate is Kyri, a two-year-old chihuahua-terrier mix named after a character in *The MoonQuest*. (See him at play in the author photo on the back cover.)

An equally significant addition to my life is my American passport. Three days into 2019 and after two decades as a legal resident of the United States, I swore the oath of allegiance to my adopted country and became a dual US/Canadian citizen. If my conscious motivation for launching the naturalization process had more to do with convenience than commitment, the powerful emotions that surged through me, first as I completed my application and later at the ceremony, reminded me that this too was an act of surrender — to my evolving, expanding self.

On a sadder note, I will no longer be able to have friendly

arguments with my sister over whose version of our shared past is the more accurate. Susan died suddenly a year ago, leaving me as the sole surviving member of my immediate family and more aware than ever not only of my mortality but of the predominant role that writing and storytelling must continue to play in my life.

That role certainly deepened through my time at Kathleen's. When I moved in, I had two books out in the world: the original editions of *The MoonQuest* and *The Voice of the Muse*. Two years later when I wrote the "Passion's Legacy" chapter of this book, I had two more: ebook-only versions of *The SunQuest* and *The StarQuest*.

The years that followed turned out to be the most creativity productive of my life to that point, and by the time I left Albuquerque in early 2018, I had published more than a dozen books; among them, new editions of both *The MoonQuest* and *The Voice of the Muse*, print editions of the *Q'ntana* sequels, five new books for writers, and *The Sara Stories*, a series of novels set in a fictionalized version of the real-life world chronicled in these pages. I had also completed the three *Q'ntana* screenplays, written early drafts of three *Q'ntana* stage musical adaptations and, just for kicks, published a couple of gay erotic romances under a pen name.

Where did that literary tsunami come from? Perhaps the lava fields a few miles from Kathleen's at Petroglyph National Monument played a role. After all, there are few natural forces more primally creative than a fiery volcano. New Mexico's may have stilled their fury long ago, but their elemental energies proved to be as transformational for me as had been those of Hawaii's and Arizona's more active volcanoes when I lived among them.

I wasn't thinking about volcanoes when I felt drawn to Portland. Yet I find myself once again living in the heart of volcano country, at the center of what geologists call the "ring of fire."

I can't know all the ways in which that fiery force will play out in my life here. I do know that the call to focus on my core passion has escalated and intensified since my arrival. I have been in Portland barely fourteen months and I have already produced two new books in an unplanned personal/spiritual growth series. In fact, so creatively fertile has the volcanic soil here been for me that the first of those *Way of the Fool* books moved from conception to publication in only ten weeks! It was a book I never expected to write, but the book I *really* never expected to write is the one I'm currently working on: a fourth, as-yet untitled *Q'ntana* book. As a result, *The Q'ntana Trilogy* is now *The Legend of Q'ntana*; you can't have a four-or-more-book trilogy! I have also released expanded editions of two of my books for writers and I am preparing both this rerelease and a new one for *Dialogues with the Divine* (see the page back of this book for a look at its new cover).

Revisiting *Acts of Surrender* for this new edition has reminded me of the many Fool-like leaps of faith I have taken over the years, an experience that both unnerved and reassured me as I thought back over my move to Portland, itself among my most daring, and frightening, leaps into the unknown.

For the first time since Hawaii and for the first time on my own, I made a conscious decision to move to a place I had never been before (unless you count a two-hour lunch stop in 2006)...a place where I knew no one, where I had no solid income-generating prospects and where I would arrive with neither a game plan nor a cushion of savings.

As with Hawaii, I would be moving somewhere considerably more expensive than the home I was leaving behind. Unlike in Hawaii where my creative projects never felt like a priority, "passion's legacy" has been operating at full tilt here: Despite monthly expenses considerably higher than any I have ever faced, the same intuitive knowingness that has initiated all my other acts of surrender continues to urge me to focus the entirety of my energy on my writerly persona, to spend no time seeking out other sources of income and to trust that all I require will find its way to me, somehow. My books, as I keep being reminded, will support me...even if the "how" is beyond my ability to see or my capacity to imagine.

So as I did early in my third Albuquerque sojourn, I have recommitted unconditionally to the heart of my passion and to the voice of my heart...to the writer and storyteller I have always been. Whether my stories are experienced by millions or by only a single person cannot matter. It is what I do because it is what I am.

"Portal land," Sander Freedman joked when I told him about my planned move, and that is what my life in Portland has turned out to be: a portal into deeper levels of trust, scarier leaps of faith and acts of more complete and absolute surrender. As Toshar puts it in the final words of his *MoonQuest* chronicle, "That is the journey. That is the quest."

Appreciation

No book is ever truly a solitary pursuit, even if it often feels that way in the writing of it. It would be impossible to acknowledge the many people who contributed to the stories that created *Acts of Surrender* — some named in these pages, most not. But there are several I must single out: Adam Bereki, who prodded me as only he can to move forward with this book; Joan Cerio, whose friendship sustained me during some of my more challenging moments; Sander Freedman, whose tough love propelled me through some of my most difficult surrenders; Kathleen Messmer, who has never stopped believing in me and my dreams (and who photographed this new edition's compelling cover image); and my daughter, Guinevere, who must still be wondering what she signed up for when she chose me as her father.

I would be remiss if I did not also thank the participants in my memoir-writing workshops, where I was as much student as teacher and learned on-the-job all I needed to know to make this book possible. I also thank the many friends I have never meet — on Facebook and across the internet — who have cheered me on over the years, on this project as on many others.

I'm grateful, too, to the energy of Albuquerque, a city in which I have birthed or completed so many of my writing projects, and to Portland, which has taken over as my creative midwife — for this new edition as for so much else.

Finally, to my Muse: Thank you for pushing me so hard to surrender to *Acts of Surrender*. It's the book I most resisted...and among the ones I am most grateful to have written.

A Journey of Singular Courage by a True Spiritual Master

When financial disaster forces Mark David Gerson from his Portland home with everything he owns packed into the back of his car, he launches an open-ended odyssey that will carry him from the Pacific to the Mississippi and back, never knowing from one day to the next whether he can muster the faith to keep going.

"A compelling read that will leave you feeling inspired and humbled."

www.ingramcontent.com/pod-product-compliance
Lightning Source LLC
Chambersburg PA
CBHW030106100526
44591CB00009B/303